Mirela Bogdani is a scholar and specialist on EU issues with a focus on EU enlargement. She has studied politics at St Antony's College, Oxford University, and was formerly Lecturer in EU Politics at Cardiff University. She has written three books, including *Albania and the European Union: The Tumultuous Journey towards Integration and Accession* (with John Loughlin, I.B.Tauris, 2007). Her website is www.mirelabogdani.com.

TURKEY AND THE DILEMMA OF EU ACCESSION

When Religion Meets Politics

MIRELA BOGDANI

I.B. TAURIS

LONDON · NEW YORK

Published in 2011 by I.B.Tauris & Co Ltd
6 Salem Road, London W2 4BU
175 Fifth Avenue, New York NY 10010
www.ibtauris.com

Distributed in the United States and Canada Exclusively by Palgrave Macmillan
175 Fifth Avenue, New York NY 10010
Copyright © 2011 Mirela Bogdani

Library of European Studies: 16

ISBN: 978 1 84885 458 1 (HB)
       978 1 84885 459 8 (PB)

A full CIP record for this book is available from the British Library
A full CIP record is available from the Library of Congress

Library of Congress Catalog Card Number: available

Printed and bound in Great Britain by
TJ International Ltd, Padstow, Cornwall

CONTENTS

ABBREVIATIONS

AKP	Justice and Development Party
B-H	Bosnia Herzegovina
CAP	Common Agriculture Policy
CDU/CSU	Christian Democratic Union/Christian Social Union
CEE countries	Central and Eastern European countries
CCEB	Candidate Countries Eurobarometer
DG	Department Generals (of the European Comission)
EB	Eurobarometer
EC	European Community
EEC	European Economic Community
EFA	European Free Alliance
EIN	European Ideas Network
ELD	European Liberal Democrat
EP	European Parliament
EPP-ED	European People Party - European Democrats
ESI	European Stability Initiative
EU	European Union
FDI	Foreign Direct Investment
FDP	Free Democratic Party
FT	Financial Times
MEP	Member of European Parliament

MP	Member of Parliament
NATO	North American Treaty Organisation
OEEC	Organisation for European Economic Co-operation
OIC	Organisation of Islamic Conference
PES	Party of European Socialists
PKK	Kurdistan Workers' Party
SVP	Swiss People's Party
TEU	Treaty of European Union
UDF	Union for French Democracy
UMP	French Union for a Popular Movement
UKIP	United Kingdom Independent Party

PREFACE AND ACKNOWLEDGMENTS

The idea to address this topic, which originally formed the subject of my thesis at St Antony's College at the University of Oxford, arose for three reasons. Firstly, there is my interest in EU politics, and in particular, its enlargement policy, on which I have written my two previous books (although these focused on one of the Western Balkan countries, Albania). I believe that enlargement is a very important policy for the EU, not only because it has to do with its very terms of membership, as well as its foreign policy, but also because it raises other significant issues related to the cultural and religious identity of Europe, European values and the EU's borders.

My reason for choosing Turkey as the focal point was that this country has become the 'thorny issue' or 'hot potato' topic of EU enlargement policy, or as I prefer to describe it 'the trendy issue of the club's enlargement'. It is proving to be the most challenging and tricky question of enlargement in the EU's whole history, and one of very great political importance for the entire EU project. Turkish accession involves the issue of a very large population (not just that of Turkey, but also that of the EU in general), and it is present constantly in public policy debates.

The third reason is related to a special interest that I have in religion, or, more exactly, in the connection of religion with politics. I am fascinated with the relation of religion not only to politics, but also to culture, history and sociology. Studies of and literature on religious and cultural issues within the political context have an appeal to me. That is why, although their ideas are considered controversial, I am attracted to the work of authors such as Samuel Huntington and Bernard Lewis, who acknowledge the significance of religious and cultural factors in shaping today's world and influencing international politics.

There is an abundance of literature on the Turkey–EU relationship and Turkey's accession, but my interest was in exploring the hidden and sensitive aspect of this accession process, namely, the impact of religion on the chances of Turkey entering the EU. In other words, whether the opposition or reluctance of Europeans was based only on concerns about the fulfilment of technical Copenhagen criteria, or, instead, on more subtle issues such as religion and culture. In the latter case, Turkish accession becomes a question of accepting a Muslim, and culturally different, people into a Western club.

Writing about religion, and especially in a political context, is always difficult. Therefore, assessing the impact of religious and cultural factors in the accession process of Turkey was certainly a difficult case to prove, both because of a lack of data, and also because of the pervasive 'political correctness' surrounding these issues, including in the 'temple of free-thought', the University of Oxford. From the outset, I was faced with 'warnings' by my professors, including my supervisor, that this project was 'un-do-able' and that I could not prove my central proposition. Nonetheless, I maintained my belief that this issue needs exploring, for one cannot ignore 'the big elephant in the room'. Ultimately, therefore, I succeeded in assessing the impact of the religious and cultural factors on Turkey's accession process and on European actors' opinions, as well as in drawing conclusions about the reasons for their reluctance to let in a country like Turkey.

Expansion of the EU to the East, and the aspiration to include a Muslim country like Turkey in a predominately atheist or Christian-rooted club, introduces into the discussion the tricky question of the compatibility of Islam with Western values, which I have also analysed in the book. However, unlike many current scholars of these issues, I know and have experienced Muslim culture and religion for real, and not merely from studying it through books and university libraries in Britain, or by spending holidays in beautiful resorts in Turkey or Tunisia. I was born and grew up in communist Albania, which at that time was officially atheist, but whose society had, nonetheless, a strong Muslim legacy, bequeathed by 500 years of rule by the Ottoman Empire. Raised in that society and with Muslim roots of my own, I am very familiar with Muslim mentality and culture. By experiencing for myself Muslim values and traditions, especially their effects on women, I have been able to compare them with Western culture and values objectively, during my recent past while living in the UK, and previously living and studying in the USA.

Despite the academic difficulties and obstacles described, I have nonetheless had the help, assistance and support of many other friends, colleagues and academics during the researching and writing of, first the thesis and subsequently the book, all of whom have given me useful suggestions, comments, ideas, data and critiques. I owe thanks to all who supported this book in different ways and at various stages. Among them, I am grateful and indebted to:

My very good friend, colleague and co-author of my two previous books, John Loughlin, Professor of Politics at Cardiff University, for his continuous academic help and support and for providing the feedback on the manuscript.

My friend and colleague, the writer Miranda Vickers, for her expertise on religious issues, her scholarship, and for her provision of very useful feedback on the manuscript.

My friend and political mentor, Jonathan Evans, Member of the European Parliament (British Conservatives), for giving me an interview, for looking over the draft of my thesis, and for providing me with much material on EU–Turkey relations.

Graham Avery, former Director at the European Commission, for giving me an interview and looking over the draft of my thesis.

Max Watson, Senior Member of St Antony's College, Oxford, for his useful comments and insights on the subject.

Professor Fatos Tarifa, former Albanian Ambassador to the USA, for his help with relevant literature, and for our exchange of interesting views on the issue of Turkey's accession to the EU and the integration of Muslim immigrants into host societies.

Andrew Baldwin, Oxford DPhil graduate, for doing the book-editing and providing interesting comments on the manuscript.

My Oxford classmate Tom (Thomas Speller) for his useful advice and comments.

My editor at I.B.Tauris, Joanna Godfrey, for her expert work and invaluable help and support.

Participants at conferences, seminars and roundtables for their contributions and expertise, from which I benefited greatly in refining my arguments. I include the five *European Ideas Network* Summer Universities (Berlin, Lisbon, Lyon, Warsaw and Rome) and in particular the EIN working group 'Geographical limits of the EU', as well as numerous events at the European Studies Centre in Oxford, the University of Cambridge, the London School of Economics, the University of London and the University of Bristol.

Last but not least, my dear friend Ilir Loka, who is always there for me with his friendship, and whom I thank for his continuous moral support.

And, most importantly, my family, Paul and Cindy, for their patience and support during my years in Oxford while I was writing my thesis, and then over the last year while I have been converting it into a book. I could not have written the book without the enormous moral and material help and support of Paul, or without the love and great inspiration of my wonderful daughter Cindy. I am also deeply grateful to my parents for supporting me in all my initiatives in life and for giving me the intellectual tools to carry out this work.

Mirela Bogdani

1

THE REVIVAL OF RELIGION
IN WORLD AND
EUROPEAN POLITICS

1.1 Religion and politics: the relationship between the two and the impact of religion on politics

Many authors have presented and analysed the relationship of religion and politics.[1] During my study of this literature, I have identified three aspects to this relationship: the first is the general impact of religion on politics; the second is the return of religious discussion to world politics; and the third is the revival of religious discussion in European politics.

With regard to the first, the general impact of religion on politics, a number of scholars recognise the important role that religion has played in world politics. Religious cultures have, in one way or another, contributed a great deal to politics. Elisabeth Hurd argues that 'Cultural and religious systems of belief and practices they engender are powerful determinants of modern domestic politics and influential contribution to contemporary international politics both in the West and outside it'.[2] Steve Bruce in his *Politics and Religion* book notes that 'the Protestant Reformation – a change in religious culture – set in chain a variety of complex developments that played a major part in the creation of liberal-democracy'.[3] He argues that Protestantism encouraged democracy in three ways: first, it played an important part in the rise of capitalism and the growth in prosperity; second it encouraged individualism and egalitarianism; third it created a context of religious diversity. Not only in the past, but still today we see many examples of the impact of religion on politics: the Evangelical upsurge in Latin America, Muslim-Christian rivalries in Africa, disputes between Arabs and Israelis, the rise of Hindu fundamentalists in India, and secularist-religious struggles in Turkey. Some of these political movements, as Peter Berger points out, are genuinely inspired by religion, while some use religion to legitimise political agendas.[4]

The importance of religious and cultural factors in shaping and influencing today's world is evident from the work of many contemporary scholars, including Samuel Huntington and Bernard Lewis, who both acknowledge the significance of religious and cultural factors for international politics. Although considered controversial, I am attracted in particular to the work of Huntington, who has been presenting the increasing importance of cultural and religious factors in international politics with considerable political intuition since the early 1990s. In his highly influential *Clash of Civilisations* thesis, he argues that world politics is entering a new phase, where the dominant sources of conflict will be not primarily ideological, political or economic, but rather cultural, that is, based on the politics of identity and culturally distinctive values, which transcend national boundaries.[5] Unlike Francis Fukuyama in his *End of History*, which argues that once ideological divisions are over the world will live 'happily ever after',[6] Huntington argues that the Velvet Curtain of Culture has replaced the Iron Curtain of Ideology, and that the great divisions among humankind and the prevailing source of conflict will be cultural. The historical events of the 1990s removed one ideological conflict, but revealed the existence of another, namely, what Huntington calls 'civilisational clashes', which, according to him, are the defining characteristics of the new era of international politics. He states, 'The fundamental source of conflict in this new world will not be primarily ideological or economic. The great divisions among humankind and the dominating source of conflict will be cultural. The principal conflicts of global politics will occur between groups of different civilisations...The clash of civilisations will dominate global politics'.[7] Huntington made this 'prediction' in 1993 and nine years later the whole world witnessed the events of September 11.

The impact of religion in shaping and influencing politics today is also reflected in what is known as 'Identity Politics', two manifestations of which are 'Political Islam' and 'Islamic Fundamentalism'. In analysing these issues in my book, I am helped by the respective work of Bernard Lewis, Caroline Cox and John Marks, Abdullahi A. An-Na'im and Tariq Ramadan. Political Islam is the use and mobilisation of religion and identity to achieve political objectives. It is undergoing a revival both in Turkey and Europe. Regarding its revival in Turkey and the subsequent creeping Islamisation of Turkish society, I refer to the work of Posch, Yavuz, White and Cagaptay. Regarding its revival in Europe and the related issue of Muslim communities in Europe, I have used Oliver Roy's 'Deterritorisation Thesis', and the work of Fukuyama, Berger, Burleigh, Leiken, Laquer, etc.

Religion has not only influenced politics, but also economics and social life. The most well-known thesis in support of a relationship between religion and economics was given by Max Weber in his 1905 book *The Protestant Ethic and the Spirit of Capitalism*, in which he argued that Protestantism provided a fertile ground for capitalism, and that Protestant values, such as the work ethic, personal discipline, hard work and a respect for learning, fostered modern economic development. Weber's thesis was, therefore, that the Reformation played a part in the rise of capitalism. Other cited examples of the impact of religion on economics are the role of Opus Dei in the Roman Catholic world (during Franco's regime), promoting a combination of rigorous theological orthodoxy with market-friendly economic openness, or the Confucian-inspired values in the economic success stories of East Asia.[8]

However, the influence of religion in social life and culture is perhaps more obvious than in politics and economics. The relationship of religion and culture, is analysed in Chapter 4.

1.2 The return of religious discussion to world and European politics

The second issue is the return of religion to world politics. Religion, despite its huge implications, has long been a neglected topic, but now, as Bruce notes, it is back on the agenda.[9] This has occurred thanks to a number of factors, the most important being contemporary religious revivals, most notably the Islamic and the Evangelical. Of these two, the revival of Islamic fundamentalism is better known, because of its more immediately obvious political implications and vast geographical scale.

Islamic fundamentalism, according to Peter Berger, refers to any sort of passionate religious movement and a return to traditional sources of religious authority.[10] It aims to bring about a restoration not only of Islamic beliefs, but of Islamic lifestyles, which in many ways contradict modern ideas, including relations of religion and the state, the role of women, moral codes of everyday behaviour, and the boundaries of religious and moral tolerance. As such, Islamic fundamentalism, as Caroline Cox and John Marks point out, is the exact opposite of Western liberal-democracy. It is a brand of totalitarianism rooted in a sacred text. It refers to radical, militantly ideological versions of Islam, in which violent actions, such as terrorism, suicide bombings or revolutions, are advocated, practised and justified, using religious terminology.[11] Abdullahi A. An-Na'im gives three reasons for the recent rise of fundamentalist political Islam: first, the failure of secular national politics; second, repeated defeats by Israel, supported and funded by US and other Western countries (the perception of Western bias undermines the credibility of liberal notions of democracy); and third, alternative Marxist and socialist ideologies are seen as discredited and have been practically abandoned. Given this political and ideological vacuum, the fundamentalists were able to present their vision of an Islamic alternative as the only natural ideology for Muslims everywhere.[12] This means using Shari'a as a framework for both national politics and international relations: in domestic policy, the strict enforcement of Shari'a by the state, and in foreign policy permanent hostile relations of the territory of Islam (Dar al-Islam) with the non-Muslim world (collectively called Dar al-harb). Islamic fundamentalism is one of the forms of Political Islam, which as mentioned before, is the use and mobilisation of religion and identity to achieve political objectives. Political Islam may be moderate or radical. While moderate Islam's aim is to bring Islamic parties to power, Islamic fundamentalism's goal is the creation of an Islamic state based on Shari'a Islamic law.

The rise of Islamic fundamentalism around the world and its implications for Europe are discussed in more details in Chapter 5.1, with political Islam being addressed in the last section of that chapter.

While the Islamic movement is gaining ground primarily in countries that are already Muslim, and among Muslim communities in Europe, the Evangelical movement, as Berger notes, is advancing in countries where this type of religion was previously unknown or marginal.[13] Conversion to Protestantism, especially in Latin America, is bringing a cultural transformation: restoration of the family, a rejection of traditional machismo, adoption of economic and work discipline (new attitudes toward work and consumption and a new work ethics), a positive attitude toward education and self-improvement, voluntary work and a concern for broad moral principles. While Islamic resurgence tends strongly toward a negative view of modernity, Evangelical resurgence is positively modernising in most places where it occurs. Evangelical congregations serve as schools of democracy and for social mobility, as Berger points out. Moreover, Evangelicals have carried forward traditions of the separation of church and state. In that respect, as David Martin argues, they are quite unlike 'fundamentalist' Muslims, who seek ideological hegemony and the total regulation society according to Islamic law. The cultural characteristics of Evangelicals, namely, participation, pragmatism, competition and personal discipline, ought in the long run to foster democracy.[14]

In their just-released book *God is Back: How the Global Rise of Faith is Changing the World*, John Micklethwait and Adrian Wooldridge, argue that despite the vocal objections of crusading atheists, religion is a resurgent force across the world. They say:

On the street and in the corridors of power, religion is surging all over the world. From Russia to Turkey to India, nations that swore off faith in the last century, or even tried to stamp it out, are now run by avowedly religious leaders, and the destabilising effects of religion can be seen far from Iraq or the ruins of the World Trade Center. Formerly secular conflicts like the one in Palestine have taken on an overtly religious cast, and religion plays a role in civil wars from Sri Lanka to Sudan. Along the tenth parallel, from West Africa to the Philippines, religious fervour and political unrest are reinforcing each other.[15]

I concur, therefore, in the sentiments with which Micklethwait and Wooldridge conclude their book: 'If you want to understand the politics of this century, you cannot afford to ignore God, whether you believe to Him or not.'

The third issue has to do with the return of religious discussion to European politics. As Katzenstein and Byrnes point out, 'religion, widely resumed to have been consigned to the political margins in Europe, is now poised to play an important role in one of the most central political processes of contemporary European life'.[16] Western Europe, they argue, may be said to have preserved Christianity only as after the manner of glimmering embers; that is, not generating much heat on its own, but, when fanned (in very different ways) by Catholic Poland, Orthodox Serbia, or Islamic Turkey, likely to flicker back into flame. The European polity is beginning to be preoccupied by these kinds of religious issues. The debate on religion in Europe resurfaced a few years ago during the preparation of the Constitutional Treaty. Disagreements between secular and Christian markers of European identity generated a long debate over whether the Preamble to the EU Constitution should recognise the Christian roots and heritage of Europe.

The return of religious discourse to European politics owes, I believe, to three factors. Firstly, the increasing Muslim population in Western Europe, and the challenges associated with this growth and subsequent issues thrown up, such as multiculturalism and integration (i.e. an 'us and them' approach). Secondly, the emergence of two independent countries in Eastern Europe with predominantly Muslim populations, Bosnia and Kosovo, which aspire to become part of the EU. Thirdly, and most importantly, the issue of Turkey's accession to the EU. With the commencement of negotiations between the EU and Turkey about eventual membership, religion now holds an important place on Europe's diplomatic agenda. Therefore, the revival of discussion of religion in European politics owes much to the enlargement of the EU towards the East. Reinsertion of religious issues into European politics is beginning to occur, brought about by trans-national communities who, after many decades, are returning to a Europe bent on enlargement.[17] The expansion of the EU towards the East of the continent, is bringing back religion into European politics, the 'return' of religion – *la revanche de Dieu*, and the debate on the relationship between politics, religion and European identity. Enlargement is bringing back into the centre of the EU what had been in its periphery: renewed attention to the dilemma of coping with the intersection between religious and secular politics, as Hurd calls it 'long dormant dilemmas of relation of politics with religion'.[18]

EU enlargement to the East, as Katzenstein and Byrnes point out, is bringing three trans-national religions, Catholicism, Orthodox and Islam, into a mutual encounter together, as well as into closer contact with the European project.[19] The Roman Catholic Church is the religious community most supportive of the prospects of European unity, but its leadership is, by its own admission, supportive only because it wants to define the integrated Europe according to its own teaching and values. Pope John Paul II's attitude towards the EU and eastward expansion was well-known: he supported Poland's accession, because EU expansion was an occasion for 'a new evangelisation flowing from East to West...a Europe not only with higher economic standards, but also with a profound spiritual life'. The Catholic Church is also interested in defining Europe, and defining what values European society should devote itself to. John Paul II was particularly fond of referring to Europe as a fundamentally Christian civilisation, and was tireless in calling on Europe to renew its civilisational identity through a renewed commitment to its Christianity. He believed that an authentic European identity and an authentic European unity were impossible without reference to the religious tradition. His successor, Benedict XVI, has spoken quite plainly about the need to acknowledge Europe's Christian roots. When he was still a cardinal, Benedict's vision of the EU was of a Christian union, rather than one in which membership is earned by meeting objective and secular criteria. In his infamous Regensburg lecture in September 2006, he accused Islam of having been 'spread by the sword'; and when he met with Conservative political parties in January 2006 he called for a restoration of Christian values at the heart of the EU.

The other religion, Islam, Katzenstein and Byrnes believe, still presents a formidable challenge to the integration of the European continent, rather than a spur towards it.[20] Grace Davie says:

> They (religious communities) perceive themselves as secular and draw boundaries of their continent – known sometimes as fortress Europe – along Christian lines. The effective barriers to entry coincide with a geographical definition of Christendom. Nations dominated by Catholic Christianity will find it easier than their Orthodox equivalents to enter the EU. Muslim states will find it harder (if not impossible) despite the existence of significant Muslim communities within most West European nations.[21]

It is not only because of the existence of Muslim communities within Europe, but, more importantly, through the possible accession of Turkey, that the EU is reaching a historical border, that of the Muslim world.

Katzenstein and Byrnes argue that religion, as a political force, is more likely to hinder than advance further integration of the European continent.[22] However, this is a paradox, given that when one looks back to the late 1940s one sees that it was Christian Democracy that laid the foundations of the European integration movement. It is difficult to imagine this integration movement without the political contribution of Robert Schuman, Alice de

Gasperi, or Konrad Adenauer, all Christian Democrats, who were the founding fathers of the European Community. Their prominent role has led some to believe in Catholic origins in the creation of the EC. Arsene Heitz, who in 1955 designed what became the European flag – 12 yellow stars on a blue background – was reportedly inspired by a reference in the New Testament's Book of Revelation to 'a woman clothed with a sun…and a crown of 12 stars on her head'. Yet, despite this Christian Democratic background, successive waves of European enlargements have been motivated by very secular interests. Some argue that Europeanisation itself is a secular phenomenon. However, as Katzenstein and Byrnes note, 'secular forces that during the last half century advanced the Europeanisation of Europe, are now joining up with a renewed political salience of religion, as Europe enlarges'.[23]

I conclude this section with Peter Berger's remark that 'those who neglect religion in their analysis of contemporary affairs do so at great peril'.[24]

1.3 Secularisation Theory, Desecularisation Thesis and European Exceptionalism

The impact of religion on politics during recent decades has been shadowed by the influence of Secularisation Theory. This theory later lost its appeal and it started to become fashionable to talk instead of Desecularisation Thesis. But let us examine in more detail this process which, in my view, involves four phases.

Secularisation Theory

First of all, what do we understand by the term 'secularisation'? According to sociologist Jose Casanova, secularisation includes three features: firstly the differentiation (separation) of state and church, secondly the marginalisation of religion to the private sphere, and thirdly the decline of religious beliefs and practices (decline of church attendance and formal adherence to religion). I would add to these, two other features: religious tolerance, and that the state cannot use its power to impose religious beliefs on individuals. As Larry Siedentop points out, secularisation is not a mere indifference, non-belief or a 'value-free framework'. It implies that there is a sphere in which individuals should be free to make their own decisions, distinguishing inner conviction from external conformity.[25] Therefore, secularisation, as Oliver Roy notes, does not mean the end of religion, but the separation of religion from other spheres of social life, a personal individual faith (the way the believer understands and practises it), versus obedience to religious scholars and clerics.[26]

Secularisation Theory was very popular some decades ago. Steve Bruce and other scholars believed that secularisation was the dominant trend of modernisation. Although the term 'Secularisation Theory' refers to works from the 1950s and 1960s, the key idea behind the theory can be traced back to the Enlightenment: modernisation leads necessarily to a decline of religion, both in society and in the minds of individuals. Steve Bruce, in *Religion in the Modern World: From Cathedral to Cults,* offers a classic statement of what has become known as Secularisation Theory, the connections between the onset of modernity and the demise of traditional forms of religious life. The key is supposedly found in the Reformation, which heralded the rise of both individualism and rationality. He says, 'individualism threatened the communal basis of religious belief and behaviour, while rationality removed many of the purposes of religion and rendered many of its beliefs implausible'.[27] As Europe's economic and political life developed, religion diminished in public significance, and religious aspirations were relegated to the private sphere. The exceptional case was the USA. It was believed that the USA was one of the last religious nations in the Western world, with an astonishing range of vibrant churches and high levels of religious belief, a phenomenon labelled as 'American Exceptionalism'. Even though there is a legal separation between church and state, the expression of religiosity in political life is mandatory (especially for politicians running for elections). In the USA 92 per cent of adults believe in the existence of God or some kind of universal spirit, 70 per cent are 'absolutely' certain of God's existence and 60 per cent believe he is someone with whom you can have a personal relationship.[28]

Desecularisation Thesis

Secularisation Theory later lost its appeal and, in the face of a global resurgence of religion, it began to be fashionable to talk instead of the 'Desecularisation Thesis'. Scholars like Peter Berger, Peter Katzenstein, George Weigel, Timothy Byrnes and others argued that, even though religion may have been reduced at societal level, it is still strong at individual level. Secularisation on the societal and institutional levels is not necessarily linked to secularisation at the level of individual consciousness, says Berger.[29] Modernisation, these scholars pointed out, has had some secularising effects, but it has also provoked powerful movements of counter-secularisation. Most of the world, not just the USA, has witnessed an explosion of passionate religious movements. Ever since the Enlightenment, intellectuals have assumed that modernisation would kill religion, and that religious America was an oddity. Yet Micklethwait and Wooldridge, in their book *God is Back*, argue that religion and modernity can thrive together, and that the American way of religion is becoming the norm. They say:

> Many things helped spark the global religious revival in the twenty-first century, including the failure of communism and the rise of globalisation; it is now being fuelled above all by market competition and a customer-driven approach to salvation. These are the qualities which have characterised America since the Founders separated church and state, creating a free market in religion defined by entrepreneurship, choice and personal revelation, and as market forces reshape the world, the tools and ideals of American evangelism are now spreading everywhere.[30]

One of the most outstanding proponents of the Desecularisation Thesis, Peter Berger, says that 'the assumption that we live in a secularised world is false. The world today, with some exceptions, is as furiously religious as it ever was.' On the international religious scene, he says, it is conservative or orthodox or traditionalist movements who are on the rise almost everywhere. They are the ones who reject an *aggioramento* with modernity. On the other hand, religious movements and institutions that have made great efforts to conform to a perceived modernity are almost everywhere in decline. In one of his essays Berger writes:

> What I and most other sociologists of religion wrote in the 1960s about secularisation was a mistake. Our underlying argument was that secularisation and modernity go hand in hand. With more modernisation comes more secularisation. It wasn't a crazy theory, there was some evidence for it. But I think it was basically wrong. Most of the world today is certainly not secular, it's very religious…A minority of sociologists of religion have been trying to salvage the old 'Secularisation theory' by what I would call the last ditch thesis: modernisation does secularise and movements like the Islamic and Evangelical ones represent last-ditch defence by religion that cannot last: eventually secularity will triumph, or to put it less respectfully, Iranian mullahs, Pentecostal preachers and Tibetan lamas will all think and act like professors of literature at American universities. I find this thesis unpersuasive.[31]

George Weigel is another proponent of this thesis. The unsecularisation of the world, he says, is one of the dominant social facts of life in the late twentieth century. This is a rapidly shrinking, non-secularised world, in which intense religious convictions and passions will constantly intersect with the world of politics and economics.[32]

European Exceptionalism from the Desecularisation Thesis
Even as the Desecularisation Thesis was becoming increasingly fashionable in the rest of the world, there was one bastion where the Secularisation Theory seemed to hold good, and that was Western Europe. Scot Thomas grants Europe an exceptional status in the resurgence of religion in world politics. Secularisation, as an inherent feature of modernisation, is, he argues, applicable to

European religion, but not to the rest of the world. According to proponents of Secularisation Theory, argued Grace Davie, 'as the world modernised, it would automatically become secularised; and what Europe did today, everyone else would do tomorrow'.[33] The example of the USA proves the opposite: a successful cohabitation of vibrant religiosity and developed modernity. So it is Europe, rather than the USA, that is exceptional – and this was labelled the 'European Exceptionalism' thesis. European Exceptionalism meant a Europe united around secular principles of democratic welfare states. Berger (1999, 2005) also accepts European Exceptionalism, and calls it 'Eurosecularity'. With increasing modernisation, he says, there has been an increase in key indicators of secularisation in Europe, both on the level of expressed beliefs (especially those that can be expressed in Protestant or Catholic terms), and on the level of Church-related behaviour: attendance at services of worship, adherence to Church-dictated codes of personal behaviour (especially with regard to sexuality, reproduction, marriage), shortage of clergy, etc. These phenomena, long observed in northern Europe, have, since World War II, rapidly engulfed the south: thus Italy and Spain have experienced a rapid decline in Church-related religion.[34] As Berger points out, there is now an overwhelmingly secular Euro-culture. Europe is perceived as the world's most secular continent, with people rarely attending church except for baptisms, weddings and funerals.[35] Berger also argues for a correlation between integration to the EU and Eurosecularity: 'countries are pulled towards secularity to the degree to which they are integrated into Europe'.[36]

The decline of European Exceptionalism

The fourth phase has seen a decline of the European Exceptionalism thesis, with authors like George Weigel, Jose Casanova, Timothy Byrnes and Grace Davie arguing that Europe is less exceptional than often thought.

Recently, it has been observed that religion is playing an important role in European politics, as a result of certain factors explained in the succeeding chapters. Critics argue that this shows that Europe is less exceptional than it is often considered to be. While many Europeans have ceased to participate in religious institutions, Davie says, they have not yet abandoned many of their deep-seated religious inclinations. She describes this attitude as 'believing without belonging'. Even in Europe, she notes, many Europeans remain grateful for, rather than resentful of their churches, recognising that the churches perform a number of tasks on behalf of the population as a whole: churches are asked, for example, to articulate the sacred at times in the life-cycle of individuals and families and at times of national crisis and celebration. Western Europeans are unchurched population, rather than simply secular. An opinion poll to observe the connection between Europe and Christianity in the UK was conducted by the BBC in 2005.[37] It confirmed the resonance of this connection: 75 per cent of respondents believed that the UK should retain Christian values. Even among the people who claimed to have no faith, 44 per cent thought that Britain should retain a Christian ethos. Jose Casanova has described the continuing public role of religion even in countries with a high degree of secularisation. With the ascendance of secularisation, European religion has not simply vanished; collective memories have provided for a reconstruction of religious traditions; partly in the churches and through churchgoers, for sure, but also in education, the media and the law.

Micklethwait and Wooldridge point out that 'the American Revolution was a unique event in modern history, a revolution against an earthly regime that was not also an exercise in anti-clericalism. The Founding Fathers saw no contradiction between the values of the Enlightenment on the one hand and religious faith on the other; their genius was to insist upon the separation of church and state. By contrast in Europe, ever since the French Revolution, religion has been equated with reaction'. They continue 'For many European liberals, American religiosity is its least attractive characteristic. They cannot believe that any modern person can be religious unless that person is either stupid or insane. But now an unsettling worry nags at Western liberals: what if secular Europe (and, for that matter, secular Harvard and secular Manhattan) is the odd one out?'.[38] Religious belief is in fact increasing – in Europe each year, 100,000 pilgrims hike to Santiago de Compostela and 6 million visit Lourdes.

One of the factors contributing to this decline of European Exceptionalism, as mentioned before, is EU enlargement. Katzenstein and Byrnes, in pointing to European enlargement, argue in favour of diminution of Europe's exceptionalism. The ongoing and inexorable enlargement of the EU, they point out, is likely to make Europe less and less exceptional as time goes on.[39] How is EU enlargement doing that? This is explored and analysed in the next chapter.

standards to countries emerging from communist and dictatorial regimes, countries in transition or with a fragile democracy, and helping them with their domestic democratisation reforms. As Olsen points out, 'the enlargement process appeals to democratic identities and values and is portrayed as consistent with liberal-democratic principles'.[2] It has helped to transform CEE countries into modern, well-functioning democracies with market economies, and more recently it has inspired far-reaching reforms in the Western Balkans and Turkey. Enlargement seems to bring advantages not only for the applicant countries, but also for the EU itself, as it increases political, economic and physical weight and military security for all Europeans.

Thus for its supporters and proponents, the enlargement policy is one of the Union's most impressive foreign policy ventures. For its sceptics and opponents, however, each enlargement inescapably widens the spectrum of divergent interests and increases internal heterogeneity. By enlarging itself, the Union becomes weaker and runs the risk of its own destabilisation.

Since the last wave of accessions in 2004, enlargement has entered a new phase: preparation for expansion to the South-East, the Western Balkans and Turkey. Among countries that aspire to join the EU, Turkey is the one attracting most attention, and has turned out to be the 'thorny issue' or 'hot potato' topic of EU enlargement policy. Efforts by Turkey to westernise and join the Union have always provoked a debate among European actors and scholars about whether Turkey is a European country and even eligible to join the 'club'. The question of Turkey's membership of the EU has brought with it controversial issues. These include not only the issues of the 'borders of the EU' and its 'geographical limits' but, even more importantly, issues of European identity, Islam's place in Europe and its role in European society. Thus, Turkey raises uncomfortable religious and civilisational questions: will including such a large Muslim country, however secular, change the basic identity of the EU? Will it affect the further deepening of European Integration? Enlargement to include Turkey is bringing back what had been on the European periphery: religion, and its relation with politics.

Against this background, principal research questions addressed in this book are: what impact do culture, religion and identity issues have on Turkey's chances of joining the EU? Are they the principal reasons and factors behind the unwillingness of European actors to accept Turkey? The hypothesis that I want to test in this book is whether religious and cultural factors *per se* constitute a primary obstacle to Turkish accession, or whether it is the interaction with other factors that is responsible for prolonging and complicating Turkey's progress towards EU membership.

2.2 The history of the Westernisation of Turkey and of its relations with the EU

Historically Turkey is considered as a bridge between East and West, a unique and exceptional country both geographically and culturally. In the fourth century, its capital Constantinople (now Istanbul) was the centre of the Eastern Roman Empire. Founded in 324 in the old port city of Byzantium by Constantine, the Roman Emperor, it gained a major Christian population and contained many churches. The area known today as Turkey remained Christian for more than 1,000 years, until 1453 when Muhammad the Conqueror overcame Constantinople and the city fell to the Muslim Ottomans. They began the process of Islamisation of state and society which continued for 623 years under the Ottoman Empire.

Turkey's unique experiment with Westernisation, that is, modernisation and Europeanisation, has consisted of a 200-year 'love-and-hate relationship' with the West. In the mid-nineteenth century the Ottomans tried to adapt a European political, economic and social-cultural paradigm. To meet the challenge of an ever more powerful Europe, Sultan Mahmud II introduced what were known as the Tanzimat reforms, which, as Ozel writes, included legal equality for all subjects of the Empire, reform of the educational system, and a restructuring of the military and the ponderous Ottoman bureaucracy.[3] These reforms were later endorsed by the Young Turks, who came to power in 1908. Even though reforms aimed at Westernisation of the Ottoman state and society, as Kazancigil explains:

> Young Turks were mainly seeking a limited introduction of Western-type modernity in administration, justice and education, while leaving untouched the Islamic communitarian lifestyle and inter-personal relations that characterised the Turkish and other Muslim groups. They viewed the Western and the Ottoman civilisation as totally incompatible.[4]

The rule of the Young Turks ended in 1918 with the defeat of the Ottoman Empire in World War I. Kemalist elites, who came to power next, led by Kemal Atatürk, pushed through far more radical reforms to create a modern state, with Europe being treated as the model. Mustafa Kemal, who founded the Turkish Republic in 1923 on the ashes of the Empire, embarked on an ambitious political, social and cultural modernisation programme. He and the other founding fathers of modern Turkey wanted to make Turkey part of the European system of states. The principles of the new Republic were modernity, militarism, statism and secularism.[5] In the area of religion, reforms included abolition of the Caliphate, separation of religion and state, and complete secularisation of the educational and legal system. They aimed at transforming all the cultural and symbolic aspects associated with the Islamic way of life, including equal rights for women, reforming the language, and the creation of a new national and cultural identity, that of being Turkish.

During the second half of the twentieth century, Turkey commenced efforts to become part of the European political space, by joining European organisations. Turkey has been a member of the Council of Europe since its inception, in 1949. It was also one of the earliest members of the OEEC (since 1961). During this period Turkey established and maintained good links not only with Western Europe, but also with the USA. In 1952, Turkey joined NATO, becoming a reliable ally of the West throughout the Cold War.

However, the question is: have all segments of Turkish society have been supportive of the country's efforts towards Westernisation? What kind of national identity, Western or Middle-Eastern, does Turkish society prefer to embrace? Turkey has two souls,[6] only one of which is Western, and which tends to be confined to the cosmopolitan Istanbul elite and other metropolitan areas. The vast Asian interior is seen as backward, impoverished and 'non-European' in its values. Central Anatolia, with its rural economy and patriarchal, Islamic culture, is the heartland of this 'other' Turkey. It has little, if any, similarity to Europe in terms of law, history, culture, religion and perspectives of change.[7] One interesting comment was that of a journalist who wrote in an article in *The Times*:

> From the West, Turkey is where Asia begins. Westerners reaching Istanbul from Europe are drawn by the Otherness of the lands at whose gates the city stands. Here we feel we leave the West. That isn't how it feels when you enter Turkey from the Middle East. Crossing into Turkey seemed somehow like coming home. Coming in from Asia, Istanbul feels like Liverpool with mosques.[8]

Many see Turkey as a bridge between these two civilisations, European and Asian, Christian and Muslim. Huntington labels Turkey a 'torn country', divided over whether its society belongs to one civilisation or another.[9] He says that its leaders wish to pursue a band-wagoning strategy[10] and make the country a member of the West, even though the history, culture and traditions of the country are non-Western.[11] He argues that Turkey is the most obvious and prototypical torn country. The late twentieth-century leaders of Turkey have followed in the Atatürk tradition and defined Turkey as a modern, secular, Western nation-state. They allied Turkey with the West in NATO, and in the Gulf War, and they applied for membership to the EC. He argues that at the same time, however, elements of Turkish society have supported an Islamic revival and have argued that Turkey is basically a Middle-

Eastern Muslim society (significant elements in society resist the redefinition of their country's identity by the elite and the public divided is on this issue). In addition, he continues, while the elite of Turkey has defined Turkey as a Western society, the elite of the West refuses to accept Turkey as such. Huntington believes that Turkey will not become a member of the EC and that the real reason, as former President Ozal said, 'is that we are Muslim and they are Christian and they don't say that'. He then says that to redefine its identity, a torn country must meet three requirements: first, its political and economic elite have to be supportive and enthusiastic about this move. Second, its public has to be willing to acquiesce in the redefinition. Third, the dominant groups in the recipient civilisation have to be willing to embrace the convert. The first two in large part exist with respect to Turkey.[12]

Having rejected Mecca, where will Turkey look if now rejected by Brussels? Some analysts say that if rejected, Turkey may look to Middle East for allies and partnership. There is a growing sense among Turks that their country, cold-shouldered by Europe and neglected by America, has no choice but to follow its Asian destiny. As Kiniklioglu points out, 'formally Turkey remains in the Western camp, but it is increasingly the odd man out'.[13] Turkey has many times faced the dilemma of whether to go West or stay East. Therefore, the question of Westernisation or EU accession is linked with debates about national identity: 'Should we look west and join the EU?' is often synonymous with 'What kind of Turkey do we want?'. On the other hand, there are some who think that Turkey is a special or unique Muslim country, in which Islam has melded with a secular democracy, and which can serve as a role model for other countries in both the Middle East and in the wider Muslim world. They believe that a modern, democratic and secular Turkey could play a constructive role in promoting understanding between civilisations.

History of Turkey's relations with the EU: a genuine process or hypocrisy of the EU?

Applying for association with the EEC as early as 1959, Turkey has indeed had the longest and the most complicated relations with the EU of all countries that have become EU members. An Association Agreement signed with the EEC in September 1963 defined Turkey's accession to the Community as a long-term goal, and Turkey has been on a mission to join the Union since that date. In 1987, Turkey made a formal application to join the EC, but was disappointed to see its consideration postponed in 1989, which was, coincidentally, at the same time as the end of the Cold War. The Commission took its decision on the grounds that the Turkish economy was not sufficiently developed and that Turkish democracy did not guarantee political and civil rights, as well because of poor relations with Greece (including the conflict over Cyprus). However, Turkish–EU relations continued to improve, and in 1996 Turkey succeeded in joining a Customs Union. The next disappointment came at the Luxembourg Summit in 1997, which officially launched the process of EU eastern enlargement, but where EU leaders declined to grant candidate status to Turkey, on the grounds that it did not meet the Copenhagen criteria (human rights, etc). At that summit, candidate status for EU membership was granted to several post-communist countries, thereafter known as the 'Luxembourg group'. Only eight years earlier, most of them had been members of the antagonistic Warsaw Pact, and one of them, Estonia, had been a republic of the Soviet Union. More significantly, even in 1997 these countries also had their own shortcomings with regard to the Copenhagen criteria, as Tarifa and Adams point out.[14] At the Helsinki Summit in 1999 the status of candidate state was finally given to Turkey. After acquiring her new status, Turkey demonstrated great determination to comply with the Copenhagen criteria in order to be eligible for the opening of the accession talks. Successive governments began implementing reforms: several political reform packages and eight constitutional amendments were enacted between 1995 and 2004. Over just ten years the prospect of Turkey's accession to the EU caused the most significant political transformation the Republic of Turkey had experienced since the introduction of multi-party politics in 1945. The reward came in December 2004, with the European Council's decision to open accession negotiations with Turkey. After almost 50 years of knocking on the gates of Europe, Turkey was finally given a green light with the beginning of negotiations on 3 October 2005.

Nobody is able to predict whether Turkey will be successful at the end, although in the history of the Union no country which has started the accession process has failed to become a member.[15] However, in the case of Turkey, some are pessimistic and believe that Europe and Turkey are heading for a 'train crash'.[16] Indeed, accession talks have since been affected adversely by a number of domestic and external problems and a crash of sorts happened. In December 2006, the Council of Ministers decided to freeze eight of the 35 chapters of membership negotiations, as a punishment for Turkey's failure to open up ports to Cyprus.[17] Countries on Turkey's side rushed to offer consoling assurances. The then British Foreign Secretary, Margaret Beckett, said that, 'there is no train crash, the train is firmly on the tracks'. Some less supportive actors, such as Spanish Foreign Minister Miguel Moratinos, merely talked of 'a slowdown'. On the opposing side, however, Austrian Foreign Minister Ursula Plassnik insisted that, 'eight central areas are going to be put into the deep freeze'.[18] According to a report by the International Crisis Group, 'Turkey and the EU should work to speed up accession negotiations, after the recent loss of momentum'.[19] Seeing 2009 as crucial, the report notes:

Turkey is entering a critical year, in which its prospects for European Union membership are at make or break stage... Both sides need to recall how much they have to gain from each other and move quickly on several fronts to break out of this downward spiral before one or the other breaks off the negotiations, which could then well prove impossible to start again.[20]

So far (October 2009), only 11 chapters out of 35 have been opened with Turkey, and only one chapter has been successfully closed (Science and Research),[21] compared to 28 opened and 12 provisionally closed with Croatia (which began talks at the same time as Turkey).[22]

In the Turkey–EU relationship, we can distinguish two main periods. The first covers 1986–97, from Turkey's formal request for membership through to the Luxembourg Summit. The later part of this period (after 1990) coincides with the membership application and accession process of the eight CEE countries,[23] plus Cyprus and Malta. The second period covers 1999–2007, from the Helsinki Summit to the present. This also coincides with the starting of the accession process for another geopolitical group of countries, the Western Balkans. Even though Turkey applied and started the process much earlier than the ten 2004 accession countries, these have managed to join, while Turkey is still waiting. Similarly, prospective accession timetables have been given to some of the Western Balkan countries which only started the process in 1999, such as Croatia (2009)[24] and Macedonia (2013), but not to Turkey. In fact, the EU has accepted countries like Bulgaria and Romania as members before they fully met the criteria. So the question is: why this 'different treatment' for Turkey? Why were its applications twice turned down? Why has Turkey required the longest period of all countries from the Association Agreement to the opening of accession negotiations (1963–2005)? Why is the prospect of Turkish membership more contentious that that of any other country? Is it simply the non-fulfilment of Copenhagen criteria, or are there other factors?

In order to analyse these questions, I have adopted a threefold analytical distinction of the potential factors influencing Turkey's process, dividing them into three broad groups:

1. Domestic political and economic factors (related to the Copenhagen criteria) and other issues (Cyprus, Armenian, Kurdish) – as 'formal obstacles'.
2. Geo-institutional and security factors – as 'semi-formal obstacles'.
3. Religious and cultural factors – as 'informal obstacles'.

2.3 Formal obstacles: domestic political and economic factors and other (Cyprus, Kurdish and Armenian) issues

These are the obstacles that have to be overcome in order to comply with the Copenhagen criteria, whose fulfilment or not determine, at least in principle, whether a candidate country is ready to join.[25] In analysing the fulfilment of these criteria by Turkey, I will also point out both the benefits and drawbacks of Turkey's accession for the EU.

Political criteria

Turkish democracy traces its origin to 1950, when, after one-party rule by the Republican People's Party since 1922, an experiment with multi-party politics led to the electoral victory of the opposition Democratic Party. The ensuing three decades, from 1950 to 1980, were characterised by alternation of pluralistic politics, three military *coups d'état* and authoritarian interludes. Since the end of military rule in 1980–83, Turkey has gradually moved towards greater civilian control of their government. Finally, in the 1990s, Turkey appeared to have a stable democratic regime. Many important political and economic reforms have been undertaken, involving liberalisation of the political system, the strengthening of civil society, development of a market economy, increase of trade and investment, and integration of the country with foreign markets. In the last decade, especially after 1999, when Turkey acquired the candidate status, reforms began to work better. The current ruling party, the Justice and Development Party (AKP), is credited with introducing pro-Western democratic and economic reforms and contributing to a rising standard of living in Turkey. However, many analysts credit the prospect of EU membership, rather than the domestic actors, as the main catalyst for domestic reforms and deepening democracy. EU-necessitated reforms have forced Turkey not only to address its shortcomings, but also to confront many of its taboos.

However, despite the practice of multi-party elections in the country for over half a century, Turkey can hardly be considered a consolidated democracy, as Cebeci points out.[26] In spite of the progress to date, Turkey continues to lag behind European standards in many aspects. The European Commission's last annual Progress Reports of 2007 and 2008 on Turkey[27] award 'bad marks', saying that reforms have slowed down since accession negotiations opened two years ago, and it points to areas needing further progress, especially as regards civilian control of the military, the independence of the judiciary and the fight against corruption. Also, the 2009 Progress Report notes that 'Little progress can be reported on effective implementation of political and constitutional reforms'.[28]

Civil-military relations, principally a reduction of the role of the military in the political arena, remains a challenge. Despite broad European sympathy for the Turkish army's secular stance, the EU is worried by its nationalistic and interventionist approach. In the past four years constitutional reforms have (in theory) reduced the army's room for political manoeuvre and made it more accountable to Parliament. However, as the 2009 report points out, despite some progress, 'the armed forces have continued to exercise significant political influence via formal and informal mechanisms'.[29] Nationalist members of the army have expressed objections to their diminished powers, and this is a concern to some observers, since the army remains very popular with the people of Turkey.

However, the main criticism of the EU has to do with human rights and fundamental freedoms. The AKP has enacted some reforms, such as the abolition of death penalty, the prohibition of torture of prisoners, and improvements in women's, children's and trade unions' rights, etc. However, the human rights argument against Turkish membership remains a major stumbling block in negotiations. The 2008 report made clear that little had been achieved on human rights reforms during 2008. It also highlights that little additional reform work has been done to ratify key human rights instruments. According to the 2009 report Turkey has yet to ratify the Optional Protocol to the UN Convention against Torture they signed in 2005, and also three additional Protocols to the European Convention on Human Rights (ECHR).[30] Both reports note that the country has made little practical progress in eliminating torture and ill-treatment, which still are a cause for great concern.[31] Another document, the Annual Report on Human Rights 2009 of the British Foreign Office, also expresses concerns with regard to prisoners' treatment and torture, as well as freedom of religion, minority rights, children's and women's rights, and guaranteeing freedom of expression.[32]

Freedom of expression and freedom of the press are also matters of concern. The number of prosecutions of writers, academics, journalists and other intellectuals has increased in the last years, with charges being laid against individuals for simply expressing a critical opinion.[33] One of the key EU demands has been for the repeal of Article 301 of the Turkish penal code, which limited freedom of expression by making it an offence to 'denigrate Turkishness'. The Turkish legal system does not fully guarantee freedom of expression in line with European standards, noted the 2008 report. Reflecting on this, on 30 April 2008 the Turkish Parliament approved a softening of the law restricting freedom of speech.[34] The recent amendment of the 'infamous Article 301' was welcomed and described as 'a step forward' by EU Presidency, European Commission and Parliament, but they added that implementation must follow and further moves should be made to change similar articles in the penal code, because this was not the only one and there are other legal provisions representing an illegitimate restriction on freedom of expression.[35] The revision of Article 301, according to the 2009 report, led to a significant decline in prosecutions compared with previous year and this article is no longer used systematically to restrict freedom of expression.[36] However, the report says that there are still some prosecutions and convictions based on this article and furthermore a number of other provisions of the Turkish Criminal Code are used to restrict freedom of expression.[37]

With regard to the freedom of press, the disproportionate fine imposed on Dogan Media Holding, Turkey's largest media group, was cited as a source of concern in the 2009 report. Frequent website bans continue to be a cause for concern, with judicial and administrative decisions blocking entire websites. YouTube has been banned since May 2008 and court cases are pending against Facebook, Google sites, and other sites.[38]

Turkey also lags behind democratic standards in freedom of religion. The European Parliament's report of 2006, and the EU Council in its document *Religious Freedom in Turkey*, considers this key to Turkey's accession.[39] They note that there are abuses and discrimination based on religious belief and practice, and report a number of religiously motivated killings, threats and attacks on non-Muslims and churches in the name of 'cleaning Turkey of non-Muslims'. One high-profile killing was that of three Christians at a publishing house in Malatya in April 2007, for which the court case is still ongoing. Minority religious communities also continue to experience difficulties in relation to property rights, training and education.[40] Regarding places of worship, non-Muslim religious communities report frequent discrimination and administrative uncertainty, as the 2009 report points out. Attacks against minority religions still occur. Members of minority religious groups have claimed that their worship activities are monitored and recorded by security forces. Missionaries are widely perceived as a threat to the integrity of the country and to the Muslim religion. Personal documents, such as ID cards, still include information on religion, leaving potential for discriminatory practices.[41] The paradox is that the headquarters of the Secretariat for the entry of Turkey into the European Union is, according to an article in the *Daily Telegraph*, in a building confiscated from the Orthodox Christian community in the 1990s. The building is located in Istanbul, in the well-known area of Ortakoy, under the first bridge over the Bosphorus. Before the seizure, the building was used as a primary school for children of the minority Orthodox of this area. Here once lived a thriving Orthodox community, now non-existent because of past purges against religious minorities.[42] But it is not just the government. A recent survey of Turkish public opinion revealed:[43]

- More than half of Turks oppose non-Muslim religious meetings;
- 59 per cent of those surveyed said non-Muslims either 'should not' or 'absolutely should not' be allowed to hold

open meetings where they can discuss their ideas;
- 54 per cent said non-Muslims either 'should not' or 'absolutely should not' be allowed to publish literature that describes their faith;
- 49 per cent of those surveyed said they would either 'absolutely' or 'most likely' not support a political party that accepted people from another religion.

Non-respect for women's rights remains a very problematic issue of Turkish society. Despite recent amendments to the country's Constitution and the establishment of a Parliamentary Committee on Gender Equality in March 2009, Turkey has a long road ahead of it in narrowing its gender gap. Gender equality, according to 2009 report remains a major challenge.[44] In a recent international study, Turkey ranked an embarrassing 105th out of 115 countries, far behind the worst-ranking EU member. Political representation of women, at both national and regional levels, is very low: Turkey has the lowest number of women in Parliament. Women's participation in the labour market is the lowest level among EU Member States and OECD countries.[45] Turkey has the highest rates of female illiteracy.[46] Women's access to education is also the lowest among the EU Member States and OECD countries.[47] Domestic violence, polygamy, honour killings, early and forced marriages, and discriminatory practices continue to be widespread.[48] Most Turkish women are still not fully aware of their rights. A European Parliament committee report called on the Turkish government to take further action ensure gender equality, in access to education and the labour market, especially in the south-eastern regions.[49] Many believe that Turkey is still a highly patriarchal society. A proof of this is the new draft Constitution,[50] which describes women as a vulnerable group needing protection. More than 80 women's groups in Turkey have condemned it, saying it sets the country back years in terms of gender equality.[51]

In the area of minority rights, Turkey's approach remains restrictive.[52] Treatment and discrimination of other minorities, such as ethnic minorities (Jews, Armenians, Greeks), religious minorities (Christians, non-Sunni Muslims, Alevis, Baha'is), racial minorities (Roma, where issues of racism are widespread) and gender minorities (e.g. homosexuals) are also of concern. The nationalists believe that implementation of minority rights would result in Turkey's dissolution. This has its roots in the Kemalist principle of a single Turkish national identity. As Posch notes, according to Kemalism, any public sign of ethnicity, such as the use of a language other than Turkish, has to be seen as a potential threat to the unity and harmony of the nation.[53] Indeed, restrictions remain, particularly on use of languages other than Turkish in TV and radio broadcasting, political life, education and contacts with public services, as the 2009 report point out.[54]

Economic criteria

Turkey also raises concerns from an economic perspective. Despite the economic progress (high growth and an increasing volume of FDI) as a result of reforms undertaken by the AKP, Turkey remains a poor country, with unstable growth, high levels of public debt and unemployment, and low GDP per capita. In the Eurobarometer No. 66, the economic concerns were the second highest for EU citizens (77 per cent; +1 point).[55] Europeans see the economics from a pragmatic/utilitarian point of view, that is, they support enlargement if they perceive the benefits to be larger than the costs. There is a perception among European people that a reallocation of resources to Anatolia would seriously strain the EU economy, and that Turkey's entry will disturb the balance of the EU budget drastically and harm the European economy more than any member in the past. The EU may need to give significant investment and financial aid to Turkey, and this means a burden to European taxpayers. Another concern, which comes especially from the recipient member states, is about EU structural and cohesion funding, which would result in huge transfer payments and subsidies from EU countries to Turkey.[56]

Turkey has a large agricultural sector, which employs 50 per cent of the active population. This would have an impact on the CAP (Common Agricultural Policy), which means an enormous burden for the EU agricultural budget, given the fact that it will add billions of Euros to the Union's farm subsidies. Both the EU's CAP and agriculture in Turkey will need further reform.[57]

Another point of concern for Europeans is the potentially massive immigration of poor Turkish job-seekers to affluent EU member states. This could have unpredictable socio-economic consequences. According to Eurobarometer 66, more than six out of ten persons fear that Turkish membership would encourage immigration to the most developed countries in the EU (66 per cent; +3 points).

For the proponents of Turkey's membership, the economics seem advantageous (as with the 2004 accession countries): a large market with much opportunity for foreign investment and supply of raw materials, as well as a young and cheap labour force, could be to Europe's benefit. However, the Eurobarometer 66 showed that one respondent out of two is sceptical about the beneficial effects of Turkish membership in terms of decreasing the average age of the European population.

Other specific issues

The Cyprus issue

The Cyprus issue has become both a cause and a symptom of the ups and downs in the EU–Turkey relationship. Turkish policy towards Cyprus, which is depicted by some as 'illegal occupation'[58] of EU territory, has been considered (at least officially) as the major obstacle in the membership negotiations. Since the invasion of the northern part of the island by Turkey in 1974 (to counter a Greek-Cypriot coup), the island has been divided into two parts: Greek-Cypriot and Turkish-Cypriot. Cyprus is recognised as a state by all countries, except Turkey, who recognises only the 'Turkish Republic of Northern Cyprus'. Turkey (backed by Britain) advocates this decision on the ground that the EU should not have accepted Cyprus before its unification. The 2004 entry of the Republic of Cyprus into the EU as a divided country imported this frozen conflict into the heart of Europe, and created an unbreakable triangle between the EU, Turkey and Cyprus. An attempt to unify the island was made in 2004 through a referendum. But the UN reunification plan, known as Annan Plan, failed when the Greek-Cypriots rejected it overwhelmingly, although the Turkish-

Cypriots voted strongly in favour.[59] Dismayed by the Greek rejection, the EU promised the north aid to lift it out of economic isolation. As 'revenge' for the continued economic isolation of Northern Cyprus and the failure of the EU to keep its promise of 2004 to end this isolation, Turkey closed its ports and airports to Cypriot ships and aeroplanes.[60] This refusal to open the ports to trade with Cyprus led the European Council to take a decision in December 2006 to suspend negotiations on eight chapters, even though Turkish officials have insisted that this issue should be left out of the talks.[61] Furthermore, due to freezes linked to Cyprus, Turkey is unable to start negotiations on at least half of the 35 candidacy chapters.

A resolution of the European Parliament in November 2007 says that 'the withdrawal of Turkish forces would facilitate the negotiation of a settlement', and urged the Turkish government 'to implement the provisions stemming from the Association Agreement and its Additional Protocol', in other words, to open up to Cypriot ships and planes.[62] Even though the Turkish Prime Minister has shown some flexibility over the island, the military is strongly opposed to any concessions. Talking about this issue, the then Greek Foreign Minister Dora Bakoyannis said in her talk at St Antony's College, Oxford:

Turkey wants to become a member of the EU, but refuses to recognise one of its members (which is a condition for EU membership), it wants to do trade with the EU, but keeps its ports closed to one of its members. It is Turkey that should adapt to the EU, not the way around, as all the member states have done.[63]

As ICG states, 'this [2009] is a critical year for Cyprus as efforts to resolve the long conflict gather steam, and for Turkey as frustration with EU enlargement fatigue weighs heavy on its chances of approaching membership'.[64] With Cyprus now a member state of the EU, and troops from NATO-member Turkey still in the northern half of the island, the inter-relationships are many. A settlement process is underway, which could lead to the reunification of the island.[65]

After five months of full-fledged negotiations, talks between the Greek and Turkish Cypriot leaders are moving consistently forward. Some areas of agreement have emerged, and Greek and Turkish Cypriot leaders concluded an initial discussion on governance and power-sharing at the beginning of 2009.[66] However, Turkey's relationship with Cyprus was considered one of the unresolved issues in the 2008 EC report, which says 'the country's continued failure to implement in full the Ankara Agreement, by not opening its ports and airports to traffic from Cyprus, remains a significant obstacle to further progress'.[67]

The Kurdish issue

Kurds, who live in the south-east of the country, are Turkey's main ethnic minority, comprising 20 per cent of the population. Historically the Turkish authorities have denied them linguistic and cultural rights and political representation. One of the main reasons for this discrimination has been fear for Turkish territorial integrity, the guiding principle behind policies towards the Kurdish minority. Speaking Kurdish in public was banned until the 1990s, as it was seen as a threat to national unity. However, since Turkey was accepted as an EU candidate country in 1999 the democratic rights of Kurds have improved. Significant measures are taken to advance Kurdish minority rights, such as political and cultural rights, and rights in education. Newspapers and CDs in Kurdish are now available, along with some radio and television broadcasts. A nationwide 24-hour public Kurdish-language television channel began broadcasting after legislation was passed in June 2008. Furthermore, in March 2009, the Turkish government commissioned the translation of the Koran into Kurdish, as part of its efforts to grant more cultural rights for the Kurdish minority. However, constraints still remain on political campaigning and education in the Kurdish language.[68] Kurdish is still banned in all state institutions and official correspondence. Ethnic Kurdish politicians who use their mother tongue are still prosecuted on a regular basis. A recent case was that of a prominent Kurdish politician and MP, Ahmet Turk, who switched languages from Turkish to his native Kurdish while giving a speech in Parliament on 24 February 2009. The live broadcast on state TV was immediately cut, as the Kurdish language is banned in Parliament. Mr Turk faced suspension, accused of fuelling separatism. But his action was praised by Kurdish people and politicians, who described the speech as a brave move, long overdue, and they called for all restrictions on the use of Kurdish to be lifted.[69]

Denial of linguistic rights to one-fifth of Turkey's population has generated Kurdish terrorism, which has plagued the country for more than 20 years. The Kurdistan Workers' Party (PKK) is considered not only by Turkey, but also by the US and the EU, as a terrorist organisation. It has been using its havens in northern Iraq to stage attacks inside Turkey. Turkey has repeatedly warned that failure inside Iraq to act against the terrorists could lead to intervention by Turkey's own armed forces. The revival of PKK terrorist activities during 2007 (including the killing of more than 30 Turkish soldiers and civilians) posed a threat to peace and stability, and not only in Turkey. In the first months of 2008 Turkey sent forces over the Iraqi border following attacks on Turkish troops by the PKK. However, the government's muscular response to the PKK's attacks risked exacerbating the geopolitical crisis in this fragile region. The EU Presidency condemned as 'terrorist violence' the attacks in Turkish territory by the Kurdish PKK, but advised Turkey not to launch military action for the fear of regional destabilisation.

The Armenian issue
The Armenian issue has become a sensitive matter for the Turkish people and government. Armenia holds Turkey accountable for a genocide supposedly committed by Ottoman forces during the World War I (in 1915), in which 2 million Armenians died, and has asked for an apology. Turkey maintains that it was not a genocide, but rather a deportation following Armenian massacres of Muslims. What is worse, this issue has become one of the

obstacles in the EU's own negotiations. French politicians have even said that Turkey must accept the alleged genocide in order to become a member of the EU. In 2006, the French Parliament approved a bill criminalising the denial of the alleged genocide. Many believe that France's 400,000-strong Armenian community, which is very powerful and well-organised, was instrumental in having the bill considered.[70] The episode caused outrage among many Turks. Some consider this to be ethnic politics at its finest, where the national interest takes a back seat to raking over animosities and events which have taken place long ago (nearly one hundred years ago in this case), far away and in a very different context (carried out by the Ottoman Empire, which no longer exists). The European Parliament has also urged Turkey to recognise the Armenian deaths during World War I as genocide, but Turkey denies responsibility, saying that the events were part of a civil war during the final years of the Ottoman Empire. Ankara has called for joint research of the events of the years of World War I, a proposal that has not been welcomed by Armenia. It is even illegal in Turkey to refer to it as the 'Armenian Genocide' – Akgunduz notes – and Turks consider the issue neither historical nor scientific, but solely political.[71] Turkey regards it as another excuse on the part of the EU, pointing out that recognition of historical events has never been a precondition for other states.

However, on 22 April 2009 the foreign ministers of Turkey and Armenia announced a framework to normalise relations, which delivered results on 10 October when they signed, in Zurich, two protocols to re-establish diplomatic relations and reopen their common border, which has been closed since 1993.[72] This new development to normalise Armenian–Turkish relations moves Turkey closer to the fulfilment of one of the conditions laid down by the EU for its accession. It was greeted enthusiastically in the recent Commission report as a historic step contributing to stability and peace in the region.[73]

2.4 Semi-formal obstacles: geography, demography, security and institutional factors

The geographic factor

Geography is sometimes mentioned as a reason why Turkey cannot be part of the EU, as only ten per cent of it lies in Europe, while the rest, including the capital, rests in Anatolia, part of Asia Minor. Those who base their opposition to Turkey on this factor say that to be part of the EU, a country should belong physically to the European continent and lie within the natural borders of Europe, defined as being from the Atlantic to the Urals[74] (*Readers Digest Universal Dictionary*, Wikipedia etc). The existing geographical definition of Europe ends at the Bosphorus and the Dardanelles, and when you pass onto the other side of Bosphorus Bridge there is a road-sign that says 'Welcome to Asia'. The *Almanac of World History* (National Geographic) specifies that Turkey is an Asian Minor country.

All the countries that have applied so far for EU membership have been situated within European territory, with the exception of Morocco, which applied for EC membership in 1987, and was rejected outright as ineligible precisely on the grounds of being not a European country, but African. Israel too has expressed some interest in joining, but it has been made clear by the EU that this is not possible, again on the grounds of geography,[75] even though Israel is closer culturally to Europe than is Turkey.

The EU treaties and legislation use the term 'European state' as a prerequisite for EU membership. Article 49 of the TEU says, 'Any European state, which respects fundamental democratic principles, may apply to become a member of the European Union'. The Lisbon Treaty, which has not yet been ratified, states that the 'Union is open to all European states respecting its values and willing to collectively further these values'.[76] Similarly, the Commission's conclusion from the frequent discussions during recent years about the ultimate borders of the European Union is that 'the term European combines geographical, historical and cultural elements'.[77]

The proponents of Turkey's membership argue that this barrier was overcome some time ago when Turkey was accepted as a candidate country. Moreover, they can point to examples of EU territories that are geographically outside the physical map of Europe. Malta (halfway towards the African coast) and Cyprus (closer to Syria and Lebanon than to Europe) are full member states. The Spanish Canary Islands are in the Atlantic off the north-west coast of Africa, but are part of the EU and use the Euro. The French *départements d'outre-mer* of Guiana on the northern coast of South America, Martinique and the Guadeloupe Archipelago in the Caribbean Sea, Réunion in the Indian Ocean, the small islands of Saint Pierre and Miquelon off the eastern coast of Canada near Newfoundland, are also all part of the EU and thus use the Euro. The Netherlands Antilles are in the Caribbean; the residents are EU citizens but have tenuous connections to the continent of Europe.[78] However, all these territories and islands are only part of the EU because they are part of member states and they did not become part of the Union through their own application. According to Eurobarometer 66, 56 per cent (+2 points) of respondents consider that Turkey belongs partly to Europe by virtue of its geography.

The demographic and 'size' factors

Turkey is a big country with a big population. The country's size is greater than the territories of the ten 2004 accession countries taken together, while its population of almost 72 million would, within ten years, likely overtake that of the EU's currently most populous country, Germany. Turkey's size has two implications for the EU: economic and institutional. When a large country is also poor, as in the case of Turkey, it has economic disadvantages for the Union. Institutional implications are explained below. Size creates another implication when combined with religion, which is analysed in the final chapter. The impact of the 'size' factor was seen when the French National Assembly approved, on 29 May 2008, a bill making referenda obligatory for accepting new EU member countries with populations accounting for over 5 per cent of the bloc's entire size, which would make it necessary to hold a referendum on Turkey's accession.

For the proponents, the demographic factor, the country's large and young population (23 per cent of which is under 15), is seen as an advantage that can compensate for the labour shortages in Western Europe, with her rapidly shrinking and ageing population.

Institutional factors

By the time of accession, Turkey is likely to be the most populous member state, which will entitle her to the largest political representation and voting weight in the EU's institutions, including the European Council and the European Parliament, in which political representation is determined by population. This has created unease among many Brussels officials and MEPs, who worry that this would affect future balances of political power in the EU institutions and voting reallocation. In the European Parliament, if accepted in 2015, Turkey will have 82 seats, the same number as Germany.[79] Jonathan Evans MEP argues that many see this as a direct challenge to the current EU voting balance between member states.[80] As a Danish newspaper points out, 'the demographic and Islamic threat is nothing compared to the frightening political power, as Turkey would be able to impose on European legislation if accepted as a member of EU'.[81]

The other reason has to do with the Union's absorption capacity as a response to the Union's 'enlargement fatigue'. Turkey's membership is associated with the fear that the Union would not function properly and would collapse administratively under its weight. Some, such as former European Commissioner Fritz Bolkestein, believe that for an overstretched Europe to include Turkey will create either chaos, or a bureaucratic monstrosity in Brussels.[82] Furthermore, if Turkey comes in, then Ukraine, Georgia, Armenia, Moldova and Belarus, countries with far better European credentials than Turkey, will want to join too. Therefore, it was agreed that, before proceeding with further enlargements, new institutional settlements should be arranged, if the EU is to avoid paralysis. The first result of this was the endorsement by the Council in December 2006 of the Union's 'absorption capacity' as an additional criterion for accession for new applicant countries. It means, firstly, the capacity of the Union to accept and accommodate more members, and, secondly, the continued acceptance of new members while at the same time maintaining the dynamic of European integration. Or, in other words, 'we should enlarge as much as it works'.[83] The term 'absorption capacity' was later replaced by a new concept: 'integration capacity'. Some argue that the trendy 'absorption/integration capacity' is just an excuse to delay the accession of new countries and, most importantly, to keep Turkey out. However, the opponents of Turkey note that 'absorption capacity' is mentioned in the Copenhagen criteria: 'The Union's capacity to absorb new members, while maintaining the momentum of European integration, is an important consideration in the general interest, both of the Union and of candidate countries', and that it is therefore not a new idea invented just for the sake of Turkey.

Security and energy

Another factor relates to security issues and EU foreign policy. Turkey's borders are contiguous with the Middle East, a region plagued by conflict, instability and terrorism. Its neighbours include Islamic regimes, such as Syria and Iran, international hotspots, such as Iraq and Afghanistan, and other problematic countries whose names end with '-stan'. Extending the frontiers of the EU to 'unsafe' territories of Central Asia, according to the opponents of Turkey's membership, would be an overstretch for the EU's security, and they therefore advise that Turkey be left as a 'buffer' to protect Europe from these troublesome countries.

On the other hand, the proponent states, such as Britain and the USA, see the security issue as an advantage, arguing that Turkey will serve as an anchor of stability in one of the most unstable and insecure regions in the world and that inclusion of Turkey may increase the soft power of the Union. Turkey can be a bridge between Europe and not just the Middle East, but also the wider

Muslim world, as well as a model for promotion of democracy in Muslim countries. However, former Director at the DG for Enlargement at the European Commission, Graham Avery, said, 'the concept of a bridge to Islamic world is very sentimental and not based on sound reason, as if Turkey joins, the EU borders will touch dangerous countries'.[84] Other proponents point to the fact that Turkey has a good relationship not only with the USA, but also with the principal US ally in the Middle East, Israel, which could alienate it from other Muslim countries.[85] Another argument in favour is that Turkey is a strong military power that could make a significant military contribution to the EU's common security and defence policies. The Turkish Armed Forces (half a million strong) are the second-largest force in NATO after the USA, and the strongest in the Muslim world.[86] These military capabilities would boost the EU's fledgling defence power.

The Eurobarometer 66 shows that only a third of European Union citizens feel that Turkish membership would strengthen security in the region (33 per cent; –2 points), while more than half (51 per cent; +3points) disagree.

Some point to another advantage, namely, energy security. They stress that Turkey is a key hub for energy-hungry European member states. It could help boost EU energy security, as new non-Russian oil and gas fields are developed in the Caucasus and Middle East, including Iraq. Turkey is set to become one of the world's most important energy-transit states. It could also become the EU's most important energy gateway, lying as it does close to 71 per cent of the world's proven gas, and 73 per cent of its oil, resources.[87] The EU is looking to cut back its dependence on Russia for gas imports following cuts to their supplies in recent years, which have left consumers in Western Europe without fuel in the dead of winter.[88] The answer lies in diversification, and Turkey may hold the key. Russia is planning two of its own new gas pipelines to Europe, the Nord Stream, which will run direct from Russia to Germany under the Baltic Sea, and the South Stream, which will run from southern Russia under the Black Sea to Bulgaria. While Russia wishes to build these two pipelines to pump more Russian gas to Europe, Turkey is planning the Nabucco[89] pipeline to pump non-Russian gas to the EU. It could also provide Iraqi oil with a valuable gateway to the EU.

At an energy summit in Prague on 8 May 2009, Turkish President Abdullah Gül signed a declaration promising to close an inter-governmental agreement in June on building the Nabucco natural gas pipeline. On 13 July 2009, four EU countries (Romania, Bulgaria, Hungary and Austria) signed an agreement with Turkey to construct the long-planned 3,300 km pipeline.[90] Once completed, the line will bring up to 31 billion cubic metres of gas a year from the Caspian Sea and the Middle East across Turkey and directly to the EU by 2025. It will provide an important alternative energy supply to Russia, which already meets 30 per cent of Europe's gas needs and will break Russia's monopoly on natural gas. According to *Voice of America* news, the signing of the agreement has raised eyebrows in Russia. Leading Russian newspapers have called the deal between Austria, Bulgaria, Hungary, Romania and Turkey a setback for Moscow's pipeline projects to Europe. The official publication of the Russian government, *Rossiyskaya Gazeta*, said, 'experts have long considered Nabucco to be stillborn, but the situation has now changed'.[91] The US Senator Richard Lugar, who represented the USA at the signing ceremony in Ankara, as well as EU Commission President Jose Manuel Barroso, welcomed the project. The latter said that Nabucco diversifies sources and brings together reliable clients, suppliers and routes.[92]

Turkey is currently stressing, and, indeed, using, the link between cooperation on energy and progress, in the accession talks.[93]

The world financial crisis

The recent financial crisis, which has plagued the whole world as well as Europe, is having its own implications on the issue of further EU expansion. It seems that the economic crisis has made national governments increasingly sensitive to claims that foreign workers from new EU countries, such as Poland or the Czech Republic, are taking up domestic jobs at a time when domestic unemployment is rising and labour markets are contracting. As a result, member states want to put on hold the further expansion of the Union, over fears of a growing backlash against migrant workers. The German and Dutch governments have effectively put a block on any further eastwards EU enlargement, fearing that it could stoke tensions over unemployment during the economic crisis; Spain, France and Belgium also share these concerns about further EU expansion. During February 2009, mass demonstrations in Ireland, the collapse of the government in Latvia, and most especially the protests at the Lindsay oil refinery in Lincolnshire, UK, over jobs taken by migrant EU workers, demonstrated the extent of the popular backlash, and set alarm bells ringing across Europe. Britain was widely seen as the EU country most open to expansion and foreign workers, so the 'British jobs for British workers' protests were seen as a turning point.[94] The UK, Ireland and Sweden were the only EU member states that allowed workers from the 2004 accession countries to have rights of work and social security benefits. Other member states had promised to do this, but, in the context of the financial crisis, some, such as Germany and Austria, have declared an extension of restrictions on the free movement of workers from the eight CEE countries of the 2004 accession, as of the end of April 2009. Eleven EU countries have already decided to extend their restrictions on the newest members, Bulgaria and Romania, until 2012. Politicians fear that issues of enlargement and free movement of workers in an economic crisis will be difficult to sell to EU electorates, and the question of jobs being lost to workers from new accession countries is expected to be a major issue in election campaigns in some member states, such as Germany.[95] Thus, the financial crisis is another factor which negatively affects the prospect of imminent EU membership for countries next in line, including Turkey.

2.5 Informal obstacles: religious and cultural factors

Turkey is a unique Muslim country, in terms of its history, culture and religion, as we saw at the beginning of this chapter. It has been a secular country since Atatürk established the Republic, and secularism has been a constitutional principle since 1937. Secular reforms even before then included abolition of Islamic institutions (the Caliphate[96] and the Ministry of Shari'a) and separation of religion from the state. So, if Turkey is a secular democratic state, why do many Europeans view or perceive Turkish as Muslim and alien? Why do they not believe that Turkey is sufficiently secular in the European sense? I attempt to offer an explanation below.

The first reason is that the guardian of secularism in Turkey is the army, rather than the political or civilian actors of the state.[97] Turkey is secular, but has its own kind of secularism, known as Kemalism, modelled after the French concept of *laïcité*. Kazancigil considers Kemalist secularism to be a mixture of French Jacobinist laicism and the Ottoman tradition of keeping religion under the control of a strong state.[98] Kemalists, as Posch points out, perceive political Islam, Kurdish nationalism and European liberalism as their main challenges.[99] This Turkish version of laicism, as Hurd argues, is an alternative trajectory of secularisation.[100] She says, 'Turkey cannot be expected to follow either a Judeo-Christian secularist model of secularisation or a laicist trajectory of secularisation, both of which evolved over the course of centuries. Although Turkey is secular in some sense, key decision makers in Europe and the majority of the European public do not believe it to be sufficiently secular in the European sense', adding that 'Turkey does not share the common cultural and religious ground that serves to anchor European forms of secularism and by extensions, European democracy'. Similarly, Oliver Roy says, 'Turkey does not share the fund of Christianity that serves as a foundation of laicism itself'.[101]

Second, secularism was forcefully imposed by the state, and thus was not embraced widely by social and political groups, which helps to explain the revival of political Islam in last decade. As Kazancigil argues, 'because it was forcefully imposed by the state, the large majority of the population considered it a violation of the liberty to practice their Islamic faith'.[102] The pluralist democracy introduced in the 1950s started to create problems for state-imposed secularism, and religious freedom became an electoral issue. After 1950 some political leaders tried to benefit from popular attachment to religion by espousing support for programmes and policies that appealed to the religiously inclined. Islamist parties appeared on the political scene in the 1970s, and were part of three coalition governments until 1980. Such efforts were opposed by most of the political elite, who believed that secularism was an essential principle of Kemalist ideology. This disinclination to appreciate religious values and beliefs gradually led to a polarisation of society, which became especially evident in the 1980s as a new generation of educated, but religiously motivated local leaders emerged to challenge the dominance of the secularised political elite. These new leaders have been assertively proud of Turkey's Islamic heritage and generally have been successful at adapting familiar religious idioms to describe dissatisfaction with various government policies. By their own example of piety, prayer and political activism, they have helped to spark a revival of Islamic observance in Turkey. In the early 1990s, the decline of the left also contributed to the rise of the political Islam.[103] By 1994, slogans promising that a return to Islam would cure economic ills and solve the problems of bureaucratic inefficiencies had enough general appeal to enable avowed religious candidates to win mayoral elections in Istanbul and Ankara, and led to the victory of the Islamist Welfare Party in 1997 and of the AKP in 2002.

The third argument is that Turkey is a secular country, but nonetheless a Muslim society; it was secularised at the official level, but religion has always remained a strong force at the mass level. Despite Kemalist secularist reforms, 623 years of Ottoman rule had left a deep legacy of Islamism. Turkey has an Islamic culture, which means a different set of values. For example, 60 per cent of Turkish women wear headscarves, including the wives and daughters of the President and Prime Minister.[104] Roy says:

> Turkey will be rejected from the EU not because the Turkish state fails to satisfy the EU demands to democratise, which would be a good reason, but because Turkish society is not 'European'...The reluctance shown by European public opinion to envisage the entry of Turkey into the EU is largely linked to it being a Muslim country.[105]

Fourth, Turkey has difficulties even at the stage of the Copenhagen criteria. The first political criterion states that the candidate country should 'guarantee human rights and the respect for and protection of minorities'. Many believe that Turkey will 'fail the exam' on this criterion alone, because of its insufficient respect for freedoms and human rights, women's rights in particular. Despite the efforts of the government (such as they have made in recent legislation on equal rights), this will be very difficult to enforce, as discrimination is rooted in society's cultural and religious social fabric. Issues of freedom of religion and freedom of expression are also related to Turkish culture and religion and, as such, are very difficult change. One of the articles of the Turkish penal code still in force, as mentioned earlier, is the notorious Article 301, which limits freedom of expression and makes it a crime to insult Turkish identity. Many writers, intellectuals, journalists and human rights activists have been prosecuted under this Article for simply expressing a critical, but non-violent, opinion, as in the prosecution of Nobel Prize winner Orhan Pamuk for defaming 'Turkishness'. The criminal charges brought against this prominent Turkish author and Europhile were for statements he made during an interview with a Swiss paper in 2005 on the Armenian and Kurdish issues, which provided grounds for allegations that Ottoman Turkey had committed genocide against Armenians during the World War I. The same Article was used to prosecute the murdered journalist Hrant Dink for commenting on the killings of Armenians by Turks in the early twentieth century. On 4 December 2008 a Turkish court sentenced politician and Sakharov Prizewinner Leyla Zana to ten years in prison for 'violating' the Turkish penal code and the Turkish anti-terror law in nine different speeches.[106]

Another form of discrimination rooted in cultural and religious mentality is that towards women. Women's rights are considered by the European Commission as a major issue in the context of EU enlargement, and as a fundamental part of human rights and of the democratisation process of any candidate country.[107] As we saw in previous sections, women's inequality, mistreatment and subjection to violence (especially domestic violence), polygamy, honour killings, early and forced marriages, low levels of participation in the labour market and in political representation, poor access of girls to education, and other discriminatory practices continue to be widespread, and most of Turkey continues to be a highly patriarchal society. Therefore, Nimet Çubukçu, Turkey's State Minister of Women's and Children's Affairs, stresses that it is not enough to adopt new laws, but that these laws also need to be implemented: 'The greatest need is for social and cultural change', she said.[108]

Thus Turkey is unable to comply with the political Copenhagen criteria, not only because this requires a fundamental review of the basic constitutional tenets upon which Turkish political society rests, but, most importantly, because these are related to Islamic values, mentality and social norms, which are rooted deeply in the social fabric of Turkish society. These limitations of fundamental freedoms, which are heavily criticised by the EU[109] and attract the highest scores of opposition in opinion polls, are related to Islamic values (see the next chapter), and therefore Turkish governments will continue to face a real challenge in addressing them.

I want to conclude this chapter with an argument of Elisabeth Hurd who, in an article that examines the cultural basis of European opposition to Turkish accession to the EU, argues that:

> Even if economic and political obstacles to Turkey's accession are lifted, even if Turkey is deemed to be in unambiguous conformity with the Copenhagen criteria, European opposition to Turkish membership will persist, because the Turkish case is controversial in cultural and religious terms as it involves the potential accession of a Muslim-majority country to an arguable, at least historically, Christian Europe.[110]

In other words, fulfilment of the Copenhagen criteria or other specific issues seems to be a fig-leaf to hide the real religion- and culture-based reservations. In the next chapters we will continue to explore and assess how true this argument may be.

3

THE COMPATIBILITY OF ISLAM WITH DEMOCRACY

3.1 Western and Muslim values: are they in harmony or do they conflict?

Talking about civilisations and the differences amongst them, Huntington argues that:

> Civilisations are differentiated from each other by history, language, culture, tradition and most important religion. The people of different civilisations have different views on the relations between God and man, the individual and the group, the citizen and the state, parents and children, husband and wife, liberty and authority, equality and hierarchy.[1]

These differences are the product of centuries, and will not disappear quickly. They are also more fundamental than differences among political ideologies.

Western values represent the values of modern Western civilisation.[2] They are often described as 'universal' values, perhaps because they represent values connected with the highest, most progressive and sophisticated form of a political regime, namely, liberal-democracy. As such, it is assumed that they should be embraced by everybody and by all countries for their own good and progress. These values are: democracy, pluralism, tolerance, fundamental freedoms,[3] human rights, equality (before the law, and between men and women), liberty, the rule of law, the separation of church and state, individualism, liberalism and constitutionalism. Modern Western societies base their philosophical principles, political and economic institutions and social structures on the values of liberal-democracy; therefore, all social, political and economic structures of these societies embody the values of tolerance, pluralism and individual freedoms. The embedding of these values has made Western societies successful, politically, economically and intellectually. Politically they enjoy freedoms, pluralism of political parties and good governance, conduct free elections, and have low levels of corruption and organised crime. Economically, their capitalist economies have proved to be a wealth-generating system, providing high standards of living for their citizens.

Some scholars attribute the formation of this Western system of values to the Christian religion. In his revised book, *Democracy in Europe*, Larry Siedentop says:

> Christianity provided the moral foundations of modern democracy, by creating a moral status for individuals, which was eventually translated into a social status or role.[4] Christian ontology provided the foundation for what are usually described as liberal values in the West: for the commitment to equality and reciprocity, as well as the postulate of individual freedom. Also the superb spread of the language of human rights throughout the world in recent decades, to the point where it has become almost a universal culture, should also be recognised for what it is, the ultimate and least resistible form of Western influence...There is a deep connection between Christianity and liberalism: the former provided, historically, the normative foundation for the latter.[5]

Similarly, Charles Taylor argues that 'Religion is part of the moral basis of Western civilisation',[6] while Cox and Marks note that 'These values were historically rooted in Ancient Greece and developed by peoples influenced primarily by Judaeo-Christian traditions'.[7]

Muslim values, on the other hand, represent values of a different civilisation. They, as Katzenstein and Byrnes note, 'were set before the division of globe into individual legal entities called states'.[8] Islam, which stands at the basis of Muslim culture and values, is an encompassing religion that addresses all aspects of individual and social life: from law to politics, from diet to socialisation. Like Judaism, Islam believes in a divine law that regulates all aspects of human activity, including even food and drink. As Tariq Ramadan states, 'Islam, more than a simple and codified link between the Believer and God, is a concept and a way of life'.[9] In particular, its traditional form represents a direct, close and continuous interaction between religion, politics, and social and educational aspects of life. For Muslims, truth is the word of Allah as recited to his Prophet Mohammed and recorded in the Koran, so the Koran, revealed over a period of 23 years (between 610–632 BC) is the Word of God. It is supplemented by the 'Hadith', which are the Prophet's teachings, that is, evidenced through his sayings and actions.[10] The Koran and Hadith both form the 'Sunnah', and constitute the Shari'as, which, as Ramadan argues, 'direct the way Muslims must be faithful to the Revealed Message…Shari'a is the way and the path to how to remain faithful to the source. It is not restricted to the penal code, it is philosophy of life'.[11] Islam, as Siedentop points out, 'emphasises the "equal submission" of believers to Allah's will, rather than "equal liberty" under the [Christian] God'.[12] A Muslim first belongs to God, second to his family (relatives and kinsfolk), and third to his community. For traditional Muslims, the criteria of truth are conformity with the words of the Koran, the Hadith and Sunnah. The aim of Islamic education is to produce devout Muslims. The main, and sometimes the only, purpose of education in traditional Islam is the study of the Koran, the Hadith and the Sunnah, as well as the history of Islam and Arabic. The major subjects taught in the West, mathematics, the natural and social sciences, engineering, arts, philosophy, economics and languages, are secondary.[13]

Cox and Marks note that Islam distinguishes between Islam as identity, Islam as faith, and Islam as political ideology.[14] The first refers to someone whose father is a Muslim and who accepts a nominal Muslim identity, but without committing himself to Muslim beliefs and practices. Islam as faith means submission or self-surrender to Allah as revealed through the message and life of his Prophet Mohammed. Islam as political ideology refers to beliefs and practices that seek to establish an Islamic state in order to enforce obedience to the Islamic law, or Shari'a. Similarly, Martin Kramer describes Islam as:

> Not merely a religion, in the Western sense of a system of belief in God. It possesses an immutable law, revealed by God, that deals with every aspect of life. It is also an ideology, a complete system of belief about the organisation of the state and the world. This law and ideology can only be implemented through the establishment of a truly Islamic state, under the sovereignty of God.[15]

Lewis also argues that Islam in one sense denotes a religion, a system of beliefs and worship, and, in another, the civilisation that grew up and flourished under the aegis of that religion. However, he says, Islam is not only a matter of faith and practice, it is also an identity and a loyalty for many – an identity and loyalty that transcend all others.[16]

Islamic societies include a very heterogeneous range of societies, cultures and people. They range from those with fundamentalist regimes, as Iran, Sudan or Afghanistan under the Taliban; to authoritarian 'traditional' regimes, such as Saudi Arabia, the Gulf States, Jordan or Morocco (these last have Shari'a law in place and prohibit most fundamental freedoms); to modern liberal Islamic countries which have adopted secular constitutions, based on secular legal systems and with some political institutions of liberal-democracy. Examples of this group include Turkey from the 1920s, Indonesia after 1945 and Egypt in the 1950s.

Politically and economically, Muslim countries lag behind Western countries. Politically, most of these countries, with the exception of Turkey or Indonesia, are not real democracies. Formal representative democracy is not always genuine. There is a lack of fundamental freedoms, functional democratic institutions and pluralism of political parties. Control is exercised over every aspect of life in the name of Islam. Religion and politics are not separated, but intertwined with each other. In some Muslim states, the legal system is dominated by Shari'a law, which is the only law, and there is no civil law. This holy law cannot be changed, as it was given by God and as such is unchangeable, unlike in democratic Western countries where the common law can be changed and evolved, according to the requests of the electorate, and where even the Church's canon or holy law can also change. Siedentop says:

> It seems likely that the difficulties Islamic nations have repeatedly encountered in trying to establish representative government and truly free institutions, derive from a moral cause, when the connection between moral equality and equal liberty is denied.[17]

Not only as regards their political and social aspects, but also from the economic point of view, Islamic societies have had less success compared to many Western countries or non-Muslim states. By all indicators from the United Nations, World Bank, etc, Muslim countries, in matters such as education, job creation, technology and productivity, lag behind the West. As a result, there is an increasing population of unemployed, uneducated and frustrated people, especially the young. If we refer to the World Bank's ranking of 200 countries according to their economic prosperity, as shown by Gross National Income per head, we can see that only seven out of 38 Muslim countries are in the top 100, while 31 are in the bottom 100. The only two Muslim countries in the top 50 are Brunei (22nd) and the United Arab Emirates (32nd), with Saudi Arabia third in 62nd place.[18] However, even the economic prosperity of these few countries is because of their huge oil reserves, rather than genuine economic development, policies and economic freedom. In addition, Islamic economies, as Cox and Marks observe, remain strongly dependent on the import of technology and science from the West, as science and education have not been given their due importance, since they are considered a departure from tradition and not in conformity with Shari'a. Their reluctance to accept and adopt new scientific ideas and innovations and new technologies from the West has been another reason for their backwardness in economic areas. Their lack of success in science is reflected in the number of Nobel prices received by Muslim scientists: 1.2 billion Muslims, who comprise about 20 per cent of the world's population, have received around half a dozen Nobel prizes in chemistry, physics and medicine. This has no comparison with Nobel winners among Western scientists, but even when compared with Jews, the figure is still very low. Jews, despite comprising only 0.2 per cent of the world's population (i.e., 200 times smaller than Muslims) have received nearly 100 prizes, almost 20 times more than Muslims. Two other reasons for poor economic progress are thought to be the lack of female higher education and high birth-rates. Unlike Cox and Marks, who argue that lack of education and science is one of the main reasons for the economic backwardness of Islamic countries, Tariq Ramadan, after accepting that 'apart from a few exceptions, the great majority of Muslims are living in deprivation and poverty', argues that the reason 'Islamic civilisation is going through a deep crisis is partly due to the forgetfulness and negligence by many Muslims of their own identity and values'.[19]

Lagging behind in political and economic development, the people of Muslim countries may feel inferior compared to Western societies. This may cause feelings of humiliation and frustration, which can sometimes make them targets for recruitment by fundamentalists (see Chapter 5). This frustration is reinforced by memories of a golden age when Islamic countries enjoyed scientific development, economic prosperity and military supremacy in the world.

To conclude, some Islamic principles and norms contradict modern and Western values, such as human rights and freedoms, the role of women and their equality with men, ideas about the relations of religion and the state, moral codes of everyday behaviour, and the boundaries of religious and moral tolerance.

Thus the Islamic and Western societies based on these respective values are very different from each other.

3.2 Is Islam compatible with liberal-democracy?

The conclusion of the previous section was that some Islamic principles and norms contradict modern and Western values. A comprehensive control, in the name of religion, of virtually every aspect of human life (individual and collective), constitutes, as Cox and Marks argue, the essence of totalitarianism, which is inherently incompatible with a principal Western value, namely, individual freedom, which lies at the heart of liberal-democracy.[20] Let us now analyse in more detail the issue of fundamental freedoms in Islam and Muslim countries. I will focus on two freedoms: freedom of religion and freedom of expression.

Religious tolerance is not something you find in Muslim countries, even in the most liberal ones. The principle of religious intolerance is enshrined in Shari'a law, in one of its main principles, which is the inequality between Muslims and non-Muslims. Throughout history, non-Muslims have been considered second-class citizens. They have been allowed to live in Muslim countries, mostly in peace, but with inferior social status and under certain limitations. Even today, discrimination against people on the grounds of their religious beliefs exists in a majority of Muslim states. The situation of Christians and Jews in contemporary Islamic societies is still a matter of concern. In fundamentalist countries like Iran and Sudan, being Muslim requires not only strict enforcement of Shari'a by the state, but also the legitimisation of particular methods of collective action against internal dissidents or external threat: Muslim dissidents are to be severely punished and repressed as heretics and traitors. Even in a democratic secular country like Turkey, as we saw earlier, religious freedom is problematic, and the rights of religious minorities are limited and circumscribed. The idea that somebody should be persecuted or even killed over the issue of religious beliefs shows the huge gap that exists between Islamic culture and mentality and the modern and democratic principles of human rights.

Freedom of expression is frequently prohibited in Muslim countries. The rationale behind this, as in dictatorial regimes, is that the dominant ideology (in this case, Islam) should be the only one. As Cox and Marks point out, 'It is very difficult for alternative views to be heard and much of the media in many Islamic countries operates under close government scrutiny and even censorship'.[21] 'From having once been an occasional event, the silencing of scholars, Professor Akbar Ahmed of Cambridge University observes, 'has increasingly become a way of life in most Muslim countries'.[22] Alongside the appearance of open information (access to e-mail and the Internet), Muslim countries have seen a more intense denial of intellectual freedom than at any time in recent history. From South Asia to North Africa, an entire generation of Muslim intellectuals is at this moment under threat, writers in particular. Many have already been killed, silenced or forced into exile. Salman Rushdie, the author of *The Satanic Verses*, was forced to change addresses 30 times in nine years after a *fatwa* was issued in Iran in 1989. Other examples include the respected Egyptian sociologist Saad Edin Ibrahim, imprisoned and on trial in 2001 for the exercise of intellectual freedom; the nuclear physicist Abdus Salam, Pakistan's only Nobel laureate; and many more. Many Muslim intellectuals, scientist and writers now live in exile in Western Europe or North America. Examples of persecution of writers and human rights activists are present even in a democratic country as Turkey, as seen in the previous chapter.

The second issue is that of equality of women. In Islamic societies, women are subject to considerable limitations and discrimination, and are in an inferior position to men, both in private and public life. They are not considered as full human beings, but as second-class citizens. Female inequality is enshrined in the Koran and Shari'a law, according to which women should stay at home, are not allowed to stay in the same room with men (even in the mosque), and should not travel without being accompanied by their husbands or other male relatives. They should be covered from head to toe, so other men cannot see their faces or bodies. Even the barbaric practice of stoning women to death for adultery is still in place in some Muslim countries. Differences from, and the supremacy of, men vis-à-vis women are enormous: a man can be married to up to four women at the same time, but a woman can only have one husband. A man can ask for divorce, but not the woman. Female illiteracy rates in Muslim countries are high, their presence in the labour force is low, and their political and public participation is the lowest in the world.

Even the moderate Afghan President Karzai, pressured by the religious conservatives of his country, signed in March 2009 the 'Shia Family Law', which appears to reintroduce the draconian policies of the Taliban era. The law includes a ban on married women leaving their homes without their husbands' permission, an article which stipulates that the wife is bound to preen for the husband as and when he desires; another which sanctions marital rape (in that the wife is bound to give a positive response to the sexual desires of her husband); and another article which endorses child marriage, with girls legally able to marry once they begin to menstruate. This law, which is in contradiction of the Universal Declaration on Human Rights, to which Afghanistan is a signatory, provoked anger and protests by women in Kabul and was widely condemned and criticised by Western governments.[23]

Phyllis Chesler, an American Professor of Psychology, who lived in Afghanistan as a wife of an Afghani man, describes her experience in the Islamic world:

I understood that it was dangerous for a Westerner, especially a woman, to live in a Muslim country…Until I arrived to Afghanistan, my husband had never once mentioned that his father had three wives and 21 children. Nor did he tell that I would be expected to lead a largely indoor life among women, to go out only with a male escort and to spend my days waiting for my husband to return, or visiting female relatives…I saw how women were forced to sit at the back of the bus and had to keep yielding their place on line in the bazaar to any man. I saw how polygamous, arranged marriages, wife-beating, marital rape led to chronic female suffering, I saw how women were not allowed to pray in mosques or visit male doctors.[24]

She continues:

> Western intellectual-ideologues have demonised me as a reactionary and racist 'Islamophobe' for arguing that Islam, not Israel, is the largest practitioner of both sexual and religious apartheid in the world and that if Westerners do not stand up to it, morally, economically and militarily, we will not only have the blood of innocents on our hands, we will also be overrun by Shari'a in the West.

Another issue to consider here is whether Islam is, as it claims, a religion of peace and harmony. Some Koranic verses are aggressive, violent, intolerant and warlike. Pope Benedict, in a speech in Regensburg, Germany, in September 2006, criticised the violent trends within Islam. He included a quote from a fourteenth-century Christian Emperor, who said, 'Show me just what Muhammad brought that was new, and there you will find things only evil and inhuman, such as his command to spread by the sword the faith he preached'. Though the Pope may have been intending to warn against religious terrorism, his remarks aroused fury throughout the Muslim world, which became actual violence in several places. Arabs in Palestinian Authority-controlled areas attacked seven Christian churches, a nun was murdered in Somalia, a call for the Pope's death was issued in London, and Iraqi groups threatened the Vatican.[25] The Pope did not apologise or retract his words, but rather expressed his 'deep regret' at its consequences and the storm it caused.

Besides the existence of violent verses, there are also two issues in the Koran that appear to be problematic from the standards and principles of liberal-democracy: jihad and apostasy.

Jihad, or the holy war,[26] is found both in the Koran[27] and collections of Hadith. It means a violent war by all Muslims towards the rest of the world until they accept Islam, or at least submit to the power of the Islamic state. Until that happens, as Bernard Lewis observes, the world is divided into two: the House of Islam (Dar al-Islam) where Muslim rule and the law of Islam prevails, and the House of War (Dar al-harb), comprising the rest of the world.[28] Between the two there is a morally necessary, legally and religiously obligatory state of war, until the final and inevitable triumph of Islam over unbelief. This war cannot be terminated by a peace, but only by a final victory. Therefore, the ultimate aim of jihad is to establish Islamic rule over the whole world. In the time of Mohammed, jihad was practised regularly against Christians and Jews, and also towards those who did not accept conversion to Islam. It lasted for nearly 1,300 years (from the seventh until the nineteenth century), conquering and converting much of Asia, Africa and a part of Europe. The final command of jihad is conquer the world in the name of Islam. As Cox and Marks argue, no subsequent Koranic verse contradicted this final command of jihad, so it must be deemed to remain a goal of Islam today.[29] At the end of the last century, the old cry of jihad against 'Crusaders' (Christians) and Jews was embraced and became a leitmotif for Islamic fundamentalists.

Wafa Sultan, an Arab-American psychologist from Los Angeles, in a TV interview with Al-Jazeera Qatar, said:

Muslims are those who began the clashes of civilisations. The Prophet of Islam said, fight people until they believe in Allah and his Messiah. They started this clash and began this war. In order to stop this war they should re-examine their books which are full of calls for fighting the infidels...Only Muslims defend their beliefs by burning down churches, killing people and destroying embassies. The Muslims must ask themselves what they can do for humankind, before they demand that humankind respect them.[30]

The second issue is that of apostasy. In Islamic law, apostasy, or conversion from Islam, is a major offence, and for men, means the death penalty. So, abandoning Islam and adopting another faith is condemned according to Islam. The person who does so is considered a traitor and, as such, should be punished with death. The idea of killing apostates has become a resurgent topic in recent years, a fact related to the increasing politicisation of Islam since September 11. Ziya Meral, born and raised in Turkey, converted from Islam to Christianity when he went to university in Britain. His parents disowned him when they heard the news, and even told people that he had died in an accident rather than bear the shame of their son leaving Islam.[31] Although some areas of the Islamic world may be moving away from imposing the death penalty for apostasy, it still remains in force in other countries.[32] A research project conducted by MERAL found that although the death penalty is rarely applied through the courts, apostates still face gross and wide-ranging human right abuses at the hands of the state, radical groups, families and local communities.[33] At the beginning of 2007, a group of men from Birmingham pleaded guilty to charges of conspiring to kidnap and behead a British Muslim soldier because they regarded him as a traitor: joining the British army was, to them, treason against Islam.[34] In 2007, the Egyptian Grand Mufti, Ali Gomaa, told the *Washington Post* that the death penalty for apostasy no longer applies. This provoked a flurry in Egypt and the wider Middle East.[35] Apostasy incites religious hatred. Therefore, any faith that still requires a death sentence for those who fall away is not appropriate in modern society.

Lack of religious tolerance, persecution and limitation of the rights of non-Muslims, non-tolerance of other social, ethnic and sexual minorities, lack of freedom of expression, persecution, killing or forcing into exile of people who criticise the regime and have alternative views, discrimination against women and treatment of them as second-class citizens, discrimination and maltreatment of homosexuals, punishing anybody who wants to choose another faith, and aiming to convert the rest of the world into Islam by force, are incompatible with the principles of liberal-democracy, in particular with human rights as enshrined in a key Western document: the UN Universal Declaration of Human Rights.

The differences in value systems and the lack of compatibility between them is perhaps the reason why democracy is so difficult to 'transport' and implement in Muslim countries. Can the promotion and spread of constitutional democracy be achieved in those countries, as is, for instance, the current US foreign policy principle? The transportation and transplantation of democratic principles, practices and institutions to Muslim countries is almost impossible to achieve, as shown by the failure to truly establish democracy in Iraq and Afghanistan. The Bush administration's view was that transplanting democracy in these countries would help to combat terrorism, as terrorism is driven by a lack of democracy. It overlooked the fact that many terrorists were radicalised in democratic European countries. It is highly naïve to think that radical Islamists hate the West out of ignorance of what the West is, as Fukuyama points out.[36] However, in my view, democracy is difficult to transplant into the Middle East, because of the difference in values and cultures with the West. Culture, unlike politics and economics, is very difficult to change, as it is a product of centuries. It requires more than granting money, dispatching troops or writing constitutions. The long-term process of social engineering, which was what Washington's neo-conservatives had in mind when invading Iraq, Roy notes, ignored sociology, history and nationalism[37] (and I would say, culture, and most importantly religion). Many Iraqis were pleased when US soldiers toppled Saddam Hussein, but they nonetheless view them as infidel invaders and occupiers and want them out. Americans are not seen as liberators and democracy is often perceived as an alien import. Western efforts to promote and propagate values of democracy, human rights and liberalism as universal and true values produce instead rejection, counter-responses and reaction against 'human rights imperialism' and a reaffirmation of indigenous values and culture. Another argument in support of this notion of incompatibility is the fact that democracy has been transplanted successfully into certain countries, notably CEE countries after the collapse of communism. I posit that the reason for success is that Western and Eastern Europe have common values and no major differences in culture.

Scholars view certain religious traditions as more conducive to democratic advancement than others. Predominantly Christian societies are often regarded as more receptive to democratisation than are non-Christian societies. Hurd argues that full secular democracy can only be fully realised in societies possessing a Judeo-Christian heritage.[38] Lipset[39] and Huntington see Islam as creating a particularly inhospitable environment for the endurance of popular rule. Even Turkey, the one major democracy in the Muslim world, they say, is prone to bouts of authoritarian politics. Although many (such as Berger[40] and others) agree that there are different strands within political Islam (ranging from moderate to radical), on the whole Islam has had a difficult time coming to terms with key modern notions such as pluralism and democracy.

The two worlds, the Muslim and the Western, are different, because the religions they are based on, Islam and Christianity, are also different. These two worlds represent different systems of values and beliefs, which do not match and are incompatible in many ways. However, despite the differences in religions, cultures and value systems, these two worlds, or civilisations in Huntington's terms, can still co-exist in peace, develop mutual respect, understanding and harmonious relationship, rather than engaging in conflicts and wars with each other. As Huntington concludes his influential *Clash of Civilisations* thesis, 'For the relevant future, there will be no universal civilisation, but instead a world of different civilisations, each of which will have to learn to co-exist with the others'.[41]

3.3 The issue of secularism: the relation of Islam and Christianity with the state

As was mentioned in the previous sections, liberal-democratic countries have constitutions and laws that can be changed, and, most importantly, changed according to the requests of the people. Even the Christian Church's canon or holy law can change. By contrast, Muslims have a divine law, called Shari'a or holy law,[42] which derives from God. As such, it is the perfect law, which means it cannot be altered or abrogated. It is not legislated, but revealed. Therefore Shari'a is called 'the law', as there is no other. According to Islam, the only law is God's law, so there should be no room for legislation and constitutions. Therefore there is no other kind of law in traditional Islamic societies. Islam emphasises strict conformity to religious law. Furthermore, Shari'a, as Tariq Ramadan highlights, is not restricted to the penal code, it is a philosophy of life. It is the way, the path to how to remain faithful to the source.[43] Shari'a is based on the Koran, the Hadith and Sunnah. Its principles of inequality, as we saw earlier, are antagonistic to the Western principle of equality. Inequality is, firstly, between Muslims and non-Muslims, and, secondly, between men and women, Shari'a principles prohibit the recognition of women and non-Muslims as full citizens of an Islamic state.

One of the main differences between most Muslim countries and Western democracies is the separation between religion and politics, or church and state. This has to do with the distinction between public and private spheres, between the secular and the sacred. The vast majority of people in Europe support the division between church and state, and believe secularism to be part of modern Europe. Secularism can be seen as one of Europe's noblest achievements. The separation of church from state started with the French Revolution and the Thirty Years War in the seventeenth century. As Katzenstein and Byrnes point out, 'Westphalia has become shorthand for an interstate system that banished religion to the domestic and private realm'.[44] Since then, all Western European countries have been built as secular states with a strict separation between church and state. The exceptions are Greece, where there is no separation between church and state, and the UK, where there is a constitutional link between the two (Britain, unique amongst Western democracies, provides for religious representation in its legislature, in the form of Church of England bishops in the House of Lords). European secularism is considered as one of its greatest achievements, with Judeo-Christianity as the foundation of this secular democracy.

For Islam, however, secularism is not acceptable. The Koran requires submission to the will of Allah. As Katzenstein and Byrnes argue, distinctions such as those between divine law and human law, between state power and religious power, so central to Western politics, are critical barriers to the realisation of

Islam's central goal: a Godly community living in harmony under Islamic Shari'a, God's law.[45] The first reason for this different definition of ideal state form is that, by contrast with Christianity, as Steve Bruce argues, Islam was founded as a political religion. The Prophet Mohammed's intention was to create a unified community that would be both religious and political in nature. He was not only a prophet and a spiritual leader, like the founders of other religions, but also a soldier, a ruler and a political leader (Mohammed himself led 27 battles). As a Byzantine emperor from the fourteenth century said, 'Muhammad spread by the sword the faith he preached'. But even after Mohammed, the leaders of Islam, under the title of 'Caliph', combined the roles of prophet and king, of spiritual and political leader. The ruler Sultan was frequently both spiritual guide and Caliph.[46] Islam did not spend its first hundred years in the wilderness; instead, its early leaders rapidly found themselves at the head of large empires. By contrast with the early spread of Islam, Christianity in its first centuries spread by persuasion, not by force of arms. It began as a religion of weakness and failure, its founder was crucified, and 250 years – ten generations – elapsed before it became the official religion of the Roman Empire. Christ was crucified, and Moses died without entering the promised land, while Mohammed triumphed during his lifetime and died a sovereign and a conqueror. Therefore, as Bruce argues:[47]

> Christianity's long period in the wilderness gave it a very good reason to take seriously the separation of church and state that Christ had suggested when he responded to a question about taxes, by saying 'one should render unto God what belongs to God and unto Caesar what belongs to Caesar'.[48]

This Biblical text exemplifies the distinction between the secular and the sacred, and thus, judging from the New Testament, early Christianity was not anti-state *per se*. Jesus saw no conflict between loyalty to God and paying the imperial Roman tax. As Lewis argues, for Christians, there is a choice between God and

Caesar, but in Islam there is no Caesar, only God and Mohammed his Prophet. Religious truth and political power were indissolubly associated: the first sanctified the second, the second sustained the first.[49] With regard to this Siedentop says, 'We have discovered that our most basic habits of thought, distinguishing between the religious and the secular, between public and private spheres, have their origins in the Christian culture of Europe'.[50]

This may lead people to believe that secularisation of Islam is difficult to achieve, untenable even, in Islamic societies. An-Na'im makes a very good point when he says that the relationship between Islam and politics in Islamic societies is so strong that strict separation between the two is believed commonly to be neither desirable in principle, nor possible in practice.[51] Distinction between religious and political authority are historically absent from the Islamic world in general and are unthinkable due to the nature of Islam itself. In this view, as Hurd argues, Muslim-majority civilisations simply do not enjoy forms of secularism and insist upon rejecting the secularism imported from the West.[52] Even where a degree of secularism has been achieved, it is associated with two phenomena: either with dictatorship, as in most of the Middle East, or as in an atypical case like Turkey, where the guardian of secularism is the military.

Roy rightly observes that, 'Europeans do not challenge Islam as a true religion, but want Muslims to be more secular-minded'.[53] Most modern Christians criticise Islam not for being 'wrong', but for not being secular enough. Europeans want to see a more liberalised Islam that incorporates Western concepts of rights and tolerance. For the European establishment, the challenge is to bring Muslims into European society without changing the foundations of their secular democracy.

It is in the realms of politics, Lewis argues, that we see the most striking differences between Islam and the rest of the world. The heads of state of Scandinavian countries and the UK do not gather in Protestant summit conferences, nor do the countries belonging to the Orthodox Church summon religious assemblies. By contrast, in 1969 an Islamic summit conference held in Morocco decided to create a body to be known as Organisation of the Islamic Conference (OIC) with a permanent secretariat in Jedda, Saudi Arabia. OIC now numbers 57 member states, two of which, Turkey and Albania, are in Europe and aspire to be in the European Union.[54]

As long as many Muslims believe that their religion should define their politics (it is not the majority that decides, but the will of God) then the chances for a consensus on democracy are remote, as Tarifa points out.[55]

3.4 An Islamic Reformation: is this necessary and possible?

Islam is considered by many, especially in the West, to be a backward and obscurantist religion. One reason for this apparent backwardness is that Islam has remained almost unchanged since its foundation in the seventh century. However, Islam, as Lewis points out, was once the leading civilisation in the world, marked as such by its great and powerful kingdoms, its rich and varied industry and commerce, and its original and creative sciences and letters.[56] During the first centuries after its birth in 622, many aspects of academic endeavour and cultural creativity flourished in Islamic societies. The period of the first 100 years, known as that of Great Imams (750–850), as Ramadan notes, 'saw the flourishing of the Islamic sciences, especially in the area of jurisprudence'.[57] For most of the Dark Ages, while Christendom was in poverty and disarray, the empire of Islam was the richest, most powerful, most creative and most enlightened region of the world. Cox and Marks state that over these centuries there were a number of outstanding Islamic contributions to the arts and science, including the development of new knowledge in mathematics, astronomy, and medicine.[58]

However, despite the outstanding achievements of Islamic scholars, no sustained scientific movement developed. After the twelfth century, the major contribution of Muslims to the later development of the world's science and culture was the preservation of Greek philosophy for medieval Europe. Many ancient works of famous Greek scientists and philosophers, such as Aristotle, Plato,

Archimedes and Ptolemy, had been lost in Europe after the fall of Roman Empire, so this preservation of the Greek texts in Arabic translation was a great contribution for humanity. But the centuries that followed did not see any further development of Islamic science and arts, nor of Muslim societies. The Islamic world lost its dominance and its leadership and fell behind the modern West. The difference in time and place between seventh-century Arabian societies and current ones has not generated dramatic changes. By contrast, Christian societies have changed and evolved over time, adapting to new developments and circumstances. Christianity itself has reformed and modernised in response to modernity and changes in humanity over centuries. Unlike Christianity, Islam has not undergone reformation, liberalisation or modernisation. Neither have Islamic societies experienced events that occurred in Christian Europe, such as the Renaissance, Reformation, Wars of Religion, Enlightenment (which shaped the new relationship between politics and religion in eighteenth-century Europe), feudalism and the Industrial Revolution. That is why the mores of the seventh century, as Joan Smith says, have no relevance in modern life.[59]

'What we need now', says Phyllis Chesler, 'is an age of Enlightenment in the Islamic world'. Without critical examination of Islam, it will remain dogmatic, fanatical and intolerant, and will continue to stifle thought, human rights, originality and truth.[60] Even the practice and interpretation of Islam continues to be literalist. The majority of Muslims believe that the Koran is the literal word of Allah; therefore, every word in the Koran has to be obeyed, rather than read in its historical context. Ramadan argues that the manner of reading of two scriptural sources depends on the margin of interpretation, degree of literality and role of reason. He says that Islam is a unity, but that its textual sources nonetheless permit a plurality of readings.[61] Many Muslim thinkers want a more modern interpretation of Islam, and have therefore welcomed the recent decision of the Turkish government to commission a revision of the Hadith. In February 2008, Turkey's Department of Religious Affairs (Diyanet) commissioned a team of theologians at Ankara University to carry out a fundamental revision of the Hadith, the second most sacred text in Islam after the Koran.[62] The Turkish state, in its efforts to modernise, has come to see the Hadith as having a negative influence on society, especially as regards the violent suppression of women. Some view this initiative as an attempt by the AKP to get into the EU. However, Fadi Hakura an analyst on Turkey at Chatham House,[63] said that:

> While the Western world has greeted this move as a door to an Islamic Reformation, Turkey's religious officials have in fact reiterated that the Turkish efforts are a 'scientific and academic' exercise, since the sacred texts are of divine origin and do not require 'revision', 'modernisation' or 'reform' (or need to be fixed by humans), but only re-interpretation.[64]

As revision of the Hadith may cause controversy among the conservative religious establishment, Turkey's top religious officials have clarified that it is not an attempt to reform Islam, but to change the way of practising it.[65]

Therefore, Islam and its sacred texts, the Koran and Hadith, as they currently stand (i.e., unreformed for 13 centuries), are filled with violent and intolerant verses, with principles of intolerance for people of different religions, and inequality for women. These principles and teachings are against some of the laws in Western democratic countries and unacceptable in Western society; they contradict the values and principles of liberal-democracy, and as such Islam, in its present form, is not compatible with it.

3.5 Can Turkey maintain a balance between secular democracy and Islamic culture?

Universal Western values, mentioned above, often have little resonance in Islamic culture. Therefore, some of the reasons behind 'Islamophobia' in Europe[66] are perhaps connected with the reluctance of Muslims living in Europe to embrace certain European values, such as freedom of speech, gender equality, women's rights, or tolerance of alternative lifestyle. Some Muslim practices and customs, such as arranged marriages (young women being forced by parents to marry men they do not know, or young men sent to their home villages in Pakistan or Anatolia to find a bride), circumcision, 'honour' crimes, female chastity or prohibition from being examined by male doctors, extended joint family, or some Islamic religious norms, such as eating of hallal, abstention from eating pork or drinking alcohol, wearing of hijab, niqab or burka, refusal to use swimming-pools or Muslim women being treated as second-class citizens in mosques in the UK, are perceived as bizarre, primitive and backward by most Europeans, especially when Muslims apply these norms and lifestyles in metropolitan Europe. In his explosive book *Reflections on the Revolution in Europe,* Christopher Caldwell argues that essential cultural differences mean a Muslim influx could destroy the very fabric of our society. He says that, 'Islam is different. Living with Muslim cultures requires larger adjustments, and they touch deeper, more essential parts of European culture...Nowhere are these adjustments trickier than in questions of family, marriage, gender and sexuality'.[67]

The failure of Islamic countries to live up to standards of democracy and human rights and their unwillingness to play by the rules of *laïcité,* is said to cause negative attitudes towards those countries in the Western world. As Abdullahi An-Na'im notes, 'when certain Islamic societies are presented as the embodiment of oppression, aggression, brutality, fanaticism and medieval backwardness, this becomes the basis for Western attitudes toward all Islamic countries'.[68] Therefore many in the West are now opposed to the promotion of more Muslim faith schools, where Muslim pupils and students are not exposed to other value systems or to intellectual argument, but instead are taught about the radical subordination of women and other human rights violations, views which run directly contrary to democratic values.

Unacceptable incidents in Islamic countries that contrast sharply with standards of democracy and freedom reinforce these perceptions about Muslims. There is the case of the British schoolteacher imprisoned in Sudan for naming a teddy bear

Muhammad,[69] the British teacher Daud Hassan Ali shot dead in Somalia because of apostasy,[70] or the woman sentenced to 200 lashes after being gang-raped in Saudi Arabia.[71] Such events and incidents, incompatible with the modern world, highlight aspects of Islam not only as they are currently practised in some Muslim countries, but also as promoted in some European mosques.[72]

These make many Europeans perceive Turkish society, whatever the secular democratic nature of the Turkish state, as very different, and indeed incompatible, in terms of its culture, values and identity. This is how an article in *Danish Affairs,* portraying Turkey as a 'Trojan horse', describes the matter:

Many Americans hardly understand why Turkey isn't embraced as a dear member of the European family. To most Europeans modern Turkey is a cheap tourist destination, a NATO ally, but also a large scale exporter of under-educated Muslims to the European welfare states. Kemal Atatürk's Western styled secular republic has not inspired the emigrating masses to wholeheartedly join Europe's core values and ethics. Instead we are witnessing self-chosen segregation, spread of Shari'a law in communities, extensive welfare dependence, and disproportional crime rates combined with higher reproduction rates than the European aboriginals.[73]

Luis Lugo argues that:

Opposition to Turkish accession is coming from secular as well as religious quarters in Europe: non-religious Europeans worry that bringing a large Muslim country into the EU could endanger the Continent's traditions of gender equality and tolerance of alternative lifestyles. For traditionalists, Turkish accession threatens the very idea of Europe as a Christian civilisation.[74]

It is true that Turkey, unlike most other Muslim countries, is a secular democracy, and has been such for almost 80 years. It has a constitution, not Shari'a law. However, as we saw in the previous chapter, there are still many limitations on fundamental freedoms, and problems with human rights, that are not in conformity with the standards of liberal-democracy. These problems are difficult for Turkey to address, as they are based in religion and embedded in the social fabric of its culture.

A study at Cologne University has revealed that Turkish attitudes differ significantly from those of EU nationals.[75] 'Two basic EU principles are not being supported, freedom of religion and gender equality', said Frederike Wuermeling, the author of the study. Only one-third of Turks backed gender equality. When it came to freedom of religion, only 16 per cent explicitly agreed to this principle, the study revealed.[76] The analysis backed the cultural hypothesis, which states that the higher the percentage of Muslims in a country and the higher the level of individual religious belief, the lower the agreement to EU principles.

The highly reliable Pew Forum on Religion and Public Life, in one of its Pew Global Attitudes surveys, found growing doubts among Turks that democracy can thrive in their country and increasing worries that Islam is playing a larger, and possibly harmful, role in politics.[77] A survey in June 2006 showed that only 44 per cent of Turks said they believed democracy could work in their country, a decline from the number in 2005 (48 per cent) and 2003 (50 per cent). 46 per cent of people said they were 'fairly' or 'very concerned' about the rise of Islamic extremism in Turkey and 28 per cent said their strongest concerns were people having fewer personal freedoms. Thus it seems to be a challenge for Turkey to maintain a balance between being both a secular democracy that respects democratic norms, and a nation with an Islamic culture.

4

WHAT PLACE DO RELIGION AND CULTURE HAVE IN THE DEBATE ON TURKISH CANDIDACY

After analysing the factors that are influencing Turkey's accession process, I now turn to the contemporary European debate on Turkey's candidacy. What are the positions and attitudes of European actors (meaning both elite and public opinion)? And what place do religion and culture occupy in the European debate? First, however, we must analyse the conceptual relationship between religion and culture.

4.1 Religion and culture: two separate concepts?

Assessing the direct impact of religious and cultural factors in the Turkish accession process is quite a challenging task. As we will see in this chapter, the words 'religion', 'Muslim' or 'Islam' are hardly mentioned in responses by people to opinion polls or on questionnaires, in official reports of EU institutions, or in statements by politicians. Rather, the terms 'culture', 'identity' and 'values' are used. So the question is: is 'culture' a code-word for 'religion? But first we must ask, what is the relation between religion and culture? Are they the same thing, or two separate concepts?

In my view, 'culture' is a broad concept that includes not only religion, but also many other elements: from customs, traditions, mentality, social norms and values, family patterns, life style, attitude and behavioural patterns, to cuisine, food and eating habits, folklore, music, dance and literature. However, I believe that religion is the principal component of a culture, because it is not only embedded, incorporated and rooted in a given culture, but also defines the other components of a culture, such as mentality, social norms or eating habits. Furthermore, cultures spring from religions. Religion is effectively embedded in a culture to an extent that persists even when people actually cease to believe. In this way, religious norms become social values and religion provides the moral fabric of a society. Roy says that 'religion is the main component of cultures, a component that can be erected as a culture in itself'.[1] Huntington's *Clash of Civilisations* paradigm is based on the premise that civilisations and cultures are founded on religion. Similarly, George Weigel notes that 'the heart of culture is religion'.[2] 'We have become aware', says Steve Bruce, 'of what a powerful role religion plays in shaping national identity, social norms and values'.[3] Katzenstein and Byrnes define religion 'as a set of ideas and practices that constitute the very content of a community's identity and religious values, practices and traditions, which shape the culture'.[4]

Religion is not only embedded in a culture, but, in the case of a 'universal' religion (such as Islam, Christianity and Buddhism), it can become trans-national, transcending the boundaries of a country, society or territory. As a result, we talk about a Muslim culture and a Muslim society, which can be found in many countries, not just in one. As with Protestant or Buddhist culture, Islam is trans-national in nature and makes universal claims on all persons, at all times, in all places. Indeed, medieval Christendom, though surely not a relevant model for modern political structures, is an indicator that European politics has not always been structured around nation-states and does not necessarily have to be structured around individual states in the future.[5] In the present day, the *Ummah*, or the Islamic people of God is not, in the perception of many Muslims, divided into national communities across the dozens of states where Muslims predominate. On the contrary, there is in Islamic thought only one Ummah, one community of Muslims. As Ramadan argues:

The Ummah is the third circle which determines the belonging of the Muslims: it is the community of faith, of feelings, of brotherhood, of destiny…To be Muslim, anywhere in the world, means to experience and develop this feeling of belonging to the Ummah as if one were an organ of a great body, as the Prophet said…The feeling of belonging to Ummah is inherent in the Islamic faith. Pilgrimage to Makka, the sacred place of gathering for millions of Muslims, is the symbol of the Ummah.[6]

The Caliphate, the human symbol of Islamic unity, even though formally abolished by the post-Ottoman Turks in 1924, is still viewed as the gathering of 52 Muslim countries. Trans-national religion is a complex category, which includes a wide variety of actors: the population belonging to that religion all around the world, the Church as a global institution, the religious leaders (i.e., the Pope), and the network of bishops, priests and imams that serve their communities all over the world. Trans-national actors, such as religious communities and religious leaders, participate in international politics and political processes and, as Katzenstein and Byrnes point out, may influence international political outcomes.[7]

Especially in this era of the resurrection of religion, what Gilles Kepel calls 'la revanche de Dieu',[8] religion provides a basis for identity and commitment that transcends national boundaries and unites civilisations. Religion becomes a sort of neo-ethnicity. For instance, many people, whatever their level of religious practice, citizenship or political activity, claim to react as Muslim against the US war in Iraq. Another example put forward by Roy is Pope John Paul II: when he campaigned for the inclusion in the European Constitution of specific mention of the Christian roots of Europe, he saw Europeans not as necessarily all being true Christians, but nonetheless as sharing a common Christian culture and, consequently, common values, even in their secularised forms.[9] Siedentop asks this good question: 'Are we as "free" of Christianity as we suppose? There is much evidence that we are still subject to its moral sway'.[10] However, the influence of religion in Islamic culture is stronger and more important than that of the Christian religion on its culture (the main reason for this being secularisation). Islam is the common connecting thread for all Muslims in the world, despite of their national cultural variances. Roy argues that 'it is difficult to find a common basis for an Islamic culture outside the tenets of the religion...the lowest common denominators in defining a Muslim culture are religious norms that can fit with, or be recast, along the lines of different cultural customs'.[11]

In the Turkish case, many, including scholars, tend to draw a distinction between religion and culture, arguing that, while Turkish culture does not constitute an obstacle to her accession, religion does, or vice versa.[12] In view of what has been said above, I posit that this is a false distinction. If culture constitutes a problem, then so does religion, since religion is the principal component of culture. Yet because, in general, Europeans prefer not to speak openly about religion, as we will see below, the word 'culture' is often used as a code-word for 'religion'.

4.2 European identity

Before examining the position of European actors with regard to Turkey, let us explain what 'European identity' is, and how Europeans view it. European identity is based on (a common) geography, history, culture and religion, which is the product of many centuries. It is a 'we feeling'. European identity is a supranational identity, which belongs to a common, Western civilisation. However, the 'European demos' is proving difficult to create, and, despite the success of the EU project, national identities have not disappeared. Not many Europeans think of themselves as generic Europeans, or swell with pride at the playing of the European anthem. Even though more Europeans feel attached to the EU (53 per cent),[13] the EU still comes a long way behind attachment to respondents' own countries. As Fukuyama notes, 'national identities in Europe, compared to that in America, remain far more blood and soil based, accessible only to those ethnic groups who initially populated the country.

Europe's old national identities continue to hang around like unwanted ghosts'.[14] Many Europeans insist that the American 'melting pot' approach to national identity is unique and cannot be replicated in Europe. European identity, by contrast, is more confused. It does not seem to have diluted the national identities of European countries, particularly of powerful ones with long and glorious histories and strong traditions, such as France or Britain. In October 2009, a country-wide debate begun in France on the issue of French identity. Public meetings took place in some 450 government offices around the country, involving campaigners, students, parents and teachers, unions, business leaders and French and European lawmakers. The debate ended with a conference in early 2010 on the twin questions of 'what it means to be French today' and 'what immigration contributes to our national identity'.[15]

However, European identity has been encouraged by the EU project, and certain elements, such as Europe Day and the EU anthem, flag and citizenship have been established since in the Maastricht Treaty in 1992. Since then, there has been an increase of awareness by Europeans of their new identity. In the Eurobarometer 67, the European flag is known to 95 per cent of Europeans and 85 per cent of them consider it a good symbol for Europe, with half of them identifying with the European flag.[16] Huntington even attributes the success of the EU to common values and identity, arguing that common culture facilitates the economic relations between countries. He says, 'economic regionalism may succeed only when it is rooted in a common civilisation: the EC rests on the shared foundation of European culture and Western Christianity'.[17] Talking about identity, he rightly observes that, in class and ideological conflicts, the key question is 'Which side are you on?', and people could and did choose and change sides. In cultural and civilisational conflicts, the question is: 'What are you?'. The answer is a given and that cannot be changed. A person can be half-French and half-Arab and have dual citizenship, but it is more difficult to be half-Catholic and half-Muslim.[18]

The Lisbon Treaty makes many references to European values, culture and identity. Its Preamble says, 'drawing inspiration from the cultural, religious and humanist inheritance of Europe, from which have developed the universal values of the inviolable and inalienable rights of the human person, freedom, democracy, equality and the rule of law'.[19] Article 1/a notes that 'the Union is founded on the values of respect for human dignity, freedom, democracy, equality, the rule of law and respect for human rights, including the rights of persons belonging to minorities. These values are common to the Member States in a society in which pluralism, non-discrimination, tolerance, justice, solidarity and equality between women and men prevail'. Article 2 stresses that 'It shall respect its rich cultural and linguistic diversity, and shall ensure that Europe's cultural heritage is safeguarded and enhanced'.[20] The European Commission's conclusion from the frequent discussions during recent years about the ultimate borders of the European Union is that 'the term "European" combines geographical, historical and cultural elements, which all contribute to European identity'.[21]

But what place does religion, more specifically Christianity, occupy in the identity of Europe? Grace Davie says:

> What we call Europe, a combination of Judeo-Christian monotheism, Greek rationalism, and Roman organisation, can be seen forming a way of life that we have come to recognise as European. The shared religious heritage of Western Europe is one of the crucial factors in the continent's development and the influence of this heritage on a whole range of cultural values.[22]

Even though Europeans do not care much about faith and religiosity, they share a cultural perception of religion, and especially Christianity, as part of European identity and history. In an interview, Graham Avery said, 'A number of historians and politicians argue that Christianity is one of the defining features of European identity'.[23] In an interview with Germany's *Sueddeutsche Zeitung* magazine, Pope Benedict XVI's private secretary, Mgr Georg Ganswein, said that 'while Christians respect Islam and desire dialogue with Muslims, they must act to protect the Christian identity of Europe'. He pointed out that 'the associated danger for the identity of Europe cannot be ignored out of a wrongly understood sense of respect'.[24] Not just religious people, but even scholars and politicians call for preservation of the Judeo-Christian spiritual and cultural heritage and its transmission it to the next generations.[25]

One phenomenon that is having an impact on European identity is multiculturalism.[26] Many people argue that in Europe it has served to dilute national identities, and individual cultures, lifestyle and religion, which have developed over centuries. Larry Siedentop, in *Democracy in Europe*, argues that the moral identity of Europe has become problematic for two reasons: a residual anti-clericalism, and a more recent phenomenon, multiculturalism. These sometimes enter into a marriage of convenience.[27] He says that 'multiculturalism converted into a political weapon by increasingly self-confident minorities, is one of the reasons that Europe's identity has become problematic'.[28] According to him:

Under the impact of multiculturalism, the Christian or post-Christian nations are confused about their moral identity to an alarming extent. That confusion has in turn two important consequences: first it makes the West a less effective defender of its own values than it ought to be; and second it prevents the West from understanding what is happening throughout the world at the most important level, the level of belief.[29]

He later says that 'Unless a coherent identity presides over the process of European integration that process will sooner or later, lead to disorder...Europe can do what it ought to do for itself and for the rest of the world only if it is secure in its own identity'.[30]

The phenomena of multiculturalism, the increasing presence of Muslim communities in Europe and the prospect of another 70 million Muslims joining, have divided Europeans over how they view European identity. People with traditional and conservative views believe that European identity is based on a common

European historical, cultural and Christian heritage. They are in favour of cultural cohesion. People with more liberal views think that European identity should be based on universal liberal political principles. They believe that cultural diversity in the EU is a strength rather than a weakness. While for the first group, European identity is a series of fixed cultural and civilisational traits, for the second it is a series of acquired characteristics. However, many Europeans agree that European identity is composed of a trinitarian legacy of faith, freedom, and rule of law, which came to them from Israel, Greece and Rome, to make up the fabric of Western civilised life. They believe that countries that want to join the Union should accept this legacy and adapt to European values and identity, rather than the other way around. In this context, some critics of Turkish EU membership suggest that Turkey will undermine an emerging European identity, since it is not European geographically, historically or culturally.[31] Hurd argues that Turkey is inherently different from Europe due to the existence of an exclusive European identity based on geography, culture and religion.[32]

Cardinal Josef Ratzinger, as Pope Benedict was then, voiced his opposition to Turkey coming into the EU on the grounds of identity and culture, on two occasions. The first was in an interview with Sophie de Ravinel, published in *Le Figaro* on 13 August 2004, where he said:

> Europe is a cultural continent, not a geographical one. It is its culture that gives it a common identity. The roots that have formed it, that have permitted the formation of this continent, are those of Christianity. In this sense, throughout history Turkey has always represented another continent, in permanent contrast with Europe. There were the wars against the Byzantine empire, the fall of Constantinople, the Balkan wars, and the threat against Vienna and Austria. That is why I think it would be an error to equate the two continents. It would mean a loss of richness, the disappearance of culture for the sake of economic benefits. Turkey, which is considered a secular country but is founded upon Islam, could instead

attempt to bring to life a cultural continent together with some neighbouring Arab countries, and thus become the protagonist of a culture that would possess its own identity, but would also share the great humanistic values that we should all acknowledge. This idea is not incompatible with close and friendly forms of association and collaboration with Europe, and would permit the development of unified strength in opposition to any form of fundamentalism.[33]

In a speech to the pastoral workers of his titular diocese, Velletri, as reported by *Il Giornale del Popolo* and by a dispatch from the news agency ANSA on 20 September 2004, he repeated:

Historically and culturally, Turkey has little in common with Europe; for this reason, it would be a great error to incorporate it into the European Union. It would be better for Turkey to become a bridge between Europe and the Arab world, or to form together with that world its own cultural continent. Europe is not a geographical concept, but a cultural one, formed in a sometimes conflictual historical process centred upon the Christian faith, and it is a matter of fact that the Ottoman Empire was always in opposition to Europe. Even though Kemal Ataturk constructed a secular Turkey during the 1920s, the country remains the nucleus of the old Ottoman Empire; it has an Islamic foundation, and is thus very different from Europe, which is a collection of secular states with Christian foundations, although today these countries seem to deny this without justification. Thus the entry of Turkey into the EU would be anti-historical.[34]

4.3 Actors in the debate

The prospect of Turkish accession has sparked a serious debate in the EU. Hidden European concerns and prejudices often come to the surface when the discussion touches upon Turkey. There is an assumption that Turkey's Islamic religious and cultural identity constitutes a significant obstacle in its membership. To assess this, I will examine the opinions and positions of four categories of actors: European citizens, EU institutions (the Commission and the Parliament), EU member-states, and European leaders and prominent politicians.

European citizens

European citizens had not had a direct say in the decision of a country's EU membership. However, former Commissioner Franz Fischler warned the European Commission in 2004 that 'we cannot continue to ignore public opinion, leaving the European construction to the diplomats'.[35] Recently there have been ideas to involve EU citizens more in deciding Europe's future direction, so it is likely that many of them will be decision makers by virtue of deciding via referenda if they want a certain country to join. One of the member-states, France, has already put in place a new constitutional clause (Article 88.5), which requires a referendum on all accessions following that of Croatia[36] (this was prior to the aforementioned bill approved by the French National Assembly last May, making referenda obligatory for accepting new EU member countries with populations over 5 per cent of the bloc's entire size, which means it would be necessary only for Turkey). However, even without the holding of referenda, public opinion will still be significant in the ongoing accession negotiations. Therefore, it is useful to know the attitude of the public, and this is the reason I am examining European citizens as a separate category.

The accession process of Turkey and its membership prospects have provoked a lively debate among European citizens. How has this debate evolved in recent years? What is the degree of support/ opposition to Turkey's candidacy? What are the main reasons behind the opposition? We saw in the previous chapter that some of the reasons are related to human rights issues, economic factors, security and institutional factors. But how about religion? Are Europeans worried about it? Do they mind the entry of a Muslim country, the accepting into the 'European club' of a culturally different newcomer? To assess these, I have traced and examined the results and findings of various public opinion sources: Eurobarometer surveys; German Marshall Fund surveys; *FT* polls; Pew Research Centre surveys; letters to daily newspapers; and reasons for rejection of the EU draft Constitution.

Eurobarometer surveys (EB)

Eurobarometer surveys are produced by various Department Generals (DG) of the European Commission. I examined the four types of EB: Standard EB, Special EB, Candidate Countries EB (CCEB) and Flash EB, from recent years (2006–2008). However, among the great number of EBs produced, there seem to be only three that provide useful information on the issue I wish to explore (the triangle: enlargement, Turkey, religion/culture variable): Standard Eurobarometer 66-2006 and 67-2007, as well as the Special Eurobarometer on Enlargement 2006.

Standard Eurobarometer 66-2006 and 67-2007

Standard EBs are produced every year by the DG for Communication to review the attitudes of European public opinion towards various issues in relation to the EU. According to Eurobarometer surveys, citizens' support for Turkey's accession to the EU is not only low, but shrinking, as the Ruiz-Jiménez and Torreblanca study shows, especially since 2001.[37] Whereas in autumn 2001, Eurobarometer 56.2 showed opposition to Turkey's membership at 46 per cent, this figure rose to 52 per cent in spring 2005 (Eurobarometer 63) and to 57 per cent in autumn 2005 (Eurobarometer 64). Eurobarometer polls show that since 2005 the share of the EU population that opposes Turkish EU membership has risen steadily, exceeding 50 per cent.[38]

I examined in more details the results of two EBs, 66-2006 and 67-2007. The EB 67 of 2007 shows that 49 per cent of Europeans are in favour of further enlargements and 39 per cent are against the idea (these figures are slightly higher than the previous EB). However, this EB did not have any specific question on Turkey.

The EB 66-2006 has a separate section on Turkey. It shows that 46 per cent of EU citizens support further enlargement, while 42 per cent continue to oppose it. But support for Turkey is less than in the previous year (28 per cent; –3 points), with 52 per cent of respondents seeing the accession of Turkey as mainly in the interest of that country. Respect for human rights is the condition that EU citizens see as the most important for Turkish membership (85 per cent; +2 points since 2005). Cultural differences also constitute a concern, with 61 per cent of interviewees feeling that the gulf between Turkey and the Member States is too important to allow it to join the EU (+6 points).

Conclusions from these surveys are that, while the overall support for enlargement has risen, support for Turkey has dropped. Public opinion supports other applicant countries, but not Turkey. Polls show that opposition has increased and that cultural differences constitute a major reason for this opposition.

Special Eurobarometer on Enlargement 2006
The Special Eurobarometer Survey is produced by the DG Enlargement, to review the attitudes and experiences of the EU population relating to the enlargement of the EU, as well as their perceptions of the advantages and disadvantages of the enlargement.

Its findings with relation to my questions are:
- 62 per cent of people think that enlargement of the EU is a good way to consolidate common European interests and values.
- Cultural diversity divides European public opinion: 71 per cent of Europeans agree that enlargement enriches Europe's cultural diversity. However, an interesting fact is that 48 per cent object to the disappearance of cultural national identities and traditions, while quite a significant number of interviewees (41 per cent) foresee this happening. The majority of British (56 per cent), Irish (57 per cent), and Greeks (57 per cent) worry about the disappearance of their cultural identities and traditions.
- Another interesting finding is that 43 per cent of Europeans think that the main challenge that applicant countries are

facing is respect for human and minority rights. 20 per cent consider the sharing of European values and principles a challenge for applicant countries.

- Of all candidate and potential candidate countries, Turkey's accession generates the most disapproval: 48 per cent are opposed and 39 per cent in favour, even if she complies with all conditions set by the EU. The strongest opposition occurs in Austria (81 per cent), followed by Germany and Luxembourg (69 per cent), Cyprus (68 per cent) and Greece (67 per cent).

- Meanwhile, 52 per cent of Europeans see the accession of Turkey as mainly in the interest of the country itself.

- 73 per cent of Austrians think that cultural differences between Turkey and the EU are too significant to allow for Turkish accession, an argument shared by 54 per cent of the EU-25 on average.

What conclusions can be drawn from these findings? Firstly, Europeans could not give any opinions about religion, because religion as a variable was not included in any of the questions. Secondly, this type of survey is done by the European Commission, and as such it reflects two things: one is the 'political correctness' of this institution with regard to tricky issues, and the other is that most of the questions are constructed around the Copenhagen criteria (political and economic issues) and *acquis communitaire*. But Turkey's accession, as we saw in the second chapter, is a complex issue that involves not just straightforward technical issues related to fulfilment of the Copenhagen criteria. This kind of opinion poll, unfortunately, does not reflect realistically what European people really think, say, discuss and worry about on this issue. There is a need for an opinion poll based on a questionnaire concerning Turkey exclusively, which should include a detailed set of questions on all the possible factors that impact on the process, in order to see what answers Europeans will give on the whole range of variables that affect her accession, including religion.

Thirdly, from the result we can see that culture, values and identity attract the attention of respondents. A large percentage of Europeans say that cultural differences are too significant to allow for Turkish accession. Also, a high percentage of Europeans want enlargement to consolidate common European values, and they object to the disappearance of national cultural identities and traditions. The notion 'different culture', as I argued before, is assumed to be meant frequently as a euphemism for 'Muslim religion'.[39] Therefore, the fact that questions on culture, values and identity attract the interest and attention of citizens means that religion would also have had such attention had it been included on the questionnaires.

Fourthly, the 'Copenhagen criteria' reasons do not seem to account fully for the high levels of opposition to the Turkish candidacy. A very interesting question is the conditional one of whether people would support membership 'once Turkey complies with all the conditions set by the EU'. It shows that nearly half of Europeans would still oppose Turkey's membership even if she fulfilled the EU 'official' conditions on the Copenhagen, Cyprus, Kurdish and Armenian issues. So, what else explain the hostility of Europeans? Religion and culture may be possible explanations.

Flash Eurobarometer 217: Intercultural dialogue in Europe 2007
Commissioned by the DG Education and Culture, the EB *Intercultural Dialogue in Europe 2007*[40] enquired about people's general attitude towards cultural diversity, and specifically the upcoming events of the Year of Intercultural Dialogue in the EU. 55 per cent of respondents expressed an attitude that suggests a preference towards cultural diversity, of being open to other cultures, but of wanting to preserve their cultural heritage as well. *'Pro diversity and keep roots'* was the most widespread attitude. However, the EB is about cultural diversity in general, without ever mentioning anything about enlargement and Turkey.

Financial Times Harris Polls
Every month the *FT* Harris Poll conducts a survey in major European countries on a variety of topics. An opinion poll conducted in June 2007 under the title *Is Europe big enough for Turkey?* said no. According to the results of the poll, conducted online in five EU countries, only 16 per cent of French voters

backed Turkish accession, while in Germany, support for Turkish membership stood at just 21 per cent.[41]

One of the few polls that had questions explicitly about religion and enlargement is that conducted in five EU countries in December 2006.[42] According to this, support for further enlargement of the European Union had fallen in the UK and Spain in the past six months, in a further sign that the policy is losing public favour. There is a question that covers both religion and enlargement, but not Turkey. To the question 'Do you feel the EU is predominantly a Christian club, or is a country's religion irrelevant to EU membership?', 35 per cent of French and Germans agree with the proposition that the EU is predominantly a Christian club. However, almost 50 per cent of Britons, French, Germans and Spaniards believe that religion is no barrier to entry to the EU.

The German Marshall Fund surveys

I examined the *2007 Transatlantic Trends Survey,* which shows that European views with regard to Turkish membership remained largely unchanged from a year before, with the largest percentage of respondents (42 per cent) viewing Turkish membership as neither a good nor bad thing, compared with 22 per cent who view it as a good thing and 31 per cent who view it as a bad thing.[43] France and Germany continued to have the highest percentage of respondents who view Turkish membership as a bad thing (49 per cent and 43 per cent respectively). These figures show a sharp decline from the results of surveys of a few years ago (in 2004, 30 per cent of the interviewees thought it was a good thing and only 20 per cent considered it a bad thing).

The Pew Forum on Religion and Public Life surveys

A Pew Forum report, titled *An Uncertain Road: Muslims and the future of Europe* says that:

> Opinion polls in most EU countries show that, despite the support of much of Europe's political elite, the continent's

populace remains sceptical of the benefits of including a largely Near Eastern and Muslim country of 70 million in Europe's grand experiment…The argument over Turkey goes beyond the geopolitical pluses and minuses of EU membership and raises the larger issue of Europe's troubled relationship with Islam. It is an old acquaintance, one stretching back more than 1,300 years.[44]

A Pew Global Attitude survey found that nearly two-thirds of the French (66 per cent) and Germans (65 per cent) oppose Turkey's EU bid, as do a majority of the Dutch (53 per cent). Support for Turkey's admittance to the EU is most substantial in Spain (68 per cent) and Britain (57 per cent). An analysis of the polling finds that opposition to Turkey's admission is also tied to growing concerns about national identity.[45]

Constitutional Treaty Referendum

Referenda are not a new phenomenon in the EU. Their use on EU issues started in the Maastricht Treaty, signifying the end of the so-called 'permissive consensus' that used to characterise public opinion attitudes during first decades of integration. However, what may be new is the idea of accepting new countries into the EU through a popular referendum. As mentioned earlier, it is likely that the accession of the next candidate countries (the Western Balkans and Turkey) will require a referendum. The application of this mechanism for new countries joining will change the policy-making process by including European citizens in the decision-making, which currently has been confined to EU institutions. Preferences of the public will be expressed on a much greater scale and not just limited to opinion polls and surveys. As Mark Leonard says, 'this new "age of referendums" changes the nature of EU debates'.[46]

The first signs of the EU public expressing their preferences as regards future enlargements were given in the referenda on the EU Constitution. In May and June 2005, voters in France and then the Netherlands rejected the Constitution. In the debate that followed, both media and political discourses often cited opposition to enlargement in general (and Turkey in particular) as a fundamental reason behind the 'nays' to the Constitutional Treaty.[47] Some voters, especially in the Netherlands, mentioned the prospect of Turkish membership as their reason for voting 'no'. However, polls carried out just after the referenda showed that the question of Turkey's accession affected only 5–6 per cent of the votes,[48] although a qualitative study carried out by OPTEM in all member states, at the initiative of the European Commission in spring 2006, showed some confusion in public opinion between the Constitution and Turkey's accession, as a majority of people thought that the accession was envisaged in the near future and not in the medium or long term, as Servantie notes.[49]

Letters in daily newspapers
Another source for the opinions of European citizens is letters to the Editorial and Opinion sections of various daily newspapers. These are particularly interesting, as the opinions are not determined according to formulation of questions, as in the case of opinion polls. One reader of the *Economist* wrote to the Editor:

> Sir, Turkey clearly does not belong to Europe. Indeed, no Muslim country does. The issue is not one of Turkish reforms failing to meet EU standards, but of an incompatible and primitive culture serving as a Trojan horse for the rest of Islam's impoverished masses.[50]

In his letter to the *Western Mail*, another person says: 'Turkey wants entry in the community, while the Turkish people and its culture will almost certainly need an extra period of time to adjust socially to the EU'.[51] In a letter in *Newsweek* magazine, a reader writes:

> The idea that a democratic Muslim nation can be just as modern and European as a Christian one is an oxymoron, as there is no example now or in the past of such a case, because the very nature of Islam is incompatible with a secular

democracy as developed by Christian Europe. The only reason that Turkey has come so far is due first to that great leader Kemal Ataturk, who introduced strong measures to curtail the influence of Islamic ideologies on Turkish society and the state. Second, the recent reforms in Turkey have been entirely due to the pressure from the EU, which no internal Turkish political force ever could have achieved.[52]

In another edition of this magazine, another person writes: 'In the wake of the global resurgence of Islam, Turks seem to have rediscovered their religious identity that lay buried under the European brand of secularism imposed by Ataturk in 1923'.[53] On the BBC News, there was this comment: 'Turkish society does not value human rights, freedom and life itself, as the Europeans do'.[54]

In conclusion, public opposition towards Turkey's accession has increased in recent years. Of course, this could change (for the better) when the time comes for Turkey to join, or member-states' governments may decide simply not to hold referenda. However, widespread public hostility is definitely having a bad impact on Turkey's accession process. Cultural differences, issues of values and identity, seem to be significant reasons for this opposition. The findings of Jiménez and Torreblanca show[55] that identity-related arguments account for the greatest opposition by Europeans, compared to post-national dimensions (democracy and human rights) and utilitarian reasons (costs and benefits).[56] Their findings show that levels of support for Turkey's accession are more likely to be based on elements connected with culture, history and geography, than with costs/benefits or universal democratic principles.[57] They conclude that the debate about Turkey's accession is and will continue to be a constitutive debate about European identity and values.

Also, in McLaren's study, rational economic self-interest does not go very far in helping to explain this opposition.[58] She argues that reasons are less economic in nature and more 'symbolic', i.e., threats to European culture and way of life, which are likely to be particularly strong in the Turkish case. Because feelings about

Therefore, while academic studies and opinion polls point to religion as a possible obstacle, the official reports and statements from the Commission do not mention this issue as an problem at all. However, even though there is no reference to religious and cultural factors, there is an ambivalence in the EU Commission's approach towards Turkey. Its policy has not been consistent over time, and the Commission has often been criticised for double standards. Many believe that the Commission has dragged out the process by finding excuses or 'inventing' conditions. Many Turks view these excuses (most notably the Cypriot and Armenian issue) as 'fig-leaves' behind which the EU hides its real religion and culture-based reservations, and suspect that they are concessions asked of Turkey, but not of other applicant countries. This differential treatment has increased frustration and sent negative messages to the Turkish people, which constitute a reason for their disappointment with the EU. It also may have a negative impact on the Turkish government, lessening its incentive for carrying out reforms. 'Putting new and even unrealistic demands on the negotiation table, without giving a clear prospect for its accession, does not help Turkey to carry on its reform process', point out Cebeci.[62] The proposals from some EU member states for alternative solution, such as 'privileged partnership', also seem to have alienated Turkish people and risk provoking a nationalist backlash. The ongoing excuses and delays seem to have damaged Turkish public support for EU membership, which the *Transatlantic Trends Survey* estimated at 40 per cent in September 2007, down from 73 per cent in 2004,[63] while the Eurobarometer 67-2007 records 43 per cent. At the same time as half of the Turkish population are expressing a negative feeling towards their European neighbours, there has been a sharp observable rise in sympathy and identification with Islamic countries (such as Iran). Furthermore, recent incidents and events in Europe, such as the hijab ban in French schools, the publication of controversial cartoons of the Prophet Mohammed in a Danish newspaper,[64] and Pope Benedict XVI's much publicised statement on Islam as a 'violent and irrational' religion,[65] have fuelled these feelings. The hostile reaction, with mass street protests, to the Pope's visit to group is divided in its position towards Turkey: in September 2006, 131 of its members voted in favour of accession and 91 for a privileged partnership. Even though the group has supported opening negotiations, it has been united in its view that there should not be a presumption of the inevitability of Turkish accession, as mentioned by Jonathan Evans MEP.[70] An important part of the EPP, led by the CDU/CSU (which has the largest number of MEPs), opposes Turkish membership. 'The Christian Democrats are the strongest opponents of Turkish entry into the EU...the views of some CDU members are that Turkey represents "an alien culture and an alien religion" and want the preservation of the EU as a "Christian club"'.[71] The chairman of the German CDU/CSU in the EP, Hartmut Nassauer MEP, points out his group's willingness to have good ties with Turkey and the AKP, but he sets limits to the relationship, saying, 'We should organise good cooperation with Turkey on the level of the customs union and all other considerations of privileged partnership. But there is, I think, no need to discuss membership'.[72] The CDU influence was also seen in the EPP summit in Val-Duchesse in 1997, which considered that Turkey does not share 'European values' as it has no Christian roots. CDU/CSU is backed by the French Union for a Popular Movement (UMP), which holds that Turkey is neither a European country nor democratic. On the other hand, many other parties, such as the Greek Neo Democracia, the Italian Forza Italia, the Spanish Partido Popular, the Finnish and Swedish parties, and in particular (and not least) the British Conservatives, are more in favour, emphasising the strategic influence of Turkey and its economic potential.[73] Parties from new accession countries are also supportive of Turkey. Even though the rejection of Turkey's candidacy is not an official position of the EPP-ED, recently they have been trying to gently close the door by increasingly endorsing the idea of a 'privileged partnership', based on the proposal of the German CDU/CSU. The EPP-ED's European Ideas Network, in its last Summer Conference,[74] established a working group called 'Europe's geographic limits', in which Turkey was the main target of discussions and its accession has been opposed. In 2005, the AKP joined the EPP-ED, and there is a hope that its presence as one of their partner parties will help to neutralise opposition to Turkish entry into the EU.

Socialists, Liberals, Greens and the European United Left are, in general, favourable, with some exceptions. The left-wing political groupings agree that the reforms made by the Turkish government need to be encouraged, and that it would be unfair to add new conditions for the country's accession. However, they believe that the country still has a lot of work to do when it comes to human rights.

The European Socialists (PES), the second-largest in the EP, have a pro-Turkish position, as they oppose the concept of a clash of civilisations and see Turkey as a bridge between Europe and the Muslim world. The leader of the European Socialists, Martin Schultz, said in a statement: 'If we succeed in including a Muslim society into our community of European values, we'd be able to refute the argument that Islam and Western values are incompatible'.[75] 'Despite the agreement on this issue within our group', said Maria Eleni Koppa, the Socialist MEP and Vice-Chairwoman of the EU–Turkey Joint Parliamentary Committee, 'there have been some differentiations and growing reservations, mainly from German and Austrian MEPs, who are more sceptical'.[76] 'My feeling is', she says, 'that the Turkish issue is not going to get better, as it is not a very positive environment in the EP. However, it is better to keep it as an open process, so that it can be a good incentive for Turkey.'

European Liberal Democrats are in favour, with exception of the Union for French Democracy (UDF) and the German liberal Free Democratic Party (FDP), who tend to be more reserved, if not opposed. Andrew Duff MEP, the Leader of the European Liberal Democrats and Vice President of the Joint Parliamentary Committee on Turkey, attacking the 'privileged partnership' proposal of the German CDU/CSU, said, 'I can see no privileges for Turkey in the so-called "privileged partnership" offered by the EPP group. A second-class membership of the Union for Turkey would make Turks second-class Europeans. We should not be satisfied with this'.[77]

The Green/EFA (European Free Alliance) is generally in favour, except for the Austrian MEPs and some German MEPs. Daniel Cohn-Bendit MEP of this group also criticises the EPP, saying that 'some of the opponents of Turkey's accession are surfing on a wave of cultural and racist prejudices'.[78]

The new Far Right grouping named 'Identity, Tradition, Sovereignty', which includes the French National Front, the Austrian Freedom Party, the Flemish nationalist Vlaams Belang from Belgium and the British UKIP, opposes Turkish accession. They are likely to push for a freeze on further EU enlargement, especially membership prospects for Turkey, principally on the grounds that it is a Muslim country. Chairman of the group Bruno Gollnisch MEP said:

> We consider Turkey as a bridge between Europe and Asia, but not as a European country. We want the EU to remain purely European. But this has nothing to do with being enemies of Turkey, just as we do not have anything against Morocco, Argentina or Canada, which are not EU members.

Another MEP from this group, Philip Claeyes, said, 'Turkey is not a European country and does not belong into Europe, and a privileged partnership would be preferable to fully fledged membership'.[79]

To conclude, while the European Commission has a unified position and supports Turkey's accession, the European Parliament is more divided on the Turkish issue and there is a diversity of positions among various political groupings and MEPs. This is confirmed by the findings of the *European Elites Survey 2006*, which shows that Commission officials felt more positive than MEPs and the general public, about Turkish membership in the EU. A plurality of EU parliamentarians and Council officials called it a 'good thing', and a majority (60 per cent) of surveyed Commission staff saw it as a 'good thing'.[80] Also, while cultural and religious issues are not mentioned at all in the Commission's position, they are articulated more in the EP, especially by individual parties and MEPs.

EU member states[81]

EU member states are divided on the issue of Turkey. Though there are national differences and varying reasons for the attitude of member states to Turkey's accession,[82] the debate seems essentially to divide along federalist and intergovernmentalist lines, with a respective divergence over deepening or widening the EU. The integrationists, who want the EU to be a supranational/federalist entity, view it as a Union with a common identity, culture, history, geography and a set of values. They believe that cultural elements, which constitute the common European heritage, should form the basis of a new common European identity. As the foundation of this European identity they see the Greco-Roman and Judeo-Christian historical, religious, cultural and political heritage. European integration and the EU project can function properly only if its members share this heritage. As Turkey lacks this heritage, it cannot be eligible to join this club. According to their view, Turkey's application should be assessed not just on the fulfilment of the Copenhagen criteria, but also on the country's compatibility with the common European values and identity. The second concern for this group is 'the workability' of the Union if Turkey is accepted. They argue that the inclusion of such a large Muslim country, with a different culture and poor economy, might make it extremely difficult for the EU to deepen its integration, and could reduce it to a simple zone of economic cooperation. They fear that further political integration along federalist lines would be impossible if the EU overstretches to include Turkey, and that her inclusion would spell the end of the federalists' dream of a political union.

This group includes France, Luxembourg, Austria, Germany, Cyprus, Hungary and Belgium, with the most voluble being Austria, France and Germany. Austria is the member state most strongly opposed to Turkey's accession.[83] It has historically served as a bulwark for Christian Europe against the Ottoman Empire and Austrians still recall the 61-day Ottoman siege of Vienna in 1683.[84] Katzenstein and Byrnes say:

Some of the trepidation expressed today about the growing presence of Muslims in Europe, or about the accession of Turkey is derived from historical memories of the great battles that took place over European religious and cultural identity in the distant, but not forgotten past. It's perhaps no accident that opposition for Turkish accession is these days strongest in Vienna.[85]

However, although some Austrians may still refer to these historical memories, the majority oppose it for contemporary reasons.[86] One significant reason is on cultural grounds, arising out of the failure of integration by Austria's 200,000 Turkish immigrants (part of its 400,000 Muslim population). Austria, like France, has declared it will put the issue of Turkey's membership to a referendum, which is likely to make it very difficult for Turkey to join.

Similarly, France is fearful of the prospect of new waves of Muslim immigration, especially given the poor integration of its existing Muslim community (of which 400,000 are Turks). Another reason relates to the influence of France's 400,000-strong Armenian community, which is very powerful and well-organised. Aside from cultural differences, a very important factor is the fear of further losing political power within the EU. The French are already worried that their country's central role in the EU has been weakened by successive enlargements.[87]

In Germany, issues of immigration and integration of a large Turkish community of three million are key ingredients of the debate about Turkish EU accession.[88] Debates on Islam and European values and the position of Turkish women have moved to the top of the German national agenda.[89] The future balance of institutional power is another concern. Therefore, Germany has come up with a Plan B, an alternative solution, known as 'privileged partnership', according to which 'there should not be new promises on EU accession beyond the Balkans'.[90]

The other group of member states with a more inter-governmentalist approach towards European integration, which sees the EU as a huge integrated market rather than a political entity, considers the debate on a common European identity unnecessary and irrelevant. They argue that the foundation of the European identity should not be based on culture and religion, but on liberal political values. As advocates of multiculturalism, they believe that cultural diversity in the EU is a strength rather than a weakness. They view the EU as a union based on universal principles of democracy and secularism that overcome religious, cultural and ethnic identities. Therefore, they support the accession of Turkey, which they view as a democratic secular country.

The greatest proponent member state is the UK (where both the two main political parties are in favour of Turkey's accession). Driven by security concerns, Italy, Spain and Portugal are also in favour. This group of member states (supported by the USA) sees Turkey's accession as a matter of foreign policy and points out the geopolitical and security advantages of making Turkey part of the EU, saying that this will make the Union a major player in global affairs, politically and militarily. They argue that accepting a big Muslim country like Turkey into the EU can be a bridge and a model, and a good way of spreading democracy in the Muslim world. However, the question is if it should be the EU's role to shape the Muslim world, and should enlargement be the instrument to do so.[91] Another argument is that Turkey can serve as a counterweight to international fundamentalist Islamist terrorism: 'America fights terrorism by invading Iraq, we fight terrorism by embracing Turkey'.[92] The opponents argue that Britain wants to dilute in-depth European integration, while the USA champions for its own interest the cause of a NATO member and American ally, and supports Turkey's entry as a geopolitical *deus ex machina*.

In his first visit as a US President to Turkey in April 2009, Barack Obama said, in a major speech to the Turkish Parliament, that Turkey's place is in Europe, and that the United States strongly supports Turkey's bid to become a member of the EU. The new president, whose dark skin and Muslim middle name Hussein have made him a hit there, went out of his way to acknowledge Turkey's pluralism in all its colours, telling Europe that in welcoming Turkey it would gain 'by diversity of ethnicity, tradition and faith'.[93] He spoke a day after telling European leaders at a summit in Prague that giving Turkey EU membership would bind the Muslim nation into the Western fold, a stance that drew opposition from French President Nicolas Sarkozy and German Chancellor Angela Merkel. France's Foreign Minister Bernard Kouchner criticised what he considered to be US intervention in EU affairs, saying that 'It's not for the Americans to decide who comes into Europe or not'. Austrian Foreign Minister Michael Spindelegger also underlined that the decision was up to European leaders alone.[94]

Hence, while the first group opposes Turkey through concern that Europe may lose much of its cultural identity, the second supports it in the hope that Turkish accession will help to bridge Islam and Europe. There are some countries where there is a mismatch between government and the public opinion position towards Turkey, most notably Greece and the UK, where the governments (and the main political parties) support Turkey, while public opinion opposes it.

It would be good if the EU could arrive at a unified position toward Turkey's membership, which it has been unable to do on past foreign issues, such as Iraq, Kosovo, etc, to show that it has a common voice in enlargement and foreign policy.

EU leaders and European politicians

The other actors, European and national leaders and politicians, also seem divided in their views about Turkey. In October 2007, fifty prominent politicians, including Joschka Fisher, Giuliano Amato, Marti Ahtisaari and Chris Patten, during the launch of a new think-tank, the European Council on Foreign Relations, appealed for the door to full membership for Turkey to be opened.[95]

Another influential group, the 'Independent Commission on Turkey', which is made up of distinguished European politicians and policy-makers, and is led by the former Finnish President and Nobel Laureate Martti Ahtisaari, is allegedly in favour of Turkey's accession. Through a hard-hitting report entitled *Turkey* turned against the idea of allowing Turkey into the EU because he was worried about the country's 'evolution in…a more religious direction'.[99] Fritz Bolkestein, former European Commissioner, is also one of the fiercest opponents of Turkey's membership, mainly because of Turkey's different culture and religion, which he expressed openly in his book *The Limits of Europe*, saying, 'If Turkey joins the Union, the relief of Vienna in 1683 will have been in vain'.[100] In a lecture given at St Antony's College, Oxford, he added, 'Turkey is not a European country and it has not gone through the historical developments that Europe did'.[101] On the same cultural grounds, former Agricultural Commissioner, Franz Fischer of Austria, opposes it by saying, 'Turkey is a *sui generis* society, far more Oriental than European', and so 'admitting Turkey as a member would be embarking on a march of folly'.[102] Similarly, the former German Chancellor Helmut Schmidt suggested that 'Turkey should be excluded from the EU due to its unsuitable civilisation'.[103] Other opponents of Turkish accession include Schmidt's successor Helmut Kohl, who declared that 'Turkey would never be granted accession while he was in power, as it represented a different culture and religion',[104] and former President of the European Commission Jacques Delors.

However, the statesman who is now leading the 'crusade' in Europe against Turkey's accession is the French President, Nicolas Sarkozy. Like his predecessor, Jacques Chirac, who proposed putting Turkey's membership to a referendum, Sarkozy made it clear during his campaign that he was not in favour of Turkey's accession, on the ground that 'largely Muslim Turkey does not culturally belong to Europe',[105] and that Europe has 'natural borders', which include the Balkans, but exclude Turkey. One of the points in his electoral programme was 'refusal of entry of Turkey permanently'.[106] He is in favour of promotion of alternative solutions such as 'associate membership/partnership'. This stance has been embraced by the German Chancellor, Angela Merkel, who has talked of a 'privileged relationship' with Ankara (initially this was proposed by centre-right politicians, such as German Interior Minister Wolfang Schäuble, and Franz Fischler). It is not clear yet what they mean by these alternatives for an advanced relationship with Turkey, but they entail a closer political, economic and strategic relationship between Turkey and the EU. However, this excludes important points in which Turkish people are interested, such as freedom of movement, employment of workers in EU countries, Turkey's access to EU structural funds, subsidies for the CAP, and participation in a common currency. Another initiative, conceived by Sarkozy during the presidential election, was the 'Mediterranean Union' as another alternative to Turkish EU membership.[107] However, matters with 'Club Med'[108] moved on, and the Turks were assured that participation will not be regarded as such an alternative.[109] Sarkozy then championed the idea of setting up a group of 'wise men' to reflect on the EU's future and its borders, endorsed in principle by the Lisbon summit. Enlargement Commissioner Olli Rehn has predicted that the group's reflections would rapidly lead them to the conclusion that enlargement is not a problem, but rather part of the solution to problems that the EU will face in the coming decades, such as energy security, climate change, cross-border crime and ageing population.[110]

In conclusion, EU leaders and prominent politicians are also divided on Turkey, with some influential people, such as Sarkozy and Merkel, opposing it. Moreover, there is currently not a positive supportive attitude on the part of EU leadership (Barroso himself is not a strong supporter of Turkey). This lack of positive political leadership, as Barysch points out, leaves the field wide open to the opponents of Turkish accession.[111]

5

REASONS FOR THE INCREASE OF EUROPEAN OPPOSITION SINCE 2001

As we saw in previous chapter, there has been a dramatic rise of European opposition towards Turkey in recent years, especially since 2001, and a growing sensitivity on cultural and religious issues. In this chapter I set out to investigate the reasons for this and I suggest there are five potential factors:

1. The rise of Islamic fundamentalism around the world and its implications for Europe.
2. The increase of the Muslim population in Western Europe and their degree of integration into European society.
3. Fear of Islamisation of Europe.
4. The prospect of a country of 70 million Muslims becoming part of the EU.
5. Political Islam as part of Turkey's mainstream politics.

5.1 The rise of Islamic fundamentalism around the world and its implications for Europe

During last century, the threats to Western societies were fascism and communism. But after the demise of the Soviet Union and Communism, as Bernard Lewis argues, Islam and Islamic fundamentalism have replaced them as the major threat to the West and Western way of life.[1] In 1991, the same year that the Soviet Union ceased to exist, bin Laden and his cohorts created al-

Qaida, which included many veterans of the war in Afghanistan. In their view, they had defeated a superpower (the Soviet Union) and now they felt ready to take on the other, America, which was a 'paper tiger' according to them. For bin Laden, his declaration of war against the USA[2] marked the resumption of a struggle for religious dominance of the world that began in the seventh century. The first terrorist organisation however, founded in 1964, was the Palestinian Liberation Organisation (PLO). Alongside the existing Islamist fundamentalist and terrorist organisations, such as the Muslim Brotherhood in Egypt,[3] the FIS in Algeria, Hezbollah in Lebanon, Hamas in Palestine, and the Taliban in Afghanistan, many new ones have been created, even outside Islamic countries. These organisations, such as the Young Ulama of Europe and the Islamic World League operate across many countries all around the world. One, a Turkish Islamist organisation in Germany called Hilafet Devleti, aims 'to declare the Caliphate State of Islam, proclaim it the legitimate government of Turkey in exile and bring to an end Turkey's existing secular government'. They aim to create the New World Order, in which 'the control of Koran will be over everybody's life, the Koran should become the constitution, the Islamic system of law should become the law and Islam should become the state'.[4] Martin Kramer highlights the global expansion of Islamist fundamentalism by saying that 'it is creating a world of thought that crosses all frontiers' and draws attention to 'the emergence of a global village of Islamic fundamentalism'.[5]

'There are many thousands of people', Cox and Marks note, 'both in Islamic countries and in most of the free countries of the world, who are working together to further the cause of Islamism and to undermine Western societies. The preservation of the latter can therefore no longer be taken for granted and will need to be defended with wisdom, courage, understanding and sensitivity'. They continue: 'the broad distinction between terrorists operating in the name of Islam and peaceable law-abiding Muslims must be respected, but it must not be allowed to cripple the effort that is needed to preserve the principles and institutions of Western societies'.[6]

In his book *The Crisis of Islam,* Bernard Lewis explains the origin of present-day Islamic fundamentalists.[7] He says that the members of the Muslim sect known as the *Assassins* (from the Arab word *Hashishija* – Hashish taker), active in Iran and then in Syria from the eleventh to the thirteenth centuries, are the true forerunners of the Islamic terrorists of today. However, Lewis explains that the Assassins were markedly different from their present-day successors. The victim was always an individual and he alone was killed (targeted assassination). An Assassin was not expected to survive his act, but in no circumstance would he commit suicide; he died at the hands of his captors. The aim of the Assassins' present-day imitators is not to defeat the enemy, but to gain publicity and inspire fear, a psychological victory. Their targets are civilians and innocents in public places. The first major example was the bombing of two US embassies in East Africa in 1998 – to kill twelve diplomats, the terrorists were willing to slaughter 200 Africans who happened to be there. The same disregard for human life, on a greater scale, lay behind the actions on US soil in 2001. Lewis argues that these are not just crimes against humanity and civilisation, they are also acts of blasphemy (from a Muslim point of view), as those who commit these crimes claim to be doing so in the name of God.

As mentioned in Chapter 3, according to fundamentalists the ultimate goal of Islam is to rule the entire world and submit all of mankind to the faith of Islam. In order to fulfil this goal, Islamic fundamentalists have proclaimed the 'jihad', the 'holy war'. It advocates a fight to the death against the West, 'the Infidel', and aims to recover lost lands or threatened territories. They claim that jihad is the only way to liberate the Muslim lands under occupation, such as Palestine, Chechnya, Kashmir, etc. For fundamentalists, the 'Qur'an is our law and Jihad is our way'. Jihad is sometimes presented as the Muslim equivalent of the Crusade; they are both holy wars for the true faith against an infidel enemy. The philosophy of fundamentalists is that:

Islam must have power in this world. It is the true religion. When Muslims believed, they were powerful. Their power has been lost in modern times because Islam has been abandoned by many Muslims. But if Muslims now return to the original Islam, they can preserve and even restore their power.[8]

Islamic fundamentalists believe that the problem of Islam is the betrayal of authentic Islamic values. The remedy is a return to true Islam, including the abolition of all laws and other social values borrowed from the West, and the restoration of Islamic Holy Law, the Shari'a. In this way, they provide a religious justification to mobilise people for jihad. In the name of jihad, martyrdom is justified, even though suicide is forbidden in the Koran. The suicide bomb, since the attack by Islamic militants on the well-defended US and French barracks in Lebanon in the 1980s, has become a popular means for fundamentalists to attack their 'enemy'. Suicide missions have been pioneered by two religious organisations, Hamas and Hisbullah, since 1982. Before then, the people who were chosen as suicide terrorists were male, young and poor. Later on, women and children were also recruited. The first female suicide bombers were Kurdish in Turkey in 1996 and then Palestinians from 2002. In Palestinian summer camps, children aged 8–12 begin the training that leads to some of them becoming suicide bombers. The suicide terrorists are offered a double reward: in the Afterlife, the delights of Paradise, and in this life, stipends for their bereaved families. Their martyrdom is subsequently celebrated and their families are given financial support.[9] Martyrs who die in the course of jihad are promised direct admission to Paradise in the Day of Judgment, and marriage to 72 beautiful virgins. This provides a great incentive and motive for suicide bombers.

The suicide terrorist dies by his own hands. The classical jurists distinguish between facing death at the hands of the enemy and killing oneself by one's own hands. This raises an important question of Islamic teachings, as the Islamic books are very clear on the subject of suicide. In Islamic faith, suicide is a major sin and is punished by eternal damnation. According to Islamic scriptures, the Prophet has said, 'Whoever kills himself with a blade will be tormented with that blade in the fires of Hell'. The suicide bomber thus takes a considerable risk on the theological nicety.[10]

Some scholars, like Oliver Roy and Francis Fukuyama, believe that radical Islamism does not come out of traditional Muslim societies, but rather is a by-product of the modernisation process itself. The radical Islamist ideology that has motivated many of the terror attacks over the past decade must be seen as a manifestation of modern identity politics, rather than as an assertion of traditional Muslim culture, argues Fukuyama.[11] Similarly, Berger notes:

> The Islamic revival is by no means restricted to the less modernised or backward sectors of society, as progressive intellectuals like to think. On the contrary, it is very strong in cities with a high degree of modernisation and in a number of countries it is particularly visible among people with Western-style higher education, in Egypt and Turkey.[12]

In this century, Islamic fundamentalism has emerged as the most dangerous threat to Western societies. Especially since September 11, 2001, the rise of Islamist international terrorism has been considered by the West as a huge security threat, hence Europe has joined forces with the USA for a common response and joint war against terrorism. The terrorist attacks in the USA in 2001 were followed by a series of al-Qaida inspired terrorist attacks in Europe over the next few years: the March 2004 train bombings in Spain, the brutal assassination of Dutch filmmaker Theo van Gogh in the Netherlands,[13] and the bombings in July 2005 on the transport system in Britain. In the past 12 months, there has been an increase in the planning of attacks in European countries, including Britain, Germany, Denmark and Austria, as a British MI5 report in 2007 confirms.[14] All these flashpoints, argue Katzenstein and Byrnes, 'have pointed to religion as a basic element of political conflict in contemporary Europe and all have involved Islam in one way or another'.[15] Lewis rightly says that most Muslims are not fundamentalists, and most fundamentalists are not terrorists; but, nonetheless, most present-day terrorists are

Muslims, and proudly identify themselves as such. In contrast, Irish or Basque terrorists do not identify themselves as 'Christian'.[16]

The rise of Islamic fundamentalism and the growing number of terrorist attacks has raised concern about internal national security. According to an *FT* Harris poll, 38 per cent of Britons, 30 per cent of Italians and 28 per cent of Germans believe Muslims in their countries are a threat to national security.[17] As the masterminds and executors of these attacks were all Muslims (in the case of the London attacks, the perpetrators were even born and raised in Britain), these events have fuelled the discussions and concerns among Europeans not only about Islamic fundamentalism, but also about Muslims and Islamic values, and they are likely to be important reasons for their increasing opposition towards entry to the EU of a candidate country that they identify as Muslim, Turkey.

5.2 The increase of the Muslim population in Western Europe and their degree of integration into European society

Muslim migration to Western Europe started after World War II, when workers from North Africa, Turkey and other Muslim countries came to work to rebuild the continent. The guest workers were supposed to stay temporarily, but they benefited from family unification programmes and became permanent residents. As Christopher Caldwell points out in his new book *Reflections on the Revolution in Europe*, immigration, intended originally as a solution to a short-term labour crisis, has become, without anyone particularly wanting it to be so, a permanent feature of the landscape.[18] Another category of Muslims came from South Asian Commonwealth countries to Britain. The current statistics of Muslim population vary from 15–20 million, up to 3–5 per cent of the EU population, and in most West European countries Muslims make up approximately 3.5 per cent of the population: France has about 5.98 million Muslims (10 per cent of the population), followed by the Netherlands with 6 per cent, Germany with about 3.4 million (3.7 per cent), then Sweden,

Map 1. Muslim populations in European countries

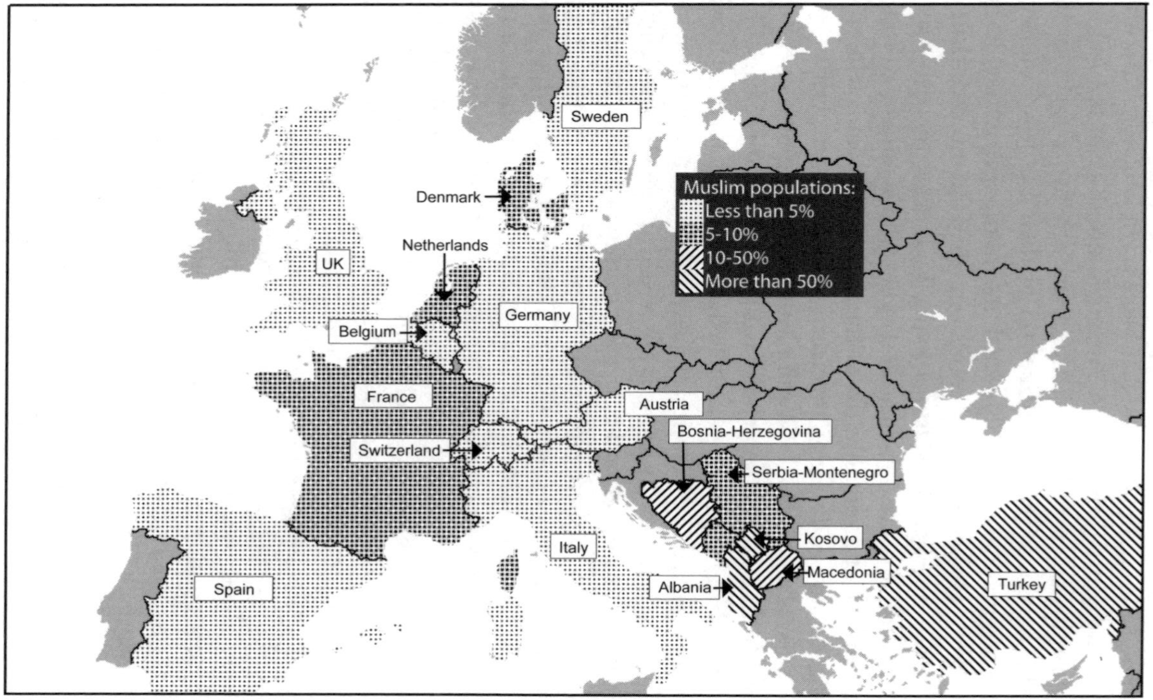

Muslim populations:
- Less than 5%
- 5-10%
- 10-50%
- More than 50%

Sweden
Denmark
Netherlands
UK
Belgium
Germany
France
Switzerland
Austria
Italy
Spain
Bosnia-Herzegovina
Serbia-Montenegro
Kosovo
Macedonia
Albania
Turkey

the UK and Italy. A study released in October 2009 by the Pew Forum on Religion and Public Life showed that there are now more Muslims in Germany than there are in Lebanon.[19] According to the Eurostat, the biggest foreign community in the EU is the Turkish one, reaching 2.419 million (this figure excludes those who have received the citizenship of their EU host country, or those with dual citizenship, which means the real number is much higher). However, as Roy points out, there are no precise figures for the number of Muslims living in Europe for two reasons: firstly, there is the difficulty of defining who should be considered a Muslim, and secondly, the European legal system is reluctant to register race and religion on census and identity papers.[20]

First of all, whom do we call a Muslim? A mosque-goer, the child of Muslim parents, somebody with a specific ethnic background (an Arab, a Pakistani)? A set of beliefs based on a revealed book? A culture linked to a historical civilisation? Roy's answer is that in the West the category 'Muslims' is often used as a neo-ethnic definition in the following terms: firstly, every person of Muslim background is supposed to share a common Muslim culture, whatever his or her real culture of origin (Turk, Pakistani or Arab), which means that religion is seen as the main component of these cultures; secondly, this culture is attributed to everybody with a Muslim origin, whatever his religious practice or level of faith; and thirdly, this culture differentiates a Muslim from others who, in the West, are never defined as members of a religious community (i.e., as a Christian), but as a pseudo-ethnic group: white, European, etc.[21] Despite the non-exact figures, one thing is for sure: the number of Muslims living in Europe has increased in less than a generation from about one million to over 15 million, and thanks to two factors – continued immigration and high Muslim fertility rates – it is predicted that this number will double by 2025. The growing presence of a Muslim community in Europe raises related issues of integration and multiculturalism.

What do we understand by multiculturalism? According to Fukuyama, multiculturalism is not just a tolerance of cultural diversity in multicultural societies, but a demand for legal recognition of the rights of ethnic, racial, religious or cultural groups.[22] Multiculturalism has now become established in all modern liberal democracies and in some of them, such as in Britain and Netherlands, there is an 'official multiculturalism'. However, most Europeans tend to see multiculturalism as a framework for the co-existence of separate cultures, rather than a mechanism for integrating newcomers into the dominant culture. Multiculturalism, as it was originally conceived in the USA, Canada and Europe, was seen as cultural diversity, as a kind of ornament to liberal pluralism that would provide ethnic restaurants, colourful dresses, and cultural and religious customs to be practised in the private sphere. Thus, the hosting societies could get along well with it as long as it did not challenge the liberal social order, and was not a threat to liberal-democracy.[23]

What is observable in recent years, however, is that certain Muslim communities are making demands or actions that simply cannot be squared with liberal principles. In some more extreme cases, some have even expressed ambitions to challenge the secular character of the political order as a whole.[24] A hostile reaction towards multiculturalism (considered by some as a euphemism for 'multi-faithism' or 'multi-racism') is on the rise, with people arguing that it has served only to dilute European countries' national identities, their own culture, lifestyle and religion, a culture that has been developed over centuries. As mentioned earlier, Larry Siedentop in his book *Democracy in Europe* speaks about 'an upsurge of multiculturalism' and a 'threat posed today by multiculturalism'.[25] Michael Nazir-Ali, Bishop of Rochester, one of the leading bishops of the Church of England, in criticising the Archbishop of Canterbury's recent claim that the adoption of some parts of Islamic law is unavoidable, points out that 'the Christian hospitality has been replaced by the newfangled and insecurely founded doctrine of multiculturalism, which has led to immigrants creating segregated communities and parallel lives'.[26] Michael Burleigh says, 'we are belatedly waking up to the divisive effects of "multiculturalism", a pernicious ideology with roots in the generic "Left University" that has undermined our confidence in ourselves'.[27] Phyllis Chesler who herself experienced an Islamic society during her years in Afghanistan says, 'We need to abandon our loyalty to multicultural relativism, which justifies, even romanticizes, indigenous Islamic barbarism, totalitarian terrorism and the persecution of women, religious minorities, homosexuals and intellectuals'.[28] Multiculturalism, argues Leiken, once a hallmark of Europe's cultural liberalism, has begun to collide with its liberalism, likewise, privacy rights with national security.[29]

While multiculturalism means the co-existence of different cultures, integration is the adoption of an ethnic community into a new hosting country identity; in this case, of Muslim communities in European societies. Francis Fukuyama considers the integration of immigrant minorities (particularly those from Muslim countries) as citizens of pluralistic societies, the most serious longer-term challenge facing liberal democracies today.[30] The integration issue is related to the revival of Islam among Muslims living in Europe.

One theory that tries to explain this is the Deterritorisation Thesis, formulated by Oliver Roy and supported by Francis Fukuyama. In his influential book *Globalised Islam*, Roy argues that the revival of Islam is not a backlash against Westernisation, but one of its consequences.[31] Neo-fundamentalism (which is just one of many forms of religious revival) is gaining ground among a rootless Muslim youth (particularly among second- and third-generation migrants in the West), ranging from support for al-Qaida to rejection of integration into Western societies. Caught between two cultures with which they cannot identify, and confronted with a sense of 'otherness', they find a strong appeal in the universal ideology offered by jihadism. Roy says that Islam thus provides a possible alternative identity to exclusion and may also offer a path to a new respectability. They break away from mainstream European values and endorse a supranational Islam, an imaginary Ummah or universal Muslim community not attached to any particular society or territory. Islam is used to bypass ethnic differences in favour of a universal, purely religious and trans-national identity. Roy argues that the root of radical Islamism is not cultural, nor is it a product of the cultural system that this religion has produced. It is a result of the fact that Islam has become deterritorialised. The question of identity does not come up at all in traditional Muslim societies. Identity becomes problematic precisely when Muslims leave traditional Muslim societies, for example, when they immigrate to Western Europe. Identity as a Muslim is no longer supported by the outside society; indeed, there is strong pressure to conform to Western society's cultural norms. Radical Islamism and jihadism, argues Roy, arise precisely in response to the quest for identity. This explains why second- and third-generation European Muslims have turned towards it. First-generation immigrants have usually not made a psychological break with the culture of their land of birth and carry traditional practices with them to their new homes. Their children, by contrast, are often contemptuous of their parents' religiosity, and yet have not become integrated into the culture of the surrounding Western society.

Fukuyama, like Roy, argues that it is their confrontation with modernity that produces the crisis of identity and radicalisation. Globalisation, driven by the Internet and the tremendous modern mobility, has blurred the boundaries between the developed world and traditional Muslim societies. The proximity brought by globalisation is inherently dangerous when cultures are different. It is not an accident that so many terrorists were either European Muslims or came from privileged sectors of Muslim societies with opportunities for contact with the West.

I agree with most of Roy's and Fukuyama's arguments. However, in my view the 'deterritorisation factor' is not the only reason for the Islamic revival in Europe. I believe that, alongside it, there are two other reasons that contribute. One is the solidarity with the Islamic cause and with 'Muslim brothers' in Palestine and Iraq, to 'protect or liberate the Islamic lands from Western occupation', as many Muslims believe there is a 'Western crusade against Muslims'. The other one is a 'classical' reason, differences in power and struggles for world military, economic and institutional power. The Western world's predominance, domination and supremacy, and Western military and economic power, have provoked hatred by fundamentalists.[32] This hatred is exacerbated even more by fond historical reminiscences about when Muslims enjoyed intellectual supremacy, economic prosperity and territorial dominance in the world. Lewis describes this hatred towards the West as 'perhaps irrational, but surely a historic reaction of an ancient rival against our Judeo-Christian heritage, our secular present and the world-wide expansion of both'.[33]

Secondly, I agree that deterritorialisation is one initial reason, but, unlike Roy, I believe that the root of radical Islamism is cultural, a product of the cultural system that this religion has produced. I do not agree, however, that religion alone is the reason that inspires and encourages the radical fundamentalist Islamism. It happens when Islamic culture comes into contact with the modernity and a different culture, and clashes because of its incompatibility with it. Thus, the whole phenomenon originates with the resilience of Muslims to integration, a process that, in my view, follows four phases:

First phase: the resilience of Muslim immigrants towards integration in the European hosting country, most typically by the first generation. This is caused by various factors, such as nostalgia for everything related with 'home' and the maintenance of powerful attachments with native cultures, as well as difficulties in adapting to the new reality, culture, lifestyle and language. Turks in Germany, Pakistanis in Britain, Moroccans in Belgium, Algerians in France, Indonesians in the Netherlands, appear to live in a parallel world within Europe, refusing to integrate, and self-segregating, socially and linguistically in housing, workplaces and schools. They gather in bleak enclaves with their compatriots and have no British, German, French friends to socialise with. As Leiken points out, 'They are European citizens only in name, but not culturally or socially'.[34] If asked, they hardly identify with their new adopted country to say 'I am British or French', but identify themselves as Muslims. Their youngsters complain about being victims and being excluded, but their social and cultural ghettoisation is mostly voluntary, as Laquer observes.[35] Amsterdam is often called the 'Satellite City' because of the huge number of reception dishes that are tuned to Al-Jazeera and Moroccan television channels. Tarifa notes:

They get their politics, religion, and culture from Arab and Turkish television channels, inter-marriages are quite rare and young men are sent to their home villages of Anatolia or Pakistan to find a bride…many Turkish women do not know German even after having lived in the country for many years.[36]

For the second or third generation, or the *beurs,* the lack of integration is more related to the crisis of identity. They are more advantaged economically and socially than were the first generation (their parents), and do not have the language barrier, but unlike their parents, they do not compare their life with that of the country of origin, but rather with that of 'white' Europeans, and subsequently feel disadvantaged.

The lack of integration of Muslim immigrants in the UK is shown in a survey carried out by the British think-tank, Policy Exchange, in 2007, entitled *Living Together Apart: British Muslims and the Paradox of Multiculturalism.* The results showed that 75 per cent of Muslims aged between 16 and 24 want women to wear the veil, one in eight of them admire al-Qaida, 40 per cent would prefer to live under Shari'a law in Britain (a legal system which, in some countries, may entail beheading, stoning to death or limb amputation), 36 per cent of the young British Muslims believe that the death penalty should apply for apostasy (thus a Muslim who converts to another religion should be 'punished by death'), and 58 per cent believe that many of the world's problems are a result of 'arrogant Western attitudes'.[37] The results of a similar poll carried out in Austria by the Muslim theologian Muhammad Korhide among 200 teachers of Islam[38] recorded similar views. Twenty-two per cent of those interviewed said they rejected democracy because it does not comply with Islam, 27 per cent did not accept human rights, and 18 per cent were in favour of death for apostasy.[39] The result of this study caused a furore amongst Austrian authorities. 'We allow religious freedom in this country', said Claudia Schmied, the Minister of Education, 'but this freedom ends where the Austrian laws begin'.

Second phase: This unwillingness to integrate, and the fact that Muslims have certain different social norms, set of values and lifestyle (which in some cases contradict the European way of life and culture), leads to the unwillingness of the hosting people to accept them into their society, which is expressed in attitudes of exclusion, xenophobia, racism, hostility, discrimination and segregation. Ayaan Hirsi Ali, the well-known Muslim dissident and former Dutch MP said in an interview:

If we do not want to adopt European values, we should expect to be criticised...you can wear whatever you want, you can give out whatever message you want, but if that message is rejected then you cannot call people Islamophobic.[40]

Similarly, Cox and Marks say, 'If they [Muslims] choose to live in Western liberal-democratic societies, they must accept the values of liberal-democracy, as Jews, Sikhs, Hindus and others have done for many years'.[41]

Third phase: as a result of this, Muslims feel ignored, despised, alienated, marginalised and estranged, not welcomed and appreciated, and their frustration gets worse over time.[42]

Fourth phase: some of them turn to neo-fundamentalism, in which they find a rewarding, universal and trans-national alternative and salvation to their identity crisis. In the words of a fundamentalist:

Islam was my salvation. They are scared of us, we are treated as fanatics, as holy madman, as violent people who do not hesitate to die or to kill. But none despise us anymore, now we are hated, but respected. This is the achievement of Islamism.[43]

The jihadists, fundamentalists and mujahedeens welcome, recruit, prepare and fund the alienated young Muslims, and encourage them to attend radical meetings, watch jihadist videos and discuss martyrdom on the Internet. There are now hundreds of websites which disseminate information about Islam and Islamist organisations. In an alarming report in November 2007, the head of Britain's MI5 said that the number of people suspected of being involved in terrorism has more than doubled in the past year, reaching a figure of 4,000, mostly young, Muslims.[44] In Britain, a group known as Islam4UK, which claimed it would march through Wootton Bassett and, in 2009, protested in Luton against a march by the Royal Anglican Regiment, had a UK ban on grounds of national security. The organisation, which has been trying to radicalise young Muslim men, advocates a worldwide Islamist system of government, and, at the same time, vehemently denounces the foreign policies of the USA and UK. Leaders and supporters of the organisation have been touring the country, holding small study circles, and arguing that Muslims owe no allegiance to the UK, but only to God, and that Muslims around the world are victims of Western aggression and British Muslims are their fellow sufferers. They also preach to followers in the UK over the Internet, justifying suicide bombings and debating whether Muslims should vote, declaring that any who did so are apostates and should be punished by death. Their website carried a picture of Buckingham Palace converted into a mosque.[45] British Muslim fanatics have often sparked fury on their websites by praising Taliban 'heroes' for sending British troops back from Afghanistan in body bags. Dozens of homegrown 'jihadis' have posted website messages in December 2009 cheering the fact that Britain's death toll has risen to 204 soldiers.

Teaching guides, who are generally supplied by public bodies in Muslim countries, such as Saudi Arabia, train teachers in Islamic educational institutions operating in Europe, particularly as regards how lessons on the Koran and the Muslim religion should be conducted. These guides pose dangers, as they seem designed to uphold Shari'a law and preach jihad, rather than respect for other people's religious beliefs, pluralism and recognition of human rights, the founding values of the European Union. Such books state that 'every Muslim is forbidden to offer allegiance or loyalty to those who do not abide by the laws of Islam and do not obey the Prophet'.[46]

However, there is another group of Muslims in Europe, who, in Tariq Ramadan's words, represent a moderate and liberal Islam.[47] There are many young and educated Muslims who are positively influenced by liberal-democratic values and try to live and behave as 'European Muslims'. They advocate political means, instead of violence, to win Muslims rights and recognition across Europe. And then, of course, there is another category, who try to integrate totally in the culture and society of hosting countries and use the opportunities the adopted country offers them, and subsequently do not have problems or crises of identity, considering themselves British, French, etc. The main character of the BBC Drama *Britz*, a young Pakistani law student born in the UK, says in his interview to join MI5: 'When my parents came to this country they had nothing, Britain took them in and fed them, and that's why I owe this country everything'. And when a friend asks him to attend a fundamentalist meeting, he says to her, 'If you don't like it here, you can leave, see if you find it better in Pakistan, where there is a military dictatorship'.[48]

Western European governments are often criticised for not having done more to integrate Muslims. This may be true, but even if they had done much more, integration would still have failed, because it is not wanted and integration is not a one-sided affair. However, with regard to this, I would argue that European governments have done a lot and have showered ethnic minorities with rights. One example is the Netherlands, a country that proclaimed multiculturalism as official and has done much to accommodate its Muslim immigrants. As Leiken notes:

Proud of a legendary tolerance of minorities, the Netherlands welcomed tens of thousands of Muslim asylum-seekers allegedly escaping persecution. It provided them with generous welfare and housing benefits, an affirmative hiring policy and free language courses. Dutch tax-payers funded Muslim religious schools and mosques, and public television broadcasts programmes in Moroccan Arabic. Mohammed Boyeri, a second-generation immigrant, was collecting unemployment benefits when he murdered Theo van Gogh.[49]

Therefore, Muslims, as Cox and Marks point out, should acknowledge that in Western societies they are better protected, more prosperous, but above all, more free to speak, to publish, to vote and to exercise numerous other freedoms, than they would be in almost any Islamic country. And should they not also acknowledge that there are few Muslim countries that offer Christians, Jews or those of other religions the freedoms that Muslims enjoy in Western societies?[50] The rights given to Muslims in European countries include even public or state support for Islamic schools. In relation to this, Siedentop argues that:

> If Islamic schools teach the radical subordination of women, do we really want public funding of such schools? For such funding amounts to a kind of endorsement of views which most of us find abhorrent, views which run directly contrary to our intuitions of justice.[51]

Some others point out that Muslims, taking advantage of one of the principles in liberal-democratic countries, the freedom of speech, are allowed to teach views that are illegal in public mosques too.

Tariq Ramadan accepts that the great majority of the millions of Muslims living in Europe enjoy freedom of worship, and organise themselves within the limits of the constitutions that protect their rights. He says that:

> The fact that after more than 40 years of presence in Europe the Muslims are generally allowed to practice their religion in peace, to build mosques and to found Islamic organisations, is clear evidence that the various European laws respect Islam as a religion and Muslims as Believers who have the right to enjoy freedom of worship. This is an indisputable fact and the increasing number of mosques and Islamic centres or institutions supports this...The great majority of Muslims in

Europe live in an atmosphere of security and peace regarding religious matters. Thus Muslims have the right to practise, found organisations and appeal to the law (after receiving unfair treatment and very often such cases are decided in their favour). Nothing within the European constitutions prevents Muslims from structuring themselves...Muslims living in Europe enjoy the right to practise their religion: there is no ban on praying, fasting or going on Pilgrimage to Makka.[52]

Fukuyama, on the other hand, believes that it is Europe's failure to better integrate its Muslims that makes a ticking time bomb that has already resulted in terrorism and violence.[53] The resolution to this problem, according to him, should be a two-fold approach, involving changes in behaviour by immigrants as well as by the national population. So, Fukuyama recommends two ways to address it:[54] firstly, due to a pervasive political correctness surrounding the whole set of issues, Europeans have not been able to address honestly and openly the problem of Muslim integration, either what immigrants owe to their adoptive society or what society owes its immigrants. The political parties on the centre-right that should drive such a discussion have been intimidated by the left's accusations of racism and old-style nationalism; they fear being tarred by the far right. Fukuyama belives that this is a huge mistake, and that the far right will make a big comeback if mainstream parties fail to take up this issue in a serious way. The return of several far-right parties in Europe has proved this, most recently with the election victory of the Swiss People's Party. Second is the issue of the Welfare State (which is also raised by Michael Burleigh).[55] Americans tend to believe, like Weber's early Protestants did, that dignity lies in morally redeeming work, rather than in the social solidarity of a welfare state, while Europeans continue to cling to the post-war welfare state and denounce the USA for its heartless social model. I agree with Fukuyama and Burleigh that the European welfare state is doing harm. The flexibility of the US labour market means that there is an abundance of low-skill jobs for immigrants to take, and most foreigners come to the USA in the search for work. In Europe a combination of inflexible work rules and generous benefits means that immigrants come in search not of work but of welfare. Europeans claim that the less generous welfare state in the US robs the poor of dignity. But the opposite is true: dignity comes through work. In many Muslim communities in Europe as much as half of the population subsists on welfare, directly contributing to the sense of alienation and hopelessness.

However, unlike Fukuyama, my view is that Muslims (and immigrants in general) should do more in terms of 'integration' and 'adoption' to their hosting country and society. Otherwise this will lead either to tensions between the sides, going through the four phases I described above, or to radical policies, such as that of the Australian government in dealing with its Muslim community. In 2007, the Prime Minister, John Howard, and his ministers criticised Muslims and threatened to throw them out of the country if they failed to integrate in their society. Treasurer Peter Costello said on National Television:

> If those are not your values, if you want a country which has Shari'a law or a theocratic state, then Australia is not for you...There are two laws governing people in Australia: one the Australian law, and another Islamic law that is false. If you can't agree with parliamentary law, independent courts, democracy, and would prefer Shari'a law and have the opportunity to go to another country, which practises it, perhaps, then, that's a better option.[56]

Education Minister Brendan Nelson later told reporters that 'Muslims who did not want to accept local values and don't want to be Australians, and who don't want to live by Australian values and understand them, well then, they can basically clear off'. Prime Minister Howard said:

> Immigrants, not Australians must adapt. Take it or leave. I am tired of this nation worrying about whether we are

offending some individual or their culture…I am not against immigration, nor do I hold a grudge against anyone who is seeking a better life by coming to Australia. However, there are a few things that those who have recently come to our country, and apparently some born here, need to understand…This idea of Australia being a multicultural community has served only to dilute our sovereignty and our national identity. And as Australians, we have our own culture, our own society, our own language and our own lifestyle. This culture has been developed over two centuries of struggles, trials and victories by millions of men and women who have sought freedom… We speak mainly English, not Spanish, Lebanese, Arabic, Chinese, Japanese, Russian, or any other language. Therefore, if you wish to become part of our society learn the language!… Most Australians believe in God. This is not some Christian, right-wing, political push, but a fact, because Christian men and women, on Christian principles, founded this nation, and this is clearly documented. It is certainly appropriate to display it on the walls of our schools. If God offends you, then I suggest you consider another part of the world as your new home, because God is part of our culture…We will accept your beliefs, and will not question why. All we ask is that you accept ours, and live in harmony and peaceful enjoyment with us. If the Southern Cross offends you, or you don't like 'A Fair Go', then you should seriously consider a move to another part of this planet. We are happy with our culture and have no desire to change, and we really don't care how you did things where you came from. By all means, keep your culture, but do not force it on others…This is our country, our land, and our lifestyle, and we will allow you every opportunity to enjoy all this. But once you are done complaining, whining, and griping about our Flag, our Pledge, our Christian beliefs, or our Way of Life, I highly encourage you take advantage of one other great Australian freedom, 'The right to leave'. If you aren't happy here then leave. We didn't force you to come here. You asked to be here. So accept the country you accepted.[57]

Speaking about the issue of integration of Muslim communities in Europe, Tariq Ramadan in his book *To Be a European Muslim* explains:

During the 1960s and 1970s the migrants arrived with the idea of returning to their country of origin as soon as they had earned sufficient money, but it became difficult, and often impossible to achieve this aim. Their sons and daughters were born in a new country, in a new environment with a new state of mind. The early simplistic conclusion was that with the passage of time, perhaps one generation, the new immigrant communities would have become assimilated, at least in their attitude to religion they would have been Europeanised. Now one generation later, the picture looks different from what observers thought. The new presence of Muslims has created problems in European societies: because of their recent social visibility and that there are now millions of Muslims residing in the West and that almost half of them are already citizens, has provoked various and contradictory reactions within the indigenous population. For some it is the obvious sign of a perilous invasion.[58] Therefore we have at one extreme, the assimilationist pattern. At the other extreme, there is the isolationist pattern which is based on the preservation of identity through the creation of an organised religious and cultural community. In the middle, it is the integrationalist pattern, which should provide both a protection to the Muslim identity and a status of citizenship.[59]

Ramadan states that, early in Islamic history, some ulama drew a specific geography of the world, distinguishing Dar al-Islam from those which were not under Islamic rule, called Dar al-harb, and stating that it was not possible for Muslims to live in Dar al-harb except under some mitigating circumstances. What bearing does this have on those Muslims who come to work and are now living in the West with their families? What about their children and their nationality? They are obviously not in the historically defined space of Dar al-Islam. There is an agreement among the ulama, which stipulates that it is not permitted for a Muslim to stay in a non-Muslim environment in three cases: without a determined need or a clear objective to justify the stay; when the settlement is based only on a selfish will (such as getting a good job or more money), or the desire to follow a Western way of life while neglecting Islamic religious prescriptions; or if the Muslim allies himself with non-Muslims for the purpose of fighting Islam or other Muslims. In all other cases, such as working, studying, trading or fleeing persecution, a Muslim is allowed to stay in a non-Muslim environment, but only under two major conditions: he should be free to practise his religion; and he ought to be useful by his work, study and other activity to his Muslim community as a whole.[60] As a minority in Europe, the Muslims obviously cannot apply all the principles and rulings prescribed by the Koran and Sunna in the field of social affairs: the specific rulings concerning marriage, death, inheritance, trade, interest, etc, are not in force in Europe (some are even contradicted by international charters). So the question is, how to remain faithful to the Koran and Prophetic teachings in new historical, social and political situations and in Europe? In other words, how to be a European Muslim? Some radical Islamic groups claim that a Muslim cannot be bound by a constitution which allows alcohol and other behaviour that contradicts Islamic teachings. Therefore, they must on the one hand respect the constitution, and, on the other, avoid all kinds of activities or involvements which are in opposition to their beliefs. They must determine which things can be done and which must be avoided: some of the latter are very clear, as in the case of what is prohibited by Islam but allowed in Western legislation, like intoxicants (alcohol and light drugs), or extramarital sexual intercourse.[61] In my opinion it is hypocrisy for many Muslim men who consider it *haram* (forbidden)to drink beer, but on the other hand take hashish, or who would stone women to death for adultery while considering it normal to have extramarital affairs themselves.

How does this analysis of the question of integration relate to this book's main argument? The failure of a proportion of the Muslims and Turks (who constitute a considerable percentage thereof) to integrate into their European hosting countries is leading to a growing hostility towards Muslims and Islamic values, and may be one of the reasons to explain the increasing opposition to Turkish EU candidacy. Thus, more than a catalyst for, this Muslim diasporic community in Europe might become a barrier to EU accession for Turkey and for other states with a majority Muslim population. The findings of McLaren's study[62] show that countries that have the highest concentrations of Turkish immigrants, such as Germany, France, the Netherlands, Austria and Belgium, exhibit the greatest intensity of opposition, because of the low degree of Turks' integration.[63] The results of various public opinion polls, as we saw in the previous chapter, confirm this. McLaren argues that some opposition can be explained by economic concerns, but that the more critical factor is probably still rooted in perceived cultural differences, especially religious differences, as some people see Turkey's candidacy as a threat to European culture and way of life. Indeed, a study of the Pew Research Centre showed that European debate over headscarves has become heated, particularly in Britain, Germany and Spain where respectively 53 per cent, 44 per cent and 45 per cent of Muslim women wear headscarves.[64] Furthermore, an ESI report showed that in Germany some 45 people have fallen victim to honour killings and similar crimes since 1996.[65] Integration of Muslims and Turks, therefore, as well as their cultural adaptation to hosting European countries, has a significant impact on European attitudes towards Turkey's candidacy.

5.3 Fear of the Islamisation of Europe[66]

As mentioned in the first section of this chapter, the events of September 11 and other attacks by Islamist fundamentalists that followed, have fuelled a backlash and feelings of Islamophobia against all Muslims, including even the majority, who are moderate, law-abiding and peaceful. However, the reasons behind Islamophobia are not solely because of the increase of Islamic fundamentalist activity. Another reason may be the growing fear among Europeans of an 'Islamic culture invasion', which has started to be perceived as a threat.[67]

The so-called 'Christian Secularism', established in Europe in the last centuries, is facing a challenge with the growth of Islam inside its territory and as the fastest growing religion in Europe. 'For the first time in history', as Osnos notes, 'Muslims are building large and growing minorities across the secular western world, more visibly in Western Europe'.[68] In East London (labelled as 'Londonistan'), in parts of Rotterdam, Berlin, Birmingham and Lyon, Muslims already constitute the majority. Islam is now the largest faith population in Europe; in some countries, such as France, Germany, the Netherlands, Denmark and Austria, it is now the second religion. There are 1,100 mosques in Britain alone, as Burleigh observes.[69] In Germany there are currently 159 mosques[70] and there are plans to construct an additional 184 mosques to accommodate the rapid rise in the Muslim population.[71] In the name of integration, so-called 'cultural centres' or 'intercultural meeting places' have been built or are planned in a growing number of towns and cities in Europe, some of the costs of which are funded from the taxes paid by EU citizens. However, these buildings can be clearly recognised as mosques from the plans alone, and some of them are being constructed in areas where scarcely any Muslims live and, moreover, without offering local residents the possibility of lodging objections.[72]

Unlike secular, moderate and liberal Europeans, many Muslims seem to take their religion very seriously. Furthermore, the children and grandchildren of Muslim immigrants in Europe are increasingly embracing Islam. In France and the UK, polls show greater commitment to daily prayers, mosque attendance and fasting during Ramadan than a decade ago.[73] Growing patterns of Islamisation are observable everywhere in Europe, as more young women wear hijab and burka and more men wear skull-caps and grow beards.[74] On many European streets, shops show signs in Arabic and other Near Eastern languages, and sell clothes and an array of exotic-looking products from the Middle East and other parts of the Islamic world. Indeed, according to a Pew Forum report, in the space of a few decades whole neighbourhoods in cities like Birmingham, Rotterdam and Paris have been transformed.[75] Islam is not only the largest faith population in Europe, but also widely considered Europe's fastest growing religion, because of the two factors mentioned earlier: immigration, and above-average birth-rates, leading to a rapid increase in the Muslim population. If Turkey joins the EU, this would seriously skew the Christian and secular nature of the European continent, given the country's population of around 80 million (almost all of them Muslim) at the time of possible accession, combined with the 17 million Muslims already in the EU. And, with a population growth among Muslims of up to 20 per cent, Islam could become the dominant religion in Europe.

Ramadan ranks five objective facts that he says can be brought to the fore regarding the reality of the Muslim presence in Europe:[76]

1. There is a revival of Islamic spirituality and practice and a feeling of belonging to a religious community amongst many young Muslims in Europe.
2. The number of indigenous European Muslims is increasing either through conversion to Islam or birth.
3. The number of places of worship has multiplied 4–5 times, although they are still insufficient.
4. The number of Islamic organisations in Europe is increasing daily. Some countries (France, UK, Germany) have already recorded more than a thousand official organisations. France has more than 2,000, and there are 120 for the small Muslim community of 200,000 living in Switzerland. There are differences between purely religious institutions and social or cultural ones, but both types are present and active today.
5. About 70 per cent of Muslims fast during the sacred month of Ramadan.

Mgr Georg Ganswein, Pope Benedict XVI's private secretary, speaking in an interview with Germany's *Sueddeutsche Zeitung* magazine about Islamic influence in Europe, said, 'Attempts at the "Islamification" of the West cannot be denied'.[77]

The fear of Islamisation of Europe is leading to three consequences: firstly to increasing Islamophobia and Turkophobia, secondly to the revival of far-right-wing parties in Europe, and thirdly to the introduction of tougher immigration policies.

With regard to the first, there is now a growing and, in some cases, very alarmist literature on the emergence of 'Eurabia'. This term was used by the Italian journalist, author and political interviewer, Oriana Fallaci, in a *Wall Street Journal* interview in 2005, where she said that 'Europe was no longer Europe, but Eurabia, a colony of Islam, where the Islamic invasion does not proceed only in a physical sense, but also in a mental and cultural sense'.[78] In the words of politicians, as Fritz Bolkestein, 'Europe is full, Europe has been oversold'.[79] These words, says Tarifa, have become endemic in the consciousness of many Europeans, who see the growing number of immigrants in their societies as 'an apocalyptic trend, an invasion by Muslims'.[80] Europeans' fear of Islamisation is leading to xenophobic and racist attitudes. A study conducted by the German Institute for Interdisciplinary Research on Conflict and Violence in 2006 in Bielefeld showed that xenophobia is on the rise in Germany: 59.4 per cent of Germans in 2006 'agreed' or 'strongly agreed' with the statement that 'too many' foreigners live in Germany, an increase of 6 per cent over 2002. In February 2008, a chain of fires on Turkish immigrants' houses and xenophobic phrases and symbols on the house walls, in several German cities (Marburg, Kreuzberg, Ludwigshafen, Herne, etc), were indications of this increasing Turkophobic atmosphere. 'As crunch time nears for one of the EU's biggest ever decisions', a journalist from the *Guardian* writes, 'Turkophobia is sweeping the region and deep-seated European prejudice is showing its true colours'.[81]

Anxieties and fear about the 'Islamisation of Europe' were clearly seen in two recent bans imposed by Europeans on Islamic symbols: minarets in Switzerland, and the burka in France.

Mosques and minaret construction projects in Sweden, France, Italy, Austria, Greece, Germany and Slovenia have been met by protests. However, the Swiss ban on minarets was one of the most extreme reactions. In November 2009, Swiss people overwhelmingly approved in a referendum a constitutional ban on minarets. More than 57.5 per cent of those voting, and 22 out of 26 cantons, voted in favour of the ban on the iconic mosque towers, thus putting Switzerland at the forefront of a European backlash against a growing Muslim population. The referendum was initiated by the nationalist Swiss People's Party, the largest party in parliament. They labelled minarets as a sign of Islamisation and symbols of rising Muslim political power that could one day transform Switzerland into an Islamic nation. Their campaign posters showed minarets rising like missiles from the Swiss flag next to a fully veiled woman. 'The minaret is a sign of political power and demand, comparable with whole-body covering by the burka, tolerance of forced marriage and genital mutilation of girls', the sponsors said. Supporters of the ban claimed that allowing minarets would represent the growth of an ideology and of the Islamic legal system, Shari'a, both of which are incompatible with Swiss democracy. Walter Wobmann, President of a Committee that backed the initiative, said its aim was not to stop people from practising their religion, but to stop political Islam and the 'further Islamisation of Switzerland'.[82] The sponsors stated that Turkish Prime Minister Recep Tayyip Erdogan had compared mosques to Islam's military barracks and called 'the minarets our bayonets' (Erdogan in fact made the comment when citing an Islamic poem many years before he became prime minister).[83] While the new law does not allow the building of any new minarets, Muslims (who comprise about 6 per cent of Switzerland's 7.5 million people – about 400,000 people, most of them immigrants from Turkey and the Balkans) could still build new mosques and continue to worship in the 200 mosques that already exist in Switzerland (according to the government, about one in 10 Muslims actively practises their religion). The ban, on the other hand, caused a strong reaction among Muslim groups in Switzerland and across the world, with condemnation of the vote as anti-Islamic and a blow to religious freedom. However, the Egyptian writer Alaa Al-Aswani rightly stated in a Swiss TV interview following the referendum that Muslims should not complain, but try to reflect a positive image of Islam. In an interview with Urs Ziswiler, the Swiss Ambassador in the USA, the interviewer, Ahmed Ghanim, an Egyptian-American writer, wondered how minarets constituted a cause for concern, yet church steeples did not. The answer of the Ambassador was that 'Christianity is deep-rooted in Switzerland, existing there for over 1,300 years. Churches are considered by many Swiss residents to be a traditional part of the landscape. Muslims residents arrived recently, most of them only in the last 25 years. Many of them found shelter in Switzerland during the conflict in former Yugoslavia'. He followed this with: 'Most of the people living in the US have a foreign background. From the beginning, the USA has been what is often called a melting pot. This is very different in Europe, where peoples and cultures have deep roots and long histories. In the past, many European cultures have been threatened by wars and aggressions. This might explain the more defensive stance of many European countries who try to defend their own specific values by asking immigrants to integrate into their societies'.[84] A heated debate continues on the meaning and implications of this referendum both for Muslims in Switzerland and in Europe in general. European right-wing groups welcomed the result in Switzerland, calling for other countries to take similar measures. The Lega Nord (Northern League), the second-largest party in Italy's governing coalition, has been against the building and opening of new mosques.

The other ban that is set to take place, in France, is of another Islamic symbol, the burka.[85] A long-running debate has been held on this issue, following the passage of a 2004 law that banned headscarves and any other 'conspicuous' religious symbols in state schools, and which received overwhelming political and public support. The debate about whether to ban the full veil was based on concerns for sexual equality and public safety. In a speech in June 2009, and in another in October, on French national identity, French President Sarkozy said the burka was not a symbol of religious faith, but rather a sign of women's subservience, and declared that the full veil was 'not welcome in French soil'. 'We cannot accept, in our country', he said, 'women imprisoned behind a mesh, cut off from society, deprived of all identity. That is not the French Republic's idea of women's dignity'.[86] A parliamentary committee of 32 lawmakers was set up to investigate the spread of the burka in France, whether women were being forced to cover themselves or doing so voluntarily, and, most importantly, if the spread was indicative of a radicalisation of Islam and whether a law should be enacted to bar Muslim women from wearing the full veil. In January 2010 a report produced by the committee said that 1,900 women wear full veils in France, and recommended a partial ban thereof in hospitals, schools and government offices and on public transport (despite the fact that opinion polls suggested a majority of French people supported a full ban).[87] The report noted: 'The wearing of the full veil is a challenge to our republic. This is unacceptable. We must condemn this excess'. Presenting it to the French National Assembly, the Speaker Bernard Accoyer, said the face veil had too many negative connotations: 'It is the symbol of the repression of women, and... of extremist fundamentalism'.[88] The Committee's 200-page report also recommended that anyone showing visible signs of 'radical religious practice' be refused a residence permit or citizenship.

A week later, the French government duly refused to grant citizenship to a foreign national on the grounds that he forced his wife to wear the full Islamic veil (the man needed citizenship to settle in the country with his French wife).[89] Commenting on this, the Immigration Minister, Eric Besson, stressed that French law required anyone seeking naturalisation to demonstrate their desire for integration.[90]

The debate on the burka ban involves important issues, such as religious freedom, female equality, secular traditions and even fears of terrorism. France is not the first country to debate and take action towards it. Some German states have introduced bans on headscarves for Muslim women teaching in public schools, and in the state of Hesse the ban applies to all civil servants. In Britain, the UK Independence Party has called for all face-covering Muslim veils to be banned. Ex-UKIP leader Nigel Farage, who leads UKIP's 13 MEPs in Brussels, said that veils were a symbol of an increasingly divided Britain, that they oppressed women, and were a potential security threat.[91] UKIP is the first British party to call for a total ban, after the anti-immigration British National Party (BNP) had already called for the veil to be banned in Britain's schools.[92] In Italy, some mayors from the anti-immigrant

Northern League have also banned the use of Islamic swimsuits. In Denmark, in 2008, the government, after pressure from the Danish People's Party, announced it would bar judges from wearing headscarves and similar religious garb in courtrooms. In Belgium, several districts have banned the burka in public places on the grounds of public safety. In Austria, the Women's Minister has said a ban should be considered in public spaces if the number of women wearing the veil increases dramatically. Similarly, in Switzerland the Justice Minister said a face-veil ban should be considered, if more Muslim women begin wearing them, adding that the veils made her feel 'uncomfortable'.[93]

This is how India Knight, a columnist at the *Sunday Times*, describes it:

> My other concern is that burkas turn women into objects – creatures, if you like. You don't think 'Oh, there's Mrs So-and-so', but you think 'There goes one of those women peering out of a grille'. It's as if there's a bird in a cage and someone has thrown a sheet over it. With the best will in the world, it's hard to see (literally) how the concepts of citizenship, freedom and democracy are working for the bird person.[94]

However, rising concerns about this issue have much to do with public safety or security. As many say, the most indisputable reason for banning the burka is that it may be used for concealing identities, and thus for purposes of terrorism. There are cases in Europe when Muslim women keep their faces covered even for their passport and driving-licence photos.

Returning to our analysis of the consequences of the fear of Islamisation: the second consequence has been the revival of far-right-wing parties in Europe, which is related to the third, the introduction of tougher immigration policies. Many European countries now have right-wing populist parties that oppose immigration on the ground of national security and demand an aggressive policy of assimilation of Muslim communities, opposing the 'multiculturalist dream of diverse communities living in harmony'. The BNP, the Freedom Party in Austria, National Front in France, the Lijst Pim Fortuyn in the Netherlands, the People's Party in both Switzerland and Denmark, are increasingly demanding new curbs on mass immigration, or even calling for a halt to it. Far-right parties are now not just part of the political spectrum, but even of governments. The most astonishing example of recent years was the victory of the People's Party in Switzerland in 2007. Despite being accused by some for a nationalistic, xenophobic, racist and Islamophobic programme and campaign, it received the highest vote ever recorded for an individual political party in Switzerland.[95] The party ran an anti-immigration election campaign which depicted white sheep standing on a Swiss flag kicking a black sheep from their midst. The slogan accompanying the image was 'More security'. Directly after coming to power, the right-wing government funded a £180,000 television advertising campaign in an attempt to deter would-be-immigrants from travelling to Switzerland.[96] The Forza Nuova is a political group in Italy that is against immigration on the grounds of national security and opposes the advance of any cultural and religious traditions that threaten Italy's cultural and religious roots. It considers Islam as an 'ancient enemy' of Western and Christian values.[97] However, tough policies on immigration and integration are not only embraced by far-right parties, but also by mainstream parties, such as the British Conservatives. They also demand the curbing of uncontrolled immigration and a tightening of procedures as regards asylum-seekers and family unification.

The increasing popularity of right-wing anti-immigration parties was seen also in the June 2009 elections for the European Parliament, where they increased their share of the vote in several European countries. In the Netherlands, the anti-immigration and anti-Islamic Freedom Party of the right-wing Dutch MP Geert Wilders, which had previously held no seats in the European Parliament, came second, wining four seats. Polls in Holland before the elections showed that EU enlargement, immigration and integration were the most unpopular government policies.[98] In Austria, the far-right Freedom Party doubled its share of the vote. There were also gains for the extreme right in Hungary and Finland. In Britain, the anti-immigration BNP won, for the first time, two seats in the European Parliament, a result that showed that voters were worried about immigration issues. Moreover, the UK Independence Party (UKIP) recorded an impressive result, finishing second and ahead of the Labour Party, and increasing its number of MEPs to 13. Its leader claimed that the party would have gained even more votes if it had been allowed to debate the European issue properly, with a focus on immigration and the Union's further enlargement, which had been largely ignored in favour of the scandal of MPs' expenses that dominated the campaign.[99]

European governments, under pressure from public opinion and political parties, have constantly revisited their domestic policies and laws in dealing with their Muslim communities, as well as with immigration; on the one hand expanding the rights of Muslims and making laws to combat discrimination and reduce segregation and unemployment, and on the other influencing the direction of Islam within its borders (deporting people engaged in terrorist or fundamentalist activities or organisations, or reinforcing secularist measures, such as the banning of head-scarves and other religious symbols in public schools in France). However, many European governments are now introducing tough policies on immigration and the integration of Muslims. According to an International Crisis Group report, Germany has introduced a very tough new citizenship test, and has proposed a new policy according to which integration should precede naturalisation: Turks and other Muslims should first integrate and demonstrate their 'German-ness' before they acquire citizenship.[100] The British have introduced a 'Life in the UK' test, which requires knowledge not just of the language, but also of the history, culture and politics of the country. The Swiss, who already have the toughest naturalisation laws in Europe, now ask the local community to give the final say in applications for naturalisation through a ballot system.[101] Applicants must get the approval of local residents, who can easily reject their application[102] even after the applicants have proved they can speak the language, understand Swiss laws and culture, and have lived in the country for at least 12 years.[103] The new law on naturalisation is very much supported by the SVP (Swiss People's Party), whose campaign poster showed black and brown hands grabbing at Swiss passports.[104] The Dutch, since the assassination of Theo van Gogh, have gone from being one of most tolerant nations in Europe, believing that Muslims could constitute another 'pillar' like Roman Catholics and Protestants, to taking serious steps towards assimilation and integration of immigrants. The Dutch government now sends out a provocative video to prospective citizens of Muslim immigrants to show them what Dutch values are like. The video includes windmills, tulips, a topless female bather, and a homosexual wedding – Welcome to the Netherlands!

The rapid increase of Islam to become the second faith in Europe may have another consequence: it may soon fill the gap created by the decline of Christianity. Faith and religion no longer play an important role in European social life. Europeans are not used to a public manifestation of religious presence in their day-to-day lives, and the majority do not practise religion. Europe has become, as Pope Benedict has said, 'empty from the inside'. Reasons for this decline have been explained in the first chapter of this book with reference to Secularisation Theory and Europe Exceptionalism. Larry Siedentop says:

> Western spokesmen, including quite often the clergy themselves, describe contemporary Western societies as secular and materialistic. This means not just that most Western people have ceased to be regular church-goers, but that Western societies are no longer grounded in shared beliefs. The implication is that what holds them together now are shared interests arising from consumer wants and the radical interdependence springing from an advanced division of labour. The pursuit of wealth, it is held, has replaced belief as the cement of society in the West.[105]

He continues, 'The future influence of Europe in the world, as well as its ability to create free pan-European institutions, will depend upon its becoming more conscious of that moral inheritance'.[106] Similarly Burleigh argues:

> Opponents of religion regard Christianity as an obstacle to a peaceful Europe, a grim record of Crusades, the Inquisition and burning witches…Europe's secularists believe that religion means intolerance, obscurantism and slaughter…But they, out of touch with the Christian roots of their liberalism often seem to lack conviction. They lose touch with the moral values generated by their religion and tradition.[107]

Bishop Michael Nazir-Ali of the Church of England has warned that 'the decline of Christian values is destroying Britishness and has created a moral vacuum which radical Islam is filling'. The Bishop of Rochester said that many Western values respected by society, such as dignity of human life, equality and freedom, are based on Christian ones. But without their Christian backbone, he said, they cannot exist forever, and new belief systems may be based on different values. Instead of the Christian virtues of humility, service and sacrifice, there may be honour, piety and the importance of saving face. Radical Islamism, for example, will emphasise the solidarity of the umma against the freedom of the individual. It is filling a void left by the collapse of Christianity in the UK.[108] The rapid increase of Islam as the second faith in Europe may spur Europeans to reassess and revisit their Christian roots.

In June 2008, a report commissioned from the University of Cambridge by the Archbishops of Canterbury and York, criticised the British government for discriminating against the Christian Churches in favour of other faiths, including Islam, and argued that British society will be infinitely poorer if the government continues to ignore the Church while focusing obsessively on the demands of minority faiths. The report said:

> While Muslim communities are courted, funded and feted, the country's majority Christian communities are barely

mosque, which would have held four times as many worshippers as Britain's largest Anglican cathedral, was inappropriate.[112]

The toleration by Europeans of other faiths and cultures, and promotion of diversity, is leading to the dilution of Christian faith, and to other faiths taking over, in particular Islam. Some believe that accommodation and tolerance of the faiths of minorities at the expense of Europe's own religion is now going to extremes. Cases observed in Europe, such as prohibition of hot cross buns or Christmas trees, out of concern about insulting Muslims, have caused anger among Europeans. In the UK, some councils around the country have banned the phrase 'Merry Christmas' from Christmas cards, replacing it with 'Holiday Greetings' or something similar. It was also suggested that school children should be discouraged from singing nursery rhymes such as 'Baa, baa, black sheep', on the basis that it sounds racist. Along with *Winnie the Pooh*, some British schools have also removed or restricted the following 'anti-Muslim' children's books: *The Three Little Pigs, Charlotte's Web, The Sheep-Pig, Olivia Saves the Circus* and *Animal Farm*. Books featuring pigs are not to be used in class in case they offend Muslims.[113] Dudley Metropolitan Borough Council has announced that, following a complaint by a Muslim employee, all work pictures and knick-knacks of novelty pigs and 'pig-related items' will be banned (workers in the benefits department at Dudley Council were told to remove or cover up all pig-related items, including toys, porcelain figures, calendars and even a tissue box featuring Winnie the Pooh and Piglet).[114] British banks are banning piggy banks because they may offend some Muslims. Halifax and NatWest banks have led the move to scrap the time-honoured symbol of saving from being given to children or used in their advertising. Prison officials in Britain have been concerned that tie pins worn by officers featuring the St George's Cross, the symbol on England's flag, could offend Muslims, who might associate it with the Crusades of the eleventh, twelfth and thirteenth centuries. Chris Doyle, Director of the Council for the Advancement of Arab-British Understanding, thinks England needs to find a new flag and patron saint.[115] In Bristol, there are separate swimming times for Muslim women (this is in addition to the Asian-only sessions). In June 2008, in an area of East Birmingham where many Muslims live, two Christians were asked by a police community officer to stop leafleting. They were told they were committing a 'hate crime' by trying to convert Muslims.[116] Additionally, in Birmingham, the city council changed its policy and let a Muslim woman have her picture on her driver's licence with her face covered. Another case was that of a British check-in worker (Nadia Eweida), who was suspended by her employer, British Airways, for wearing a cross necklace at work in 2006. She accused the airline of fostering a culture of disrespect for its Christians employees and treating them with contempt; subsequently, 200 colleagues signed a petition to support her.[117]

The decision of the European Court of Human Rights in Strasbourg not to allow the display of crucifixes in Italian schoolrooms has caused a backlash and a heated debate in Italy and other European countries. In November 2009, the European Court, based on a complaint made by a Finnish-Italian woman, Soile Lautsi,[118] found unanimously that the display of crucifixes violated the principle of secular education and might be intimidating and disturbing for children from other faiths. Italian courts had ruled earlier that the cross was a symbol of Italy's history and culture, prompting Lautsi to take her case to the European Court. The judgment sparked anger in predominantly Catholic Italy. Even though the Vatican in Rome, which has been the seat of the Catholic Church for most of its 2,000-year history, did not officially respond to the ruling, the Conference of Bishops said in a written statement that 'It does not take into account the fact that in Italy the display of the crucifix in public places is in line with the recognition of the principles of Catholicism as part of the historical patrimony of the Italian people'.[119] The decision was condemned from across the political spectrum, which considered it as an assault on the country's Roman Catholic identity. Foreign Minister Franco Frattini, speaking during a visit to Morocco, said the European Court's verdict was an attack on Italy's Christian identity and that the government would appeal the decision. 'At a time when we're trying to bring religions closer together, this is a blow to Christianity', he said. Italian public opinion also reacted with outrage, saying that the crucifixes are an integral part of Italy's national identity and that generations of Italian children have grown up studying in classrooms in which a wooden or metal crucifix looms above the blackboard. Even though Italy has been transformed in the past two decades from a country that exported migrants to one that has accepted around 4.5 million economic refugees and asylum-seekers from Eastern Europe, Africa and Asia, as the Education Minister said, 'the Christian cross is a symbol of the country's Roman Catholic religion and cultural identity'.[120]

The Church of Greece also reacted angrily after the news that the European Court of Human Rights had ruled that the presence of crucifixes in classrooms was a breach of human rights. Greece's Orthodox Church fears that the Italian case will set a precedent, and is therefore is urging Christians across Europe to unite in an appeal against the ban on crucifixes in classrooms in Italy. Although the Greek Orthodox Church has been at odds with Roman Catholicism for 1,000 years, the judicial threat to Christian symbols has acted as a unifying force. The head of the Greek Church, Archbishop Ieronymos, echoed Catholic complaints that the Court is ignoring the role of Christianity in forming Europe's identity.[121] He added that it is not only minorities that have rights, but the majority also. However, it seems that, despite the Strasbourg Court decision, the Church is highly unlikely to concede the removal of icons or crucifixes from public buildings.

As a result of such cases, some right-wing European parties are increasingly asking for a halt to 'political correctness' and the fostering of the indigenous religion, culture, national identity and values. In its 2009 European election manifesto, the BNP stated: 'Stop wasting money on handouts for PC minorities. Promote OUR culture, celebrating our Saints George, Andrew, David and Patrick...Make sure that British people are put first and our own people aren't turned into second-class citizens'.

In a speech held at the American Enterprise Institute, entitled 'A Sermon for the West', the Italian writer and journalist, Oriana Fallaci, said:

President Bush has said, 'We refuse to live in fear'. Beautiful sentence, very beautiful. I loved it! But inexact, Mr. President, because the West does live in fear. People are afraid to speak against the Islamic world. Afraid to offend and to be punished for offending the sons of Allah. You can insult the Christians, the Buddhists, the Hindus, the Jews. You can slander the Catholics, you can spit on the Madonna and Jesus Christ. But, woe betide the citizen who pronounces a word against the Islamic religion...I call my book a sermon – addressed to the Italians, to the Europeans, the Westerners. And along with the rage, this sermon unchains the pride for their culture, my culture. That culture that in spite of its mistakes, its faults, even monstrosities, has given so much to the world. It has moved us from the tents of the deserts and the huts of the woods to the dignity of civilisation. It has given us the concept of beauty, of morals, of freedom, of equality. It has made the unique conquest in the social field, in the realm of science. It has wiped out diseases. It has invented all the tools that make life easier and more intelligent...Socrates and Aristotle and Heraclitus were not mullahs. Jesus Christ, neither. Leonardo da Vinci and Michelangelo, and Galileo, and Copernicus, and Newton and Pasteur and Einstein, the same...My book is also a *j'accuse*. To accuse us of cowardice, hypocrisy, demagogy, laziness, moral misery, and of all that comes with that. The stupidity of the unbearable fad of political correctness, for instance. The paucity of our schools, our universities, our young people, people who often don't even know the story of their country, the names Jefferson, Franklin, Robespierre, Napoleon, Garibaldi.

She continued:

The problem is that the solution does not depend upon the death of Osama bin Laden. Because the Osama bin Ladens are too many, by now: as cloned as the sheep of our research laboratories...In fact, the best trained and the more intelligent do not stay in the Muslim countries...They stay in our own countries, in our cities, our universities, our business companies. They have excellent bonds with our churches, our banks, our televisions, our radios, our newspapers, our publishers, our academic organizations, our unions, our political parties...Worse, they live in the heart of a society that hosts them without questioning their differences, without checking their bad intentions, without penalizing their sullen fanaticism. If we continue to stay inert, they will become always more and more. They will demand always more and more, they will vex and boss us always more and more. Till the point of subduing us. Therefore, dealing with them is impossible. Attempting a dialogue, unthinkable. Showing indulgence, suicidal. And he or she who believes the contrary is a fool.[122]

In Europe, we have freedom of religion, but also we have freedom of expression, two of the fundamental freedoms of Western democracy. In dealing with Muslims, these two seem to contradict each other. The key liberal principle of freedom was articulated by John Stuart Mill in his essay *On Liberty*, in which he stated that the only legitimate reason for coercing someone against their will was to prevent harm to others. When a Danish newspaper publishes cartoons of the Prophet Mohammed and Muslims feel insulted and start attacking Danish embassies, burning Danish flags or boycotting Danish products, is freedom of expression threatened? When, after the Pope quotes a Christian Emperor about Mohammed, fury arises throughout the Muslim world, developing into actual violence in several places, such as Arabs in Palestine attacking Christian churches, a nun being murdered in Somalia, a call for the Pope's death being issued in London, and Iraqi groups threatening the Vatican, is freedom of speech threatened?[123] It is understandable that freedom of speech and expression must be applied with care and responsibility when Europeans are in Muslim countries, especially in those where Shari'a is in place (as with the British teacher in Sudan), but the question is: should this freedom be circumscribed even in Europe?

Should Europeans sacrifice one of their fundamental freedoms because this may insult the religious feelings of Muslims, or may display 'lack of respect for Islam'?

The British government came under fire after banning the Dutch MP Geert Wilders from entering the UK over anti-Islamic remarks, on 12 February 2009.[124] Geert Wilders, the Freedom Party MP, had been invited to a House of Lords screening of his film *Fitna*,[125] which among other things, draws attention to the danger of Islamisation of Europe and gives warning of a 'tsunami' of Islam swamping the Netherlands. The final words of the film are 'Stop Islamisation, defend our freedom';[126] and Wilders has described the film as a call to shake off the creeping tyranny of Islamisation. He considers the Koran to be a book full of totalitarian ideology that incites violence. The film shows a selection of Suras from the Koran, interspersed with newspaper clippings and media clips, arguing that Islam encourages, among other things, acts of terrorism, jihad, anti-Semitism, apostasy, violence against women and homosexuals, and Islamic universalism. This 17-minute-long documentary was released in March 2008 and was posted on the Internet by the author, and has since caused has controversy and outrage and waves of protests across the Muslim world.[127] Because of this, the Dutch government banned the film, and an Amsterdam court put the author on trial for inciting hatred and religious discrimination (to which Wilders reacted by calling the prosecution an 'attack on the freedom of expression'). The court's decision was welcomed by Muslims, who make up one million of the Netherlands' 16 million population. Defending Wilders, Robert Spencer, a scholar of Islamic history and the director of Jihad Watch said, 'If they succeed in doing this, we will be rendered mute, and thus defenceless, in the face of the advancing jihad and attempt to impose Shari'a on the West'. Wilders, however, has become a 'globally famous figure' with thousands of people watching the film on the Internet. The decision of the British Labour government to refuse to allow 'the flying Dutchman' to enter the UK to be present at the screening of his film (even though Wilders was barred from entering the UK, his film was nonetheless shown in the House of Lords), has been criticised by political parties and has provoked outrage among citizens, on the grounds of a violation of freedom of speech. Keeping Wilders out agitated feelings among the non-Muslim majority and angered many of the silent majority, and thus proved as inflammatory as letting him in would have been.[128] Crossbench peer Baroness Cox, who hosted a later screening for the media, accused the British government of 'succumbing to threats of intimidation' and said it was 'a very sad and a very disturbing day for British democracy when a European parliamentarian has not been allowed into this country'. Lord Pearson told the BBC it was a 'matter of free speech' and the film would only be offensive to violent Islamists. The Dutch government and media also criticised the British government for this decision.[129] 'London used to be a refuge for extremists and radicals who came from all corners of the world and other radical Muslim groups were allowed to settle there... and now they are refusing entry to an MP of another EU country', said a reputable Dutch newspaper.[130] On the other hand, Muslim groups in Britain praised the Government for deporting him and reacted angrily to Wilder's comments, labelling him 'an open and relentless preacher of hate'.

I take the view that democracy means differences, debate and alternative views, and that to ban or exclude people simply because of their views breaches one of the most valuable and profound commitments of liberal-democratic countries, which is freedom of expression. That is the most precious freedom of all, because all the other freedoms depend on it. As Michael Burleigh says, 'Most Europeans are by definition cultural Christians, so are we seriously being expected to downplay that fact to appease a minority of 15 million Muslims in Europe and to omit 1500 years of our cultural heritage?'[131]

After assessing the factors from 'within', let us turn to the outside factor, a Muslim country of 70 million, with a party of Islamic roots in power, which aspires to join Europe.

5.4 The prospect of a country of 70 million Muslims becoming part of the EU

Turkey is a big country with a big population. The current population is almost 72 million, and by the time of accession it will be the most populous country in the EU. Turkey is also a big country in terms of its territory, which is larger than the territories of the ten 2004 accession countries combined. The High Representative for the Common Foreign and Security Policy (CFSP) Javier Solana, in a talk at Oxford University, said that 'the problem for Turkey is its size'.[132] However, the concern of Europeans has little to do with size or numbers by themselves. Most did not seem concerned when Poland, another big (and not rich) country of almost 40 million, was a candidate for joining the EU. Numbers, it seems, start becoming a concern when a big nation is different in terms of culture, religion and values. Poland was Christian and not perceived as different religiously and culturally. Turkey's accession would change the religious balance within the Union from roughly 3 per cent Muslim to nearly 20 per cent, as 99 per cent of Turkey's population are Muslims (the majority of whom are Sunni). What is more worrying is that most Turks cite Islam as a central part of their identity. In a survey by the Turkish Economic and Social Studies Foundation, 45 per cent of Turks identified themselves first as Muslims rather than Turks, compared to 36 per cent in 1999.[133] As one German Foreign Ministry official said, 'Berlin is already the second-largest Turkish city in the world. We do not want it to become the largest'.[134] Therefore, it is the combination of large size with the Muslim religion, the prospect of bringing 70 million Muslims into a secular club with Christian roots, which seems to cause the problem and provoke concern among Europeans.

Another argument in support of this view can be observed when comparing Turkey's case with four Eastern European countries, all viewed as having large Muslim populations, which are also aspiring to join the EU: Bosnia-Herzegovina, Albania, Macedonia and Kosovo. Bosnia-Herzegovina is 40 per cent Muslim. Albania is still perceived by Europeans as a Muslim country, although official figures are not accurate, being based on a poll conducted in 1929, according to which 70 per cent of the population were Muslim, 20 per cent Greek Orthodox and 10 per cent Roman Catholic. In Kosovo, now an independent state, Muslims constitute almost 90 per cent. In Macedonia, 25 per cent of the population (Albanians and a Turkish minority) are Muslim. Along with Turkey, these countries are next in line to join the EU, as part of a new geopolitical region, called the 'Western Balkans'. They have started the process much later than did Turkey, only in 1999, within the framework of a regional strategy called the 'Stabilisation and Association Process' (SAP), and currently Macedonia is a candidate country, while Albania and Bosnia-Herzegovina are potential candidates.

The point I want to make here is that although two of these countries, Albania and Bosnia-Herzegovina, have or are viewed as having Muslim-majority populations, there is no strong opposition from European citizens (and a much smoother accession process at the level of EU institutions) to letting them in once they have fulfilled the Copenhagen criteria. One of the main reasons for this is that they have small populations: Albania, three million and Bosnia-Herzegovina, four million. For example, in the Special Eurobarometer on Enlargement (2006), support by Europeans for Macedonia, Bosnia-Herzegovina and Albania is respectively 49 per cent, 48 per cent, and 42 per cent, compared to 38 per cent for Turkey. Turkey therefore attracts the lowest support compared to all other applicant countries. The main reason for that is the unfortunate combination of (large) size and (Muslim) religion, which weighs heavily against Turkey's bid to join the Union. This is reflected in a concise way in the opinion of many Western Europeans that Turkey is 'too big, too poor and too different'.

5.5 Political Islam as part of Turkey's mainstream politics

Islamic parties in power in secular states, as in the case of Turkey, represent one variant of 'political Islam'. Political Islam is a movement that began in the late 1920s, after secular governments failed to secure economic independence, prosperity and good governance in the Muslim world. Convinced that a return to the sovereignty of Islamic law was the only hope for progress in the Muslim world, proponents of 'political Islam' started to advocate Islamic governments. An-Na'im defines 'political Islam' as the mobilisation of Islamic identity in pursuit of particular objectives of public policy, both within an Islamic society and in its relations with other societies.[135] According to this definition, political Islam can be seen as a legitimate right of Muslim people to self-determination. However, there are other variants of political Islam, such as: fundamentalist regimes (as in Iran and Sudan); authoritarian 'traditional' regimes (such as Saudi Arabia, the Gulf States, Jordan, Morocco); Islamic/fundamentalist movements seeking political power (as in Algeria and Egypt). Political Islam, which can be described as the use and mobilisation of religion and identity to achieve political objectives, may be moderate or radical. While moderate Islam's aim is to bring Islamic parties to power, Islamic fundamentalism's goal is the creation of an Islamic state based on Shari'a Islamic law.

The party that has been since six years in power in Turkey, the AKP, represents moderate political Islam. Its Islamic ideological background is a source of concern for many Europeans, who question Turkey's commitment to secular democratic politics. The existence of a neo-Islamist party in power in a country which aspires to join the EU highlights a key question, with repercussions throughout the Muslim world and the West: what role should Islam play in political, social and public life?

However, the most intriguing issue is the so-called 'Turkish paradox'. Turkish politics and society are bifurcated: on one side is the army,[136] the sentinel of secularism and a defender of nationalism, but non-sympathetic to the EU. On the other side is the AKP,[137] a neo-Islamic party, but in favour of Europe and Europeanisation. The question is, which one is better for Turkey: nationalist military secularism or pro-EU moderate Islam? This paradox has to do with three issues: first, the guardian of secularisation in Turkey is the army; secondly, military intervention in politics; and thirdly, the identification with Western modernity, which used to be 'Kemalist philosophy', is now embraced by the AKP in the form of EU membership and Europeanisation. However, as Katzenstein and Byrnes note 'Atatürk's pursuit of 'Westernisation' was not the same thing as Erdogan's acceptance of 'Europeanisation'.[138] On the question of how democracy, Islam and modernity can co-exist under the rule of law, the two sides have radically, perhaps irreconcilably, different views. On the question of EU membership, by contrast with Central and Eastern European countries and also Balkan countries, there is no cross-party consensus. Moreover, taking into account Turkey's turbulent political history, it may be difficult for all groups in Turkish society to reach agreement on fulfilling the political Copenhagen criteria.

Who are the AKP? The party was created as a result of a split in the Islamist movement in the 1990s. It emerged from the ashes of the Islamist Welfare Party, and came to power in 2002. Its leader, Recep Tayyip Erdogan, served time in prison in 1999 for reciting a poem in public that made reference to Turkey's Islamic heritage. Even though the AKP retained links and support from the traditional constituencies of the Islamist parties, the younger generation (Erdogan and his allies) broke away from the more conservative and ideological (and also anti-EU) group. It became extremely popular in rural Turkey, as well as with the new urban, religious-conservative middle-class. It now has a growing number of supporters among the middle-class entrepreneurs and businessmen, who have prospered and benefited from the economic reforms of liberalisation and openness. Despite many shortcomings, the AKP has made progress on EU accession, political and economic reforms, civilian control of the military, and consolidation of the rule of law. However, in the eyes of some, especially the army, the AKP remains suspect because of its origin, and the ideologically motivated and faith-based cultural preferences of its leaders, whose wives wear Islamic headscarves, long banned in public offices and universities.[139] The secular establishment are afraid that the AKP, which draws much of its support from poor and pious Muslims, would use the state to promote Islam in all aspects of Turkish life.[140] Many are sceptical of the AKP's real intentions and of its leaders' commitment to secularism, and accuse them of having an Islamist 'hidden agenda' to redefine Turkish identity and the nature of the Turkish state.

For their part, AKP leaders say that Turkey and the AKP have become the symbol of 'moderate secular Islam', and they have no intention of taking any formal steps to Islamise the country. They say they are opposed to Shari'a or Islamic law and point out that its legislative agenda has been far more economically liberal and pro-Western than that of its secularist opponents. The AKP, since coming to power, has been caught up in a life and death struggle with the military.

The Turkish military is considered the country's most respected institution. It has served as the primary guardian of the secular republican order and therefore has not hesitated to intervene whenever the 'Atatürk legacy' of secularism has been threatened. Thus it has carried out four military interventions, in 1960, 1971, 1980 and 1997, when Turkey elected its first pro-Islamic party to government, the Welfare Party (an Islamic fundamentalist party). Generals threw it out of office and the following year banned it on the grounds of being a threat to Turkey's secularism. But despite the efforts of the establishment (the country's ruling elite and the army) it seems that Islamic parties are popular in Turkey, and in 2002 the AKP won a landslide victory.[141] The army tolerated its position in government, but the prospect of one of its members taking up the highest post in the country, the presidency, caused great concern. The secular elite believed that the nomination of Foreign Minister Abdullah Gül (a one-time Islamist activist whose wife wears the headscarf)[142] for the presidency, hitherto a bastion of secular power, would have Atatürk turning in his grave. The militarist old guard threatened to intervene to crush what they see as a threat to secular values. Referring to an 'Islamic reactionary mentality that was engaged in endless efforts to disturb the fundamental values of the Republic', they initiated the most serious clash with a government in a decade.[143] This time, the AKP refused to give up. Enjoying a majority in Parliament and widespread popularity, Erdogan called for an early general election in July (the parliamentary elections had been scheduled for November). This triggered a serious political crisis, with each side accusing the other: the government depicting it as a 'military intervention in the democratic process', and the generals calling it a 'threat to secular values'. The months before the elections were a tense period, with mass demonstrations in Istanbul, Ankara and Izmir, in support of secularism and against the government. However, one of the slogans featured in demonstrations was 'Neither Shari'a, nor a putsch',[144] which reflected equal popular antipathy to the prospect of military intervention.

Binyon notes that, for some, this election was considered the most important since the death of Atatürk.[145] Many outsiders viewed elections as an ideological contest between secularists and Islamists. At stake was more than a row over whether an Islamist could be elected President. The elections were important for determining the nature of Turkish democracy and the identity of the Turkish state, whereas across the Muslim world they were perceived as a test case for political Islam. Elections took place on 22 July and the AKP won a great majority, with about 46.5 per cent of the vote. More importantly, the generals accepted the result and did not attempt any coup. The next victory came with the election of Gül as the country's President. Another victory for the AKP came in October, when Parliament approved its proposed constitutional amendment for direct presidential elections.

The AKP's victory proved that the party continued to enjoy widespread popular support. The elections demonstrated the electoral power and the consensus that the AKP enjoys among the Turkish electorate. Does this mean that the Turkish public supports the progressive Islamisation of the public and political space in Turkey? According to the Power and Interest News Report, there are a series of structural and contingent factors explaining how the AKP has strengthened its popular support during the past few years.[146] From a structural viewpoint, the first factor is that the AKP has an impressive and widespread party machine, and a strong network of local administrators. These two elements give the party a deep-rooted presence in the country. A second structural factor is the presence of many AKP mayors with control over local administrations, which was strengthened after the local elections in 2004. This has given the party a fundamental instrument for creating consensus networks using welfare and local services to reinforce clientele networks based on the lavishing of jobs in the public sector and the redistribution of wealth, above all in the less developed areas of the country. Furthermore, there is the presence of a new, different middle class, characterised by its Islamic roots, in search of political representation; the so-called 'green capitalists', united under the Independent Industrialists' and Businessmen's Association (MUSIAD), who promote an Islamic, conservative vision of society associated with a liberal and market-oriented vision of the economy. The emergence of such a social and political actor is one of the more durable results of the economic liberalisation process and the market-oriented reforms implemented by the Turgut Ozal-led government in the 1980s. Among the contingent factors is the economic growth rate of the country, close to 5.5 per cent in 2006, and the overall economic record of the AKP government in the past five years. These elements are thought to have had a fundamental role in its victory. Moreover, the performance of the AKP as a reformist party during its first term has caused liberal sectors of the society to look with favour on the AKP, since they also do not agree with an active role for the military in politics. The final factor is the lack of electoral depth of the AKP's political adversaries. The concern, which still exists in some sectors of Turkish society and has been expressed by the military and the nationalist parties, over the possible existence of a hidden and radical Islamist agenda of the AKP, has not been as strong among the greater part of the electorate.

The AKP had promised not to take any formal measures to Islamise the country and declared that all it intended was a reconciliation of Islam with democratic values. However, as Posch notes, 'Islamisation of Turkish everyday life is becoming a fact, primarily affecting small and medium-sized towns'.[147] Moreover, many parts of Istanbul, as Abramowitz describes, now look more and more like the Middle East: boys and girls separated in many public places, and women covered from head to foot.[148] In July 2008 a court found a woman guilty, giving her a five-month suspended prison sentence, for 'exhibitionism', wearing what was termed 'improper clothing'.[149] About 70 women protested in Istanbul chanting: 'It's not exhibitionism, it's male abuse'. Women protesters say finding the woman guilty of 'exhibitionism' is disturbing proof that conservative thinking is on the rise in Turkey. They called for the law on exhibitionism to be overturned, as it reinforces the patriarchal order in Turkey and discriminates against women. There is also a noticeable enforcement of religious elements in daily existence: liquor is getting harder to come by, and many shops that once sold pork have been closed, bringing Turkey's pork industry to the brink of extinction.[150] Newspaper advertisements are being photoshopped to lengthen sleeves and skirts. Erdogan has called on women to have at least three children, and his cabinet includes just one woman. Under the AKP, the share of women in the workforce has dropped, from 29 per cent in 2000 to 22 per cent in 2006.[151] People think that the AKP is led by devout Muslims and that Turkey is becoming more conservative under the rule of what they call the 'religious government'.[152] Even more worrying is that religion is becoming the key to promotion in public institutions and high-level positions, favouring people who practise Islam or have Muslim credentials. These signs of Islamisation of Turkish politics and society are perceived as a 'loss of Atatürk's legacy'. These developments have allowed Islam, its symbols and its cultural and social values, to play a stronger role in the public discourse and to be a fully recognised part of the Turkish political mainstream. Yavuz (2003), White (2002) and Cagaptay (2006) come to the conclusion that Turkey is experiencing a revival of religion in the public sphere that challenges the European universalist norms regarding the secularist division between religion and politics, upon which Kemalism was modelled. Pew surveys have found that Turks believe Islam is playing a larger role in the nation's political life. About half the population (47 per cent) thinks religion's role in national political life has grown in recent years.[153]

Another move which came right after the election victory was the decision of Prime Minister Erdogan to change the Constitution to lift the ban on Muslim headscarves in schools and institutions. Two constitutional amendments were passed speedily by Parliament in January 2008.[154] AKP leaders justified it on the grounds that the ban represents a violation of human rights and freedoms and deprives some women of the right to higher education, while their opponents viewed it as a violation of secularism and as a political symbol of an Islamic lifestyle. Opinion polls suggest there is also strong public support for lifting the ban.[155] On the other hand, 30 per cent of Turkish people believe that allowing headscarves (which they see as a sign of backwardness) will lead to further Islamisation of the country.[156] Because of this pressure, the ban on headscarves being worn at universities, introduced by a parliamentary vote, was overturned. On 5 June, Turkey's Constitutional Court annulled Parliament's decision, on the grounds that it violated the secular principles of the Turkish Constitution.[157]

The Islamic-favoured agenda of the AKP was reflected even in foreign policy. Despite Ankara's relatively strong security relationship with Tel Aviv in recent years, Erdogan has long made clear his criticism of Israeli treatment of the Palestinians and his support for the inclusion of Hamas in peace talks. In early 2009, Erdogan caused another distraction with tough talk against Israel in Brussels and a walk-off from a stage in the World Economic Forum in Davos. In both places, he tried to focus world condemnation on Israeli actions in Gaza, but instead European and American audiences focused on whether the forthright style in which he did it proved that he was an Islamist, or that Turkey was turning away from the West.[158]

The rift between the AKP and secularists continued. In March 2008, the Chief Prosecutor in Ankara called for the end of the AKP on account of anti-secular activity,[159] and on 31 March the Constitutional Court decided unanimously to hear the full case for the dissolution of the AKP. Following this, the country's chief prosecutor petitioned the court to outlaw the AKP and ban 71 of its members from politics for 5 years, including Erdogan, on the alleged grounds that they are trying to destroy secularism and create an Islamic state in Turkey.[160] However, to ban a party that seems to be easily the most popular in the country seems nonsensical. On 30 July, ten of Constitutional Court's eleven judges found the AKP guilty of being a 'focal point of anti-secular activities', but did not go as far as banning the party as requested by the opposition, the Republican People's Party (CHP), and the Chief Prosecutor.

The AKP responded by trying to defeat the 'militaristic ghosts' of the past. In June 2008, when an arms cache and apparent series of coup plots linked to serving and retired security forces personnel were uncovered, the conflict morphed into a court case known as 'Ergenekon',[161] a conspiracy to overthrow the government. In a case described as the most important in Turkey's history, 142 defendants were charged. The so-called 'Defendants of Atatürk' included retired generals, journalists, academics and businessmen. All were said to be members of the shadowy 'Ergenekon' network of ultra-nationalists believed to have been behind a series of assassinations and disappearances in the last decade and now accused of plotting to overthrow the government of the AKP. For some, the arrest of highest ranking officers in Turkey's 63-year history of multi-party democracy was a critical blow against a once-untouchable military. For others, the charges were an invention of the ruling AKP to weaken the secular army and open the way for the country's Islamisation. Outside the courtroom in Silivri, hundreds of the defendants' supporters waved national flags and portraits of Atatürk, chanting 'The patriots are in prison'.[162] A secular opposition politician compared the 'Ergenekon' investigations to the 1979 Islamic Revolution in Iran.[163] Concerns have been raised about effective judicial guarantees for all the suspects[164] and, according to a ICG article, 'Unscrupulous judicial methods resulted in some clearly unjust detentions among the defendants'.[165]

Political Islam in mainstream Turkish politics, the government's anti-secular activities, and the creeping Islamisation of the country's politics and society, are likely to make Turkey look more religious and different in the eyes of Europeans. In any case, the rise of Islamist populism in a country that is aspiring to be part of secular democratic Europe is likely to worry Europeans. It raises doubts that Turkey has not yet completed its progress from the religious Islamic past to a secularist European present, which for some is enough to question Turkey's eligibility for EU membership.

In conclusion, I would say that these five factors have contributed to the rise of negative perceptions and views amongst the population in the EU about the role and impact that religion and cultural factors have on the chances of Turkey joining the club, and, as a result, have increased that population's reluctance to accept Turkey into the EU.

CONCLUSION

The EU is approaching a new phase of expansion, that towards the South-East, the Western Balkans and Turkey. However, of all the countries hoping to join the EU, Turkey is the one attracting the most attention, turning out to be the 'thorny issue' or 'hot potato' topic of EU enlargement policy. The prospect of Turkey's membership has forced the discussion of controversial issues, including not only 'the borders of the EU' and its 'geographical limits', but critical questions of European identity, Islam's place on the Continent and its role in European society. An analysis of Turkey's relationship with the Union shows that Turkey has had the longest and most complicated relations with the EU of all countries that have become EU members. Also Turkey has received 'different treatment' in comparison with CEE and Western Balkan countries. How is this explained? Is it simply non-fulfilment of the Copenhagen criteria, or other factors?

The first part of this book set out to analyse the complex range of factors that are influencing Turkey's accession process. I assessed these factors by adopting a three-set analytical typology: formal obstacles, such as domestic political and economic factors (related to Copenhagen criteria) and other (Cyprus, Armenian and Kurdish) issues; semi-formal obstacles, such as geo-institutional and security factors; and informal obstacles, such as religious and cultural factors. I started from the assumption that religious and cultural factors *per se* do not constitute a primary obstacle to Turkish accession, but that their interaction with other factors is prolonging and complicating Turkey's progress towards EU membership. It is clear that that Turkey faces many challenges in fulfilling the Copenhagen criteria. There are the political challenges, most notably on human rights, including women's and minority rights, freedom of expression and religion, military intervention in politics, etc. There are the economic challenges of being a poor agricultural country, which has implications for the EU budget and structural funds, and raises the prospect of a large immigration (although economics can be portrayed as bringing benefits, as it was with the 2004 accession countries). Other issues that are Turkey-specific, such as the Cyprus, Kurdish and Armenian problems, many Turks and outside observers consider as 'fig-leaves': invented excuses to keep Turkey out.

The obstacles in the second group are even more intrinsically contentious. They involve security (whether the EU should risk overstretching its frontiers to the Middle East), institutional factors (should the EU be willing to allow a poor and culturally different country to have the highest representation in its main institutions) and geography (whether Turkey, which territorially lies mostly in Asia, is eligible to be part of a European entity). So there are many obstacles even before moving onto the third, most controversial group of issues, the religious-cultural fabric of Turkish society. Turkey has been a secular state for 80 years, but is still perceived by many Europeans as not secular enough, as Muslim and alien. Why is this? I have offered several possibilities. Firstly, the sentinel of Kemalism (Turkish secularism) is the army. Secondly, secularism was forcefully imposed by the state, and thus was not embraced widely by social and political groups, which helps to explain the revival of political Islam in last decade. And thirdly, Turkey is a secular country but nonetheless a Muslim society; it was secularised at the official level, but religion has always remained a strong force at the mass level (600 years of Ottoman rule left a longstanding legacy of Islamism).

The assumption of many is that even if Turkey formally fulfils the Copenhagen criteria, resolves Armenian and Kurdish issues and recognises Cyprus, the EU will 'invent' other reasons, such as 'popular referenda', 'integration capacity', or 'privileged partnership'. However, Turkey is likely to 'fail the exam' even at the stage of the Copenhagen criteria (the political obstacle), as important elements, such as human rights and freedoms, are related closely to social values. Women's and minority rights, freedom of religion and expression (limited by the notorious Article 301), all of which are heavily criticised by the EU and attract the highest scores of opposition in opinion polls, are related to Islamic values and rooted in the social fabric of Turkish society, and therefore the Turkish government faces a real challenge in addressing them.

This brings us to the tricky question of the compatibility of Islam with Western values and its ability to accommodate democracy and secularisation. I have suggested arguments which explain why it is difficult for some Islamic values to be reconciled with European ideas of democracy, pluralism, human rights, equality, fundamental freedoms, and relations of religion and the state. I argue that Islam and its sacred texts, the Koran and Hadith, as they currently stand (i.e., the same as they were thirteen centuries ago) are filled with violent and intolerant verses, with principles of discrimination against people of different religions, women's inequality with men, teachings of jihad and apostasy. As such, they contradict the values and principles of liberal-democracy, and cannot be compatible with it. It is true that Turkey, unlike most other Muslim countries in the world, is a secular democratic country and has been so for almost 80 years. It has a constitution and not Shari'a law. However, there are still limitations on fundamental freedoms and problems with human rights, which are not in conformity with the standards of liberal-democracy, and these issues are difficult for Turkey to address, as they are based in its religion and embedded in the social fabric of its culture. In this context, it seems to be a challenge for Turkey to maintain a balance between being both a secular democratic country that respects democratic norms and a nation with an Islamic culture.

I next assessed the contemporary debate on Turkey's candidacy from the European angle. What are the positions and attitudes of European actors towards Turkey's candidacy? I examined four actor categories: European citizens, EU institutions (the Commission and the Parliament), EU member states, and European leaders and prominent politicians. I included European citizens in my analysis because many of them are likely to have a say on the next round of enlargements via referenda. To this end, I examined several sources of opinion polls, such as Eurobarometer surveys, Marshall Fund surveys, *FT* polls and Pew Research Centre surveys. I obtained two interesting results: firstly, citizens' support for Turkey's accession is not only the lowest among all applicant countries, but also shrinking: opposition to Turkish EU membership has risen steadily over the last decade, exceeding 50 per cent. Secondly, polls show that opposition has risen markedly since 2001. I set out to investigate the reasons for this and was able to identify five potential factors. The first is connected with the rise of Islamic fundamentalism around the world and its implications for Europe. The terrorist attacks in the USA in 2001, followed by a series of al-Qaida-inspired terrorist attacks in Europe over the last few years, all masterminded and executed by Muslims, have fuelled discussion and concern among Europeans not only about Islamic fundamentalism, but also about Muslims and Islamic values. This is likely to be an important reason for the increasing opposition towards admission to the EU of a candidate country whom Europeans identify as Muslim.

The second factor, I argued, is the increase of the Muslim population in Western Europe and the issue of their integration. Europe is now home to a large and rapidly growing Muslim community, and many Europeans are beginning to see its presence as a problem, or even, in some cases, as a threat. There are now around 20 million Muslims in the EU (5 per cent of its population), and Turks constitute a considerable percentage thereof. The failure of a portion of these Muslims and Turks to integrate into their European hosting countries is leading to a growing hostility towards Muslims and Islamic values, and may explain the increasing opposition to Turkish candidacy. The findings of various studies and surveys show that countries with the highest concentrations of Turkish communities, such as Germany, France, Austria and the Netherlands, score the highest opposition. Therefore, integration of Muslims and Turks and their cultural adaptation to hosting European societies has a significant impact on European attitudes towards Turkey's candidacy.

The third factor is the fear of Islamisation of Europe. Islam is now Europe's fastest growing religion. This has led to increasing Islamophobia and Turkophobia, tougher policies on immigration, and a revival of far-right wing parties in Europe. This fear of Islamisation, I argue, may be another factor responsible for European opposition towards Turkey.

After assessing factors from 'within', I then argue that there are two outside factors, directly related to Turkey: namely that it is a Muslim country of 70 million, and that it has a party with Islamic roots in power. The AKP, in power since 2002, represents moderate political Islam and, as such, is viewed with suspicion both inside Turkey, by the military and secularist groups within society, and from outside, by those Europeans who question Turkey's commitment to secular democratic politics. However, the AKP has shown itself very committed to reforms (although more economic than political and cultural ones), as well as to the EU accession process. There has been an ongoing conflict in the last few years between the AKP (a neo-Islamic but pro-European party) and the military (the guardian of secularism, but also deeply nationalistic and unsympathetic to the EU). This is seen by many as an ideological conflict between Kemalism (Turkish secularism) and moderate political Islam. This conflict culminated in 2007 in a serious political crisis. The elections that followed confirmed the AKP in power and allowed one of its leaders to be elected Turkey's President. Despite the AKP's promises not to take any formal measures to Islamise the country, there are signs of creeping Islamisation of politics and society, one of the most recent being the decision of Prime Minister Erdogan to change the Constitution to lift the ban on Muslim headscarves in schools and institutions. Political Islam in mainstream Turkish politics, the government's anti-secular activities and the rise of Islamist populism are likely to make Turkey look more religious and more different in the eyes of Europeans. Moreover, when this is the country aspiring to be part of secular democratic Europe, Europeans are likely to be worried that Turkey has not yet really progressed from her religious Islamic past to a secularist European present.

I also addressed the place that religion and culture occupy in the European debate. I must admit that this was not an easy task. From the outset I was faced with 'warnings' that assessing the impact of religious and cultural factors in the accession process of Turkey is 'un-do-able'. It was certainly a difficult case to prove, because of a lack of data and the pervasive 'political correctness' surrounding these issues. I started with European public opinion surveys, from which I obtained the following findings:

First, it was very hard to trace attitudes on religion among Europeans, as hardly any questionnaires contained questions about it, those by Eurobarometers in particular. Second, the reasons that questions on religion are not present in Eurobarometers is because this type of survey is organised by the European Commission and, as such, it reflects two things: the political correctness of this institution with regard to tricky issues, and the fact that most of the questions are constructed around the Copenhagen criteria (which concerns political and economic issues) and the *acquis communitaire*. Turkey's accession, however, is a complex issue involving more than just purely technical issues related to fulfilment of the Copenhagen criteria. Most opinion polls do not realistically reflect European concerns on this issue.

Third, while 'religion', 'Muslim' or 'Islam' are hardly mentioned in questionnaires, the terms 'culture', 'identity' and 'values' are used. Interestingly, questions on culture, values and identity attract the attention of respondents. A large percentage of Europeans say that the cultural differences are too significant to allow Turkish accession, and that they want enlargements to consolidate common European values. The notion of a 'different culture' in the Turkish case is assumed to be used frequently as code-word or euphemism for 'Muslim religion'. Why do I say this? I have argued here that 'culture' is a broad concept, including not only religion but also many other elements: from customs, traditions, mentality, social norms and values, family patterns, life style, attitude and behavioural patterns, to cuisine, food and eating habits, folklore, music, dance and literature. However, I believe that religion is the principal component of a culture, because it is not only embedded, incorporated and rooted in a given culture, but also defines the other components of a culture, such as mentality, social norms and eating habits. Religion may continue to be effectively embedded in a culture even when people cease to believe in the religious faith. Therefore I do not agree with those who say that Turkish culture does not constitute an obstacle to her accession but religion does, or vice versa. If culture constitutes a problem, then so does religion, since religion is the main component of culture. Because, in general, Europeans prefer not to speak openly about religion, they often use 'culture' as a code-word for 'religion'. The fact that questions on culture, values and identity attract the interest and attention of citizens means that religion would also have had such attention had it been put on the questionnaires.

Finally, the 'Copenhagen criteria' reasons do not seem to account fully for the high levels of opposition to the Turkish candidacy. The very interesting question of whether people would support membership 'once Turkey complies with all the conditions set by the EU', produced the result that nearly half of Europeans would still oppose it, even if Turkey fulfils the EU's 'official' conditions, such as the Copenhagen criteria and resolution of the Cyprus, Kurdish or Armenian issues. So, what else explains the hostility of Europeans? Religion and culture may be possible explanations. Elisabeth Hurd says:

> Even if economic and political obstacles to Turkey's accession are lifted, even if Turkey is deemed to be in unambiguous conformity with the Copenhagen criteria, European opposition to Turkish membership will persist because the Turkish case is controversial in cultural and religious terms, as it involves the potential accession of a Muslim-majority country to an arguable, at least historically Christian Europe.[1]

Findings from other sources, such as the Pew Forum, *FT* and Marshall Fund surveys, and especially opinions expressed by citizens in their letters to daily newspapers, yielded similar results.

A Pew Forum report notes that 'the argument over Turkey goes beyond the geopolitical pluses and minuses of EU membership and raises the larger issue of Europe's troubled relationship with Islam'.[2]

Having explored public opinion, I then turned to analysing the position of the European elite with regard to these variables. With the exception of the Commission, which is very favourable to Turkey and unified in its position, the EU actors are divided on the Turkish issue. In the Parliament, there is a diversity of positions, not only among the various political groupings, but even within them. The MEPs I interviewed confirmed that the Turkish issue has created such splits. I examined the position of four political groupings: the EPP-ED, the European Socialists, the European Liberal Democrats, and the Far Right. The biggest grouping, the EPP-ED, even though it formally supported the opening of accession negotiations, is divided internally, with the influential German CDU favouring a 'privileged partnership', while others (led by the British Conservatives) support Turkish membership. Socialists, Liberals, Greens and the European United Left are, in general, favourable, with some exceptions, while the far right strongly opposes it. While cultural and religious issues are not mentioned at all in the Commission's position, they are articulated more in the Parliament, especially by individual parties and MEPs.

Member states are also divided, interestingly along federalist and intergovernmentalist lines. Integrationists oppose Turkish membership, fearing that Turkish entry would spell the end of the federalists' dream of a political union. They view the EU as a union with a common identity, culture, history, geography and a set of values, and argue that cultural elements, which constitute the common European heritage, should form the basis of a common European identity. Austria, France and Germany lead this group. The intergovernmentalists see the EU as a huge integrated market rather than a political entity. They argue that European identity should not be based on culture and religion, but on universal principles of democracy and secularism. Britain leads this camp, backed by Italy and Spain. They believe that Turkey within the EU can act as a bridge, a model, and a means of spreading democracy within the Muslim world.

European and national leaders and politicians are also divided, with proponents pointing out the benefits Turkey will bring to the EU (mainly as regards the EU's foreign policy, as well as Turkey's role as a counterweight to international fundamentalist Islamist terrorism), while opponents claim that Turkish cultural and religious differences represent a threat to Europe's culture and way of life. French President Sarkozy is leading the 'crusade' in Europe against Turkey's accession and, together with other leaders (Merkel, etc), promotes alternative solutions to full membership. In recent years, Merkel and Sarkozy have poured cold water on Turkey's hopes for membership.[3]

Two main conclusions can be drawn from my research. As with some previous studies, the findings of this research show that opposition to Turkey is not purely for economic reasons or democratic principles. Therefore, I suggest that religion is a partial explanatory variable. However, because of the lack of availability of data, we do not know the exact extent to which religion counts in this opposition and, without a survey to include these variables, the conclusions remain probabilistic rather than conclusive. I see this as a gap; a survey exclusively on Turkey, based on a questionnaire offering all possible independent variables (as shown in second chapter), including religion, would be beneficial, and might produce interesting results.

The second conclusion: if it is true that religion is a significant reason for European opposition, how is it then that other Muslim countries that are also EU applicants do not attract the same kind of opposition? For Bosnia-Herzegovina, Albania and Macedonia, which have or are viewed as having Muslim-majority populations, all European actors seem ready to accept them once they have fulfilled the Copenhagen criteria. The reason is that they are small, 3–4 million each, compared to 72 million in Turkey. Thus religion *per se* does not constitute a major problem. Nor does size in itself. Europeans did not seem concerned when Poland, another big (and not rich) country of almost 40 million, was a candidate for joining the EU. Poland was Christian and not perceived as 'different religiously and culturally'. But the combination of (Muslim) religion with (large) size seems to create the problem. This is reflected in a concise way in the opinion of many Western Europeans that Turkey is 'too big, too poor and too different'. The interaction of religion and size seems to be the reason for high opposition: for Europeans, being Muslim and small causes fewer worries than being Muslim and huge. This book suggests therefore that it is this unfortunate combination of size and religion (being Muslims, or 'culturally different' in the words of politically correct Europeans), which weighs most heavily on Turkey's bid to join the Union.

Despite the 'true' reasons responsible for this long and complicated journey, for Turkey the most important thing is the continuation of the accession process, even with its ups and downs, setbacks and drawbacks, because this ensures the country's continuation of reforms in all fields, political and economic. As in other things, here too, the process is more important than the outcome itself.

APPENDIX I

Muslims in Europe: Country Guide

ALBANIA

Total population: 3.1 million

Background: Officially, Albania is perceived as a country with a majority Muslim population. However, the official figures for Albania are not accurate, as they are based on an outdated poll conducted in 1929, according to which 70 per cent of the population were Muslim, 20 per cent Greek Orthodox and 10 per cent Roman Catholic. Originally, Albania was a Christian country (Illyrians, the predecessors of Albanians, converted to Christianity while under the Roman Empire) and, after the Great Schism between Rome and Constantinople in 1054, it was split into a Roman Catholic north and an Orthodox south. After the Ottoman invasion, Albanians started their conversion from Christians into Muslims. Thus the biggest religious shift happened during Ottoman rule and, by the end of seventeenth century, the majority of Albanians were Muslims. Unlike most of their neighbours, who remained Christian, Albanians easily abandoned their religion and massively embraced the new one. The majority of Albanian Muslims are Sunnis, the branch which, in contrast to the Shi'ites, is most open to western influences such as in dress and social habits. The other Muslim tradition in Albania is Bektashism, a form of Shi'ite Islam close to the Sufis (best known for the practice of the 'whirling dervishes'). The Bektashis are one of the least dogmatic expressions of Islam and open to collaboration with other faiths. However, Islam has never been a strict and traditional form in Albania. Most Muslim Albanians have a long secularist tradition, being very moderate and liberal (in the sense of marrying someone of another religion, drinking alcohol or eating pork, etc). In 1967 the Albanian communist leadership, inspired by the Chinese model of the Cultural Revolution, abolished all religions. Albania proclaimed itself the 'first atheist state in the world'. All religious practices were banned and many priests and imams were imprisoned. Churches and mosques were destroyed. Nobody was allowed even to have a copy of the Bible or Koran and even the very thought of belief in God could not be expressed openly. The ban was lifted in 1991 after the collapse of communism. In addition to other freedoms, Albanians were at last free to practise any kind of religion they wished and there has been a modest religious revival. However, it has tended to favour conversions to Christianity rather than Islam, reinforced by the wish of Albanians to join the European family, which is viewed as a 'Christian club'. In Albania there is little evidence of Islamic fundamentalism, or even Islamisation. Most young Albanians today conform to the more hedonistic and secularist life-styles of their western counterparts. The situation in Albania is unlike Kosovo or Macedonia where religion has been an important element of their national identity for the ethnic Albanian populations. Another specific feature is that Albania historically did not have a single national church, powerful and influential, as had its neighbouring countries Greece and Serbia.

Source: Bogdani, M. and Loughlin, J. *Albania and the European Union: The Tumultuous Journey towards Integration and Accession.* London and New York: I.B.Tauris, 2007.

AUSTRIA

Total population: 8.2 million

Muslim population: 339,000 (4.1 per cent)

Background: Large numbers of Muslims lived under Austrian rule when Bosnia-Herzegovina was annexed by Austria-Hungary in 1908. Many of Austria's Muslims have roots in Turkey and others arrived from the Balkans during the 1990s wars – partly because of historical ties. Islam has been recognised as an official religion in Austria for many years, meaning that it has a role in the religious teaching in schools. Vienna has historically been regarded as the place where the Islamic world reached its most western point, a critical battle in Austria in the sixteenth century marking the beginning of the decline of the Turkish Ottoman Empire.

Sources: Total population – Statistics Austria, 2005 figures; Muslim population – Statistics Austria, 2001 figures.

BELGIUM

Total population: 10.3 million

Muslim population: 0.4 million (4 per cent)

Background: Islam is one of seven recognised religions in Belgium, a status that brings it a number of subsidies and official roles, such as providing teachers. Despite this there have been complaints of discrimination. Unemployment and poor housing have been one such cause of tension. There have also been claims of discrimination against women in traditional dress. A majority of Belgium's Muslims are of Moroccan or Turkish origin; many others are from Albania. (Citizenship is available after seven years).

Sources: Total population – Statistics Belgium 2001; Muslim population – US State Department.

BOSNIA-HERZEGOVINA

Total population: 3.8 million

Muslim population: 1.5 million (40 per cent)

Background: Bosnia-Herzegovina is still recovering from the bloody inter-ethnic war of 1992–95. Around 250,000 people died in the conflict between Bosnian Muslims, Croats and Serbs. Almost 8,000 Muslims were killed by Bosnian Serbs at Srebrenica in 1995 – Europe's worst atrocity since World War II. Many Muslims were displaced, as were members of other communities. A peacekeeping force remains in the country, whose frontiers have long been considered the western borders of the Islamic faith in Europe.

Sources: Total population – Agency for Statistics Bosnia and Herzegovina, 2003 figures; Muslim population – US State Department.

DENMARK

Total population: 5.4 million

Muslim population: 270,000 (5 per cent)

Background: In the 1970s Muslims arrived from Turkey, Pakistan, Morocco and the former Yugoslavia to work. In the 1980s and 1990s the majority of Muslim arrivals were refugees and asylum-seekers from Iran, Iraq, Somalia and Bosnia. Access to housing and employment have been sources of concern for Muslims in Denmark. (A minority have citizenship).

Sources: Total population – Statistics Denmark, 2004 figures; Muslim population – US State Department.

FRANCE

Total population: 62.3 million

Muslim population: 5–6 million (8–9.6 per cent)

Background: The French Muslim population is the largest in western Europe. About 70 per cent have their heritage in the former north African colonies of Algeria, Morocco and Tunisia. France favours integration and many Muslims are citizens. Nevertheless, the growth of the community has challenged the French ideal of strict separation of religion and public life. There has been criticism that Muslims face high unemployment and often live in poor suburbs. A ban on religious symbols in public schools provoked a major national row as it was widely regarded as being a ban on the Islamic headscarf. Late 2005 saw widespread and prolonged rioting among mainly immigrant communities across France.

Sources: Total population – National Institute for Statistics and Economic Studies, 2004 figures; Muslim population – French government estimate.

GERMANY

Total population: 82.5 million

Muslim population: 3 million (3.6 per cent)

Background: The majority of the Muslim population is Turkish, with many retaining strong links to Turkey. Others arrived from Bosnia and

Kosovo during the Balkan wars. Until recently Muslims were considered 'guest workers', who would one day leave the country – a view that is changing. Racist violence is a sensitive issue, with the authorities trying a range of strategies to beat it. Steps are being taken to improve integration.

Sources: Total population – Federal Statistical Office, 2004 figures; Muslim population – Federal Ministry of the Interior estimate.

ITALY

Total population: 58.4 million

Muslim population: 825,000 (1.4 per cent)

Background: The Muslim population is diverse, the largest group coming from Morocco. Others are from elsewhere in North Africa, south Asia, Albania and the Middle East. Most arrived from the 1980s onwards, many of them as students. Italy is working to formalise relations between the state and the Muslim community. Up to 160,000 Muslims are Italian-born. Most Muslims have the right to reside and work in Italy, but are not citizens.

Sources: Total population – Italian National Statistical Institute; Muslim population – UK Foreign Office.

KOSOVO

Total population: 1.8 million

Muslim population: about 90 per cent

Background: The late 1990s saw devastating conflict after the Kosovo Liberation Army, supported by the majority ethnic Albanians – most of whom are Muslim – came out in open rebellion against Serbian rule. Yugoslav President Slobodan Milosevic began 'ethnic cleansing' against the Kosovo Albanian population. Thousands died and hundreds of thousands fled. NATO intervened between March and June 1999 with a 78-day bombing campaign to push back Serb forces. Kosovo gained its independence from Serbia in 2008, and a growing number of countries have recognised it.

Sources: Total population – UK Foreign Office; Muslim population – US State Department.

MACEDONIA

Total population: 2.1 million

Muslim population: 630,000 (30 per cent)

Background: Macedonia's largest religion is Macedonian Orthodox, but almost one-third of the population describe themselves as Muslim. Macedonia was spared the inter-ethnic violence that affected much of the Balkans following the break-up of Yugoslavia. But in early 2001 rebels staged an uprising demanding greater rights for the ethnic Albanian minority – a group which includes most Muslims. With EU and NATO support a deal was reached offering them greater rights, although some have been unhappy with the pace of change. The US State Department suggests that religious freedom is generally respected and that 'societal discrimination is more likely to be based upon ethnic bias' than religion.

Sources: Total population – UK Foreign Office; Muslim population – UK Foreign Office.

NETHERLANDS

Total population: 16.3 million

Muslim population: 945,000 (5.8 per cent)

Background: The integration of Muslims remains a concern for the Dutch government, particularly after a filmmaker critical of Islam was murdered in 2004 by a radical Islamist. Further tensions surround the view held by some that there is a high level of crime among Muslim youths and a problem with unemployment. In the 1950s Muslims arrived from the former colonies of Suriname and Indonesia. One of the most important groups is the substantial Somali minority. Others are from Turkey and Morocco. The Netherlands favours multiculturalism, essentially the accommodation of different groups on equal terms.

Sources: Total population – Statistics Netherlands, 2005 figures; Muslim population – Statistics Netherlands, 2004 figures.

SERBIA AND MONTENEGRO

Total population: 8.1 million

Muslim population: 405,000 (5 per cent)

Background: Within Serbia and Montenegro the predominant religion is Serbian Orthodoxy. Islam is the second-largest faith, with Muslims accounting for about 5 per cent of the population, rising to about 20 per cent in Montenegro. The Muslim community is considered one of seven 'traditional' religious communities. Religion and ethnicity remain closely linked across the country and discrimination and tensions continue to be reported.

Sources: Total population – UK Foreign Office; Muslim population – US State Department.

SPAIN

Total population: 43.1 million

Muslim population: 1 million (2.3 per cent)

Background: Almost eight centuries of Moorish rule over Spain came to an end in 1492, providing the country with a strong Islamic legacy, particularly in its architecture. The modern Muslim population started to arrive in significant numbers in the 1970s. Many were Moroccans coming to work in tourism and subsequent growth came when their families joined them. The state recognises Islam, affording it a number of privileges including the teaching of Islam in schools and religious holidays. There have been some reports of tension towards Muslim immigrants. Spain was shaken in 2004 when terror attacks by suspected radical Islamists killed 191 people on Madrid commuter trains.

Sources: Total population – Spanish National Institute of Statistics, 2005 figures; Muslim population – US State Department.

SWEDEN

Total population: 9 million

Muslim population: 300,000 (3 per cent)

Background: The Muslim population is broad – with significant groups from Turkey, Bosnia, Iraq, Iran, Lebanon and Syria. The size of the Muslim population is such that representative bodies receive state funding. Sweden favours multiculturalism and immigrants can become citizens after five years. Sweden prides itself on its tolerance, but there has been criticism that Muslims are too often blamed for society's problems.

Sources: Total population – Statistics Sweden, 2005 figures; Muslim population – US State Department.

SWITZERLAND

Total population: 7.4 million

Muslim population: 310,800 (4.2 per cent)

Background: Official figures suggest the Muslim population has doubled in recent years, but some sources say there are also about 150,000 Muslims in the country illegally. The first Muslims arrived as workers in the 1960s, mostly from Turkey, the former Yugoslavia and Albania. They were joined by their families in the 1970s and, in recent years, by asylum-seekers. (Comparatively few have citizenship.)

Sources: Total population – Swiss Federal Statistical Office, 2003 figures; Muslim population – Swiss Federal Statistical Office, 2000 figures.

TURKEY

Total population: 68.7 million

Muslim population: 68 million (99 per cent)

Background: Although Turkey is a secular state, Islam is an important part of Turkish life. Its application to join the EU divided existing members, some of which questioned whether a poor, Muslim country could fit in. Turkey accused its EU opponents of favouring a 'Christian club'. Membership talks were formally launched in October 2005, with negotiations expected to take 10 years. Most Turks are Sunni Muslim, but a significant number are of the Alevi branch of Shias.

Sources: Total population – Turkish State Institute of Statistics, 2003 figures; Muslim population – US State Department.

UNITED KINGDOM

Total population: 58.8 million

Muslim population: 1.6 million (2.8 per cent)

Background: The UK has a long history of contact with Muslims, with links forged from the Middle Ages onwards. In the nineteenth century Yemeni men came to the UK to work on ships, forming one of the country's first Muslim communities. In the 1960s, significant numbers of Muslims arrived as people in the former colonies took up offers of work. Some of the first were East African Asians, while many came from south Asia. Permanent communities formed and at least 50 per cent of the current population was born in the UK. Significant communities with links to Turkey, Iran, Iraq, Afghanistan, Somalia and the Balkans also exist. The 2001 Census showed one-third of the Muslim population was under 16 – the highest proportion for any group. It also highlighted high levels of unemployment, low levels of qualifications and low home ownership. The UK favours multiculturalism, an idea shared by other countries which, in general terms, accepts all cultures as having equal value and has influence over how government engages with minorities.

Sources: Total population – Office for National Statistics, 2001 figures; Muslim population – Office for National Statistics, 2001 figures.

APPENDIX II

Some Islamic Terminology

Shari'a   As word means 'the way', the 'path leading to the source'. It determines 'how to be a Muslim'. Is the corpus of general principles of Islamic law extracted from its two fundamental sources: the Koran and Sunna.

Hadith   What the Prophet said, did, or approved.

Umma   Community of faith, spiritual community, uniting all Muslims thorough the world in their attachment to Islam.

Ulama   Islamic elders, a scholar in a broad sense.

Mujtahidun   A scholar working on scriptural sources.

NOTES

Chapter 1

1   Peter Berger, Oliver Roy, Steve Bruce, Bernard Lewis, Samuel Huntington, Michael Burleigh, Grace Davie, Francis Fukuyama, Peter Katzenstein, Timothy Byrnes, Robert Leiken, George Weigel, David Martin, Jonathan Sacks, Jose Casanova, Abdullahi A. An-Na'im, Elisabeth Hurd and others.

2   Elisabeth Hurd, "Negotiating Europe: The politics of religion and the prospects for Turkish accession to the EU", *Review of International Studies*, Vol. 32, no. 3, July 2006, p. 418.

3   Steve Bruce, *Politics and Religion* (Cambridge: Polity Press), p. 254.

4   Peter Berger (ed), *Desecularisation of the World: Resurgent Religion and World Politics* (Washington: Ethics and Public Policy Centre, 1999).

5   Samuel Huntington, "The clash of civilisations", *Foreign Affairs* vol. 72, Summer 1993, p. 31.

6   Francis Fukuyama, "The end of history", *National Interest*, 1989.

7   Huntington, "The clash of civilisations", p. 22.

8   Berger, *Desecularisation of the World*.

9   Bruce, *Politics and Religion*, p. 13.

10 Berger, *Desecularisation of the World*.

11 Caroline Cox and John Marks, *The West, Islam and Islamism: Is Ideological Islam Compatible with Liberal-democracy?* (London: Civitas: Institute for the Study of Civil Society, 2003), p. x.

12 A.A. An-Na'im, "Political Islam in National Politics and International Relations", in Berger, *Desecularisation of the World*, pp. 104–106.

13 Berger, *Desecularisation of the World*, pp. 9–14.

14 David Martin, "The Evangelical upsurge", in Berger, *Desecularisation of the World*, p. 39.

15 John Micklethwait and Adrian Wooldridge, *God is Back: How the Global Rise of Faith is Changing the World* (London: Allen Lane, 2009).

16 P.J. Katzenstein and T.A. Byrnes, "Trans-national religion in an expanding Europe", *Perspectives on Politics*, vol. 4, no. 4, December 2006, p. 679.

17 Ibid., p. 690.

18 Hurd, "Negotiating Europe".

19 Katzenstein and Byrnes, "Trans-national religion in an expanding Europe", p. 686.

20 Ibid., p. 689.

21 Grace Davie, "Europe: The Exception", in Berger, *Desecularisation of the World*, p. 39.

22 Katzenstein and Byrnes, "Trans-national religion in an expanding Europe". p. 689.

23 Ibid., p. 684.

24 Berger, *Desecularisation of the World*, p. 18.

25 Larry Siedentop, "Do you realise Europe is in the throes of civil war?" *The Times*, 27 February 2007.

26 Oliver Roy, *Globalised Islam: The Search for a New Ummah* (New York: Columbia University Press, 2004), p. 334.

27 Steve Bruce, *Religion in the Modern World: From Cathedral to Cults* (Oxford: Oxford University Press, 1996).

28 Micklethwait and Wooldridge, *God is Back*.

29 Berger, *Desecularisation of the World*, p. 19.

30 Micklethwait and Wooldridge, *God is Back*.

31 Ibid., p. 12.

32 George Weigel, "Roman Catholicism in the Age of John Paul II", in Berger, *Desecularisation of the World*, p. 35.

33 Davie, "Europe: The Exception", p. 76.

34 Peter Berger, "Religion and the West", *National Interest* 8, 2005, pp. 112–19.

35 Berger, *Desecularisation of the World*, p. 9.

36 Berger, "Religion and the West".

37 BBC News World Edition, "Britons backed Christian society", BBC Poll, 29 November 2005.

38 Micklethwait and Wooldridge, *God is Back*.

39 Katzenstein and Byrnes "Trans-national religion in an expanding Europe", p. 693.

Chapter 2

1   Mirela Bogdani and John Loughlin, *Albania and the European Union: The Tumultuous Journey Towards Integration and Accession* (London and New York: I.B.Tauris, 2007), p. 88.
2   J. Olsen, "The many faces of Europeanization", *Journal of Common Market Studies*, Vol. 40, no. 5, 2002, p. 928.
3   S. Ozel, "Turkey faces west", *Wilson Quarterly*, vol. 31, no. 1, 2007, p. 20.
4   A. Kazancigil, "High stateness in a Muslim Society: The case of Turkey", in M. Dogan and A. Kazancigil (eds), *Comparing Nations: Concepts, Strategies, Substance* (Oxford: Blackwell 1999), p. 224.
5   Democracy was not named as one of the principles underpinning the ideology of Kemalism.
6   European Stability Initiative (ESI), *Islamic Calvinists. Change and Conservatism in Central Anatolia.* Report, 19 September 2005.
7   Some see Turkey as a divided map: the liberal coastline, the conservative inland, the ultra-nationalist middle and the Kurdish nationalist southeast.
8   Matthew Parris, "A distant view of the hills and the news", *The Times*, 21 May 2009.
9   Huntington, "The clash of civilisations", p. 42.
10 'Band-wagoning' in IR theory is to attempt to join the West and accept its values and institutions.
11 Huntington argues that the central axis of world politics in the future is likely to be the conflict between 'the West and the Rest' and the responses of non Western civilisations to Western power and values. Those responses take one or a combination of three forms: at one extreme, non-Western states can, like Burma, and North Korea, attempts to pursue a course of isolation, to insulate their societies from penetration by the West and to opt out of participation in the Western dominated global community. The costs of this course are high and few states have pursued it. A second alternative, the equivalent of 'band-wagoning' in IR theory, is to attempt to join the West and accept its values and institutions. The third alternative is to attempt to balance the West, while

preserving indigenous values and institutions, to modernise but not Westernise.

12 Ibid., p. 44.

13 Suat Kiniklioglu, *International Herald Tribune*, 7 September 2006.

14 F. Tarifa and B. Adams, "Who's the sick man of Europe: A wavering EU should let Turkey in", *Mediterranean Quarterly*, vol. 18, no. 1, 2007, p. 56.

15 One exception is Norway, which has twice both started and completed accession negotiations, but has not gone on to become a member. However, unlike in Turkey's case, this was not because of European public opinion, or of EU unwillingness to accept Norway, but because its own population who rejected EU membership in referenda.

16 Kirsty Hughes, Talk at the European Studies Centre, Oxford, 21 January 2008.

17 BBC News, November–December 2006.

18 Stephen Castle, *Independent*, 12 December 2006.

19 Enlargement Newsletter, 13 January 2009.

20 Ibid.

21 Delegation of the European Commission to Turkey's website: http://www.avrupa.info.tr/AB_ve_Turkiye.html

22 Delegation of the European Commission to the Republic of Croatia's website: http://www.delhrv.ec.europa.eu/en/static/view/id/27

23 Plus Bulgaria and Romania, which joined the EU three years after these ten.

24 It had been hoped that Croatia could complete accession negotiations in 2009, but this was delayed because of a minor border dispute with neighbouring Slovenia in the first nine months of 2009. Already an EU member, Slovenia could have blocked Croatia's admission. However, on 2 October 2009 the two countries finally reached an agreement. Croatia is near the finishing line, aiming to conclude negotiations with the EU by the end of 2010 and to join the block within 2012.

25 Established by the European Council in 1993 and laid down in Articles 6 (1) and 49 of the EU Treaty, these require that the candidate countries ensure:
1. Stability of institutions guaranteeing democracy, the rule of law,

human rights and the respect for and protection of minorities (the political criteria);

2. The existence of a functioning market economy, as well as the capacity to cope with competitive pressure and market forces within the Union (the economic criteria);

3. Ability to take on the obligations of membership, including adherence to the aims of political, economic and monetary union (the administrative-technical criteria).

26   M. Cebeci, *The EU's Security Impact on Turkey: Democratisation as desecuritisation*. Lecture at European Community Institute. 2006.

27   European Commission, *Turkey 2007 Progress Report*, Brussels, 6 November 2007; and European Commission, *Turkey 2007 Progress Report*, Brussels, 5 November 2008.

28   European Commission, *Turkey 2009 Progress Report*, Brussels, 14 October 2009, p. 9.

29   Ibid., p. 10.

30   Ibid., p. 13.

31   Ibid., p. 16.

32   UK Foreign and Commonwealth Office, *Annual Report on Human Rights*, March 2009.

33   David Charter, *The Times*, 7 November 2007.

34   Enlargement Newsletter, 15 May 2008.

35   Enlargement Newsletter, 2 June 2008.

36   European Commission, *Turkey 2009 Progress Report*, p. 17.

37   Ibid., p. 18.

38   Ibid.

39   EU Council, *Religious Freedom in Turkey*, Report, 8 June 2006.

40   UK Foreign and Commonwealth Office, *The Annual Report on Human Rights*, March 2009.

41   European Commission, *Turkey 2009 Progress Report*, pp. 21–22.

42   Damian Thompson, "Headquarters of Turkish campaign for EU membership is…a confiscated Christian building", Telegraph.co.uk, 12 December 2009.

43   Ibid.

44   European Commission, *Turkey 2009 Progress Report*, p. 23.

45   The Employment Package adopted in 2008 aims at addressing unemployment challenges, with a specific focus on the promotion of job opportunities for women (Enlargement Newsletter, 25 March 2009).

46   European Stability Initiative, *Sex and Power in Turkey: Feminism, Islam and the Maturing of Turkish Democracy*, 2 June 2007.
47   European Commission, *Turkey 2009 Progress Report*, p. 23.
48   European Commission, *Turkey 2007 Progress Report*; Enlargement Newsletter, 25 March 2009; European Commission, *Turkey 2009 Progress Report*, p. 23.
49   European Parliament, *Second Report on Women's Role in Social, Economic and Political Life in Turkey*, EP Women's Rights Committee, 20 December 2006 (in Enlargement Newsletter, 12 January 2007).
50   A new civilian Constitution is being prepared to replace the current one, which was introduced in 1980 after a military coup.
51   Sarah Rainsford, BBC News, 24 January 2008.
52   European Commission, *Turkey 2009 Progress Report*, p. 27.
53   Walter Posch, *Crisis in Turkey: Just Another Bump on the Road to Europe?*, p. 10.
54   European Commission, *Turkey 2009 Progress Report*, p. 29.
55   European Commission, Eurobarometer Survey No. 66: *Public Opinion in the European Union*, 2006.
56   Interview with Jonathan Evans, 5 April 2008.
57   Kirsty Hughes, "Turkey and the EU: Just another enlargement?" A *Friends of Europe* Working Paper, June 2004.
58   Corrado Pirzio-Biroli, "Does Muslim Turkey belong in Christian Europe?" Debate at the National Press Club, Washington DC, 13 January 2005.
59   Alex Spillius, *Daily Telegraph*, 14 December 2006.
60   Daniel Dombley, *Financial Times*, 11 December 2006.
61   Nicholas Watt, *Guardian*, 12 December 2006.
62   Enlargement Newsletter, 5 November 2007.
63   Dora Bakoyannis "Does Europe have a message for the world?"Annual Lecture of South Eastern European Centre, St Antony's College, University of Oxford, 6 November 2007.
64   International Crisis Group, *"Solving the EU–Turkey-Cyprus Triangle"*, Istanbul/Brussels, 23 February 2009.
65   Enlargement Newsletter, 23 February 2009.
66   Hugh Pope, *"The EU–Turkey–Cyprus Triangle: Setting the Stage"*, ICG, 23 February 2009.
67   European Commission, *Turkey 2008 Progress Report*.
68   UK Foreign and Commonwealth Office, *The Annual Report on Human Rights*, March 2009.

69 Sarah Rainsford, "MP breaks language law in Turkey", BBC News, 25 February 2009.

70 K. Barysch, *What Europeans Think about Turkey and Why* (London: Centre for European Reform, 2007), p. 3.

71 A. Akgunduz, *The Ottoman State as a Muslim State*. Lecture at Marmara University, 3 December 2006.

72 Turkey closed its border with Armenia during the latter's conflict with neighbouring Azerbaijan over the disputed mountain region of Nagorno-Karabakh.

73 European Commission, *Turkey 2008 Progress Report*.

74 Europe is bounded to the north by the Arctic Ocean, to the west by the Atlantic Ocean, to the south by the Mediterranean Sea, to the southeast by the Caucasus Mountains and the Black Sea and the waterways connecting the Black Sea to the Mediterranean. To the east, Europe is generally divided from Asia by the water divide of the Ural Mountains, the Ural River, and by the Caspian Sea.

75 Jose Manuel Barroso, Lecture at St Antony's College Oxford, 11 October 2007.

76 Conference of the Representatives of the Governments of Member States, *Treaty of Lisbon*, 3 December 2007.

77 European Commission, *Enlargement Strategy and Main Challenges 2006–07*, 8 November 2006.

78 Tarifa and Adams, "Who's the sick man of Europe: A wavering EU should let Turkey in", p. 5.

79 Kirsty Hughes, "Turkey and the EU: Just another enlargement?".

80 Interview with Jonathan Evans, 5 April 2008.

81 Danish Affairs, "Why Europeans don't want Turkey in EU", 9 May 2008.

82 Fritz Bolkenstein, *Financial Times*, 31 May 2006.

83 The recommendations of the European Ideas Network Working Group on "Geographic Limits of the EU". Lyon, 2006.

84 Interview with Graham Avery, 4 March 2008.

85 However, during the world Economic Forum at Davos in 2009, Turkey's Prime Minister, Erdogan, was very critical of the recent Israeli operation into Gaza and fiercely debated this with Israeli President Shimon Peres (*Newsweek*, "Interview with Erdogan on the passions and power politics currently rolling the Middle East", 9 February 2009).

86 Turkey was the only Muslim nation that was a founding member of NATO, it fought bravely by the side of the US in Korea, and

has been a staunch ally up until the US invasion of Iraq in 2003. It is the only Muslim country that has a genuinely close relationship with Israel and it cooperates with Tel Aviv in many areas.

87 Tony Lodge, "Turkey is key for the EU's energy-hungry states", *Independent*, 21 April 2009.

88 The disruptions have been caused by Russia cutting supplies to Ukraine following a number of disputes over how much Ukraine must pay for its gas. This has had a knock-on impact on suppliers to Western Europe, as most of the pipelines from Russia currently run through Ukraine.

89 The Nabucco project is named after the opera by Italian composer Giuseppe Verdi that deals with the subject of liberation.

90 BBC News, "Europe gas pipeline deal agreed", 13 July 2009.

91 Peter Fedynsky, "Nabucco Pipeline Competition for Russian Gas", *Voice of America News*, 14 July 2009.

92 Ibid.

93 Enlargement Newsletter, 15 May 2009.

94 'British jobs for British workers' was adopted as the campaign slogan of the British National Party (BNP) for the 2009 European elections. In their election manifesto it was stated: 'Our money shouldn't be wasted on expanding Europe, so that millions of Muslims in Turkey can join the invasion of foreign job-snatchers'.

95 Bruno Waterfield, "EU expansion halted over fears of unrest", *Daily Telegraph*, 25 February 2009.

96 Abolition of the Caliphate, the symbol of Muslim unity, in 1924, was seen by bin Laden and other fundamentalists as a humiliation and disgrace that Islam has lived with for more than 80 years.

97 The military issue is explained in more details in Chapter 5.

98 Kazancigil, "High stateness in a Muslim Society", p. 232.

99 Posch, *Crisis in Turkey*, p. 3.

100 Hurd, "Negotiating Europe", pp. 408–409.

101 Oliver Roy, *Globalised Islam: The Search for a New Ummah* (New York: Columbia University Press 2004), p. 16.

102 Kazancigil, "High stateness in a Muslim Society", p. 233.

103 Posch, *Crisis in Turkey*, p. 5.

104 Sarah Rainsford, BBC News, 24 January 2008.

105 Roy, *Globalised Islam*, p. 16.

106 Enlargement Newsletter, 13 January 2009.

107 Enlargement Newsletter, 25 March 2009.

108 Enlargement Newsletter, 15 May 2009.

109 Thirty Members of the European Parliament sent a letter of protest to the Turkish Prime Minister and Minister of Justice on 18 December 2008, condemning the sentence handed down by the court to Leyla Zana, saying that 'We, as Members of the European Parliament, strongly condemn this court decision which is a major set back for the democracy process in Turkey'.
110 Hurd, "Negotiating Europe", p. 409.

Chapter 3

1 Huntington, "The clash of civilisations", p. 25.
2 The term 'Western' is now inappropriate geographically, but is widely used to refer to a constellation of societies that, while they may differ from each-other in many aspects, generally share fundamental philosophical, political and social characteristics.
3 Fundamental freedoms include: freedom of thought, freedom of expression, freedom of press, freedom of religion, freedom of assembly and association.
4 Larry Siedentop, *Democracy in Europe*, Ch. 10, "Europe, Christianity, and Islam", p. 193.
5 Ibid., p. 210.
6 Quoted in Hurd, "Negotiating Europe".
7 Cox and Marks, *The West, Islam and Islamism*, p. 2.
8 Katzenstein and Byrnes, "Trans-national religion in an expanding Europe", pp. 686–87.
9 Tariq Ramadan, *To Be a European Muslim* (Leicester: Islamic Foundation, 1999) p. 20.
10 According to Islam, the Koran was revealed to Mohammed over a period of 20 years, from about 610 until his death in 632. However, the writing down of the Koran did not start until soon after the death of Mohammed in 632 and was completed only around 650; even then it continued to evolve over the next two centuries. The writing down of the Hadith took place between 850–975.
11 Ramadan, *To Be a European Muslim.* p. 46.
12 Siedentop, *Democracy in Europe*, p. 207.
13 Cox and Marks, *The West, Islam and Islamism*, p. 21.
14 Ibid., p. 5.

15   Martin Kramer, "Islam vs Democracy", in *Commentary*, January 1993, p. 38–39.
16   B. Lewis, *The Crisis of Islam: Holy War and Unholy Terror* (London: Weidenfeld & Nicolson 2003), pp. 3, 17.
17   Siedentop, *Democracy in Europe*, p. 193.
18   Cox and Marks, *The West, Islam and Islamism*, p. 42.
19   Ramadan, *To Be a European Muslim*, p. 57.
20   Ibid., p. 31.
21   Cox and Marks, *The West, Islam and Islamism*, p. 41.
22   Akbar Ahmed and Lawrence Rosen, "Islam and freedom of thought", *Islam for Today*, 15 July 2008.
23   Tom Coghlan, "Karzai backs down over abhorrent marital rape law", *The Times*, 28 April 2009.
24   Phyllis Chesler, *The Times*, 7 March 2007.
25   Hillel Fendel, "Another Islam–Christian Blow-up on the horizon?" IsraelNationalNews.com, 29 July 2007.
26   This is further explained in Chapter 5 in the section 'Islamic fundamentalism'.
27   Some of the verses in the Koran that speak about Jihad are: 'Fight those who believe not in Allah', 'Fight with them until there is no more tumult and oppression. And there prevail justice and faith in Allah all together and everywhere'. Bin Laden, in his letter addressed to the USA in 1998, said Muslims must 'fight and slay the pagans wherever you find them'.
28   Bernard Lewis, *The Political Language of Islam* (Chicago: University of Chicago Press, 1988), pp. 72–73.
29   Cox and Marks, *The West, Islam and Islamism*, p. 34.
30   Wafa Sultan, TV interview with Al Jazeera (Qatar), 21 February 2006.
31   BBC News, "When Muslims become Christians", 21 April 2008.
32   Hashem Aghajari, a history professor in Tehran, was sentenced to death for apostasy in November 2002.
33   Ibid.
34   Ibid.
35   Ibid.
36   Francis Fukuyama, "Identity, Immigration, and Liberal-democracy", *Journal of Democracy* 17/2, 2006, p. 12.
37   Roy, *Globalised Islam*, p. 338.
38   Hurd, "Negotiating Europe, p. 409.
39   Seymor Martin Lipset, "The centrality of culture", in Larry

Diamond (ed), *The Global Resurgence of Democracy* (Baltimore: Johns Hopkins University Press, 1996).

40   Berger, *Desecularisation of the World*, p. 8.
41   Huntington, "The clash of civilisations", p. 9.
42   However, (full) Shari'a is in place only in some Muslim countries, such as Saudi Arabia, the Gulf States, Sudan, Afghanistan, Iran, and not in all the countries with a majority Muslim population.
43   Tariq Ramadan, *To Be a European Muslim*, p. 60.
44   Katzenstein and Byrnes, "Trans-national religion in an expanding Europe", p. 689.
45   Ibid., p. 282.
46   The Ottoman Sultan had been Caliph of the Islamic world for 407 years.
47   Bruce, *Politics and Religion*, p. 240.
48   Matthew 22:21–22.
49   Lewis, *The Crisis of Islam*, p. 6.
50   Siedentop, *Democracy in Europe*, p. 199.
51   An-Na'im, "Political Islam in National Politics and International Relations", p. 115.
52   Hurd, "Negotiating Europe", p. 410.
53   Roy, *Globalised Islam*, pp. 28, 115.
54   Lewis, *The Crisis of Islam*, p. 13.
55   Fatos Tarifa, *Facing Tomorrow's Global Challenges: What Role for Social Science?* Paper presented at the 2006 Annual Conference of the Association for Applied and Clinical Sociology. California, October 2006, p. 13.
56   Lewis, *The Crisis of Islam*, p. 4.
57   Ramadan, *To Be a European Muslim*, p. 34.
58   Cox and Marks, *The West, Islam and Islamism*, p. 17.
59   Joan Smith, "Islam and the modern world don't mix", *Independent*, 28 November 2007.
60   Chesler, *The Times*, 7 March 2007.
61   Ramadan, *To Be a European Muslim*, p. 238.
62   Robert Piggott, BBC News, 26 February 2008
63   Interview with Fadi Hakura, 11 April 2008.
64   See also Mustafa Akyol, *Turkish Daily News*, 1 March 2008.
65   Tom Heneghan, *Washington Post*, 29 February 2008.
66   Further explored in Chapter 5.3
67   Christopher Caldwell, *Reflections on the Revolution in Europe* (London: Allen Lane, 2009).

68 An-Na'im "Political Islam in National Politics and International Relations", p. 112.
69 British teacher, Gillian Gibbons was arrested and found herself in prison in Khartoum, accused of a crime that it carries a penalty of up to 6 months in jail or 40 lashes, according to Article 125 of the criminal code, which covers insults against faith and religion. Her 'offence' was to name a teddy bear Muhammad, though the name was chosen by her pupils (BBC News, 26 November 2007).
70 BBC News, "When Muslims become Christians", 21 April 2008.
71 In Saudi Arabia there is a strict interpretation of Shari'a law, according to which women are not allowed in public in the company of men other than their male relatives (*Independent* ,"In the name of God: The Saudi rape victim's tale", 29 November 2009).
72 Smith, "Islam and the modern world don't mix".
73 *Danish Affairs*, "Why Europeans don't want Turkey in EU", 9 May 2008.
74 L. Lugo, "Does Muslim Turkey belong in Christian Europe?" Debate at the National Press Club, Washington DC, 13 January 2005.
75 Deutsche Welle, "Study shows Turkish values don't coincide with EU ideals", 3 July 2007.
76 The study was based on data from the "European Values Survey".
77 Pew Forum on Religion and Public Life, *Can Secular Democracy Survive in Turkey?*, 4 May 2007.

Chapter 4

1 Roy, *Globalised Islam*, p. 126.
2 George Weigel, "Roman Catholicism in the Age of John Paul II", in Berger, *Desecularisation of the World*, p. 35.
3 Bruce, *Politics and Religion*, p. 9.
4 Katzenstein and Byrnes, "Trans-national religion in an expanding Europe", p. 689.
5 Ibid., p. 685.
6 Ramadan, *To Be a European Muslim*, p. 158.
7 Katzenstein and Byrnes, "Trans-national religion in an expanding Europe", p. 684.

8   Quoted in Huntington, "The clash of civilisations", p. 26.
9   Roy, *Globalised Islam*, p. 330.
10 Siedentop, *Democracy in Europe*, p. 100.
11 Roy, *Globalised Islam*, p. 129.
12 See also Luis Lugo, Jonathan Davidson, Corrado Pirzio-Biroli, and Omer Taspinar, "Does Muslim Turkey belong in Christian Europe?" Debate at the National Press Club, Washington DC, 13 January 2005.
13 European Commission, Eurobarometer Survey No. 67: *Public Opinion in the European Union*, November 2007.
14 Fukuyama, "Identity, Immigration, and Liberal-democracy", p. 17.
15 Telegraph.co.uk, "Nicolas Sarkozy pushes for burka ban in France", 12 November 2009.
16 European Commission, Eurobarometer Survey No. 67: *Public Opinion in the European Union*, November 2007.
17 Huntington, "The clash of civilisations", p. 27.
18 Ibid.
19 Conference of the Representatives of the Governments of Member States, *Treaty of Lisbon*, 3 December 2007.
20 However, the Treaty drops all reference to the symbols of the EU, although the flag, the anthem and the motto will continue to exist.
21 European Commission, *Enlargement Strategy and Main Challenges 2006–07*, 8 November 2006.
22 Davie "Europe: The Exception", p. 66.
23 Interview with Graham Avery, 4 March 2008.
24 Peter Seewald, "Interview with Georg Ganswein", *Sueddeutsche Zeitung Magazin*, 27 July 2007.
25 Cox and Marks, *The West, Islam and Islamism*, p. 71.
26 Multiculturalism is developed further in Chapter 5.2.
27 Siedentop, *Democracy in Europe*. p. 189.
28 Ibid.
29 Ibid., p. 109.
30 Ibid., p. 189.
31 Hughes, "Turkey and the EU", p. 28.
32 Hurd, "Negotiating Europe", p. 410.
33 Jihad Watch, 18 October 2004.
34 Ibid.

35   Ian Traynor, *Guardian*, 22 September 2004.

36   This is how Katinka Barysch describes the importance of a public referendum for Turkey: 'Imagine this: Nicolas Sarkozy drops his election pledge to keep Turkey out of the EU; the Cyprus issue is resolved; the EU unblocks the eight frozen chapters in the accession negotiations; successive Turkish governments plough slowly, but surely through the massive reform agenda required for EU membership; an accession treaty is signed in, say 2015. But a year later, after 20 EU countries have already ratified, the French and Austrians vote against the accession in national referendums. The EU is in crisis, Turkey is enraged' (K. Barysch, *What Europeans Think About Turkey and Why*).

37   A. Ruiz-Jiménez and J.I. Torreblanca, *European Public Opinion and Turkey's Accession: Making sense of arguments for and against.* European Policy Institutes Network, 16 May 2007.

38   A study of Wolfgang Zaunbauer, November 2005 (quoted in Barysch, *What Europeans Think About Turkey and Why*, p. 1).

39   Omer Taspinar, "Does Muslim Turkey belong in Christian Europe?" Debate at the National Press Club, Washington DC, 13 January 2005.

40   European Commission, Flash Eurobarometer 217: *Intercultural dialogue in Europe 2007.* December 2007.

41   *Financial Times* Harris Poll, *Attitudes toward Muslims mixed in Europe and the US*, 23 August 2007.

42   *Financial Times* Harris Poll, *Religious views and beliefs vary greatly by country*, 20 December 2006.

43   The German Marshall Fund of the USA, *Transatlantic Trends Survey*, 2007.

44   Pew Forum on Religion and Public Life, *An Uncertain Road: Muslims and the future of Europe*, Report, October 2005.

45   Pew Global Attitude Survey, *Islamic Extremism: Common concern for Muslim and western publics*, 14 July 2005.

46   Mark Leonard, *Democracy in Europe: How the EU can survive in an age of referendums*, CER essay, March 2006 (quoted in Barysch, *What Europeans Think About Turkey and Why*).

47   Ruiz-Jiménez and Torreblanca, *European Public Opinion and Turkey's Accession*, p. 4.

48   Special Flash Eurobarometer conducted two days after the referenda in France and the Netherlands: Eurobarometer 171/2005 and Eurobarometer 127/2005.

49   A. Servantie, "European public opinion on Turkey", *The Bridge: A quarterly review on European integration*, 2007.

50   *Economist*, 21 December 2002.

51   Hugh Prosser, *Western Mail*, 3 November 2007.

52   Russell Armitage, *Newsweek*, 12 February 2007.

53   Sharad C. Misra, *Newsweek*, 3 December 2007.

54   Spyros Athens, BBC News, January 2007.

55   Ruiz-Jiménez and Torreblanca, *European Public Opinion and Turkey's Accession*.

56   The study is based on data from Eurobarometers.

57   According to this view the EU would be a geographically delimited entity, with a strong sense of common identity, history, culture and traditions, a 'value-based' community with a common history, geography and a set of values – whether Christian or secular – forming the 'European way of life' (Jiménez and Torreblanca, *European Public Opinion and Turkey's Accession*, p. 6).

58   L. McLaren, "Explaining Opposition to Turkish Membership of the EU", *European Union Politics*, no. 8, 2007.

59   Ibid., p. 18.

60   Enlargement Newsletters are monthly online publications of the Commission, prepared by the Information Unit of the Enlargement Directorate General. They reflect and report all events, activities, policies and declarations of the European institutions with regard to applicant countries.

61   Expressions used in the declarations and speeches of President Barroso and the Commissioner of Enlargement, Olli Rehn (Enlargement Newsletter, 24 May, 13 June and 18 July 2007).

62   M. Cebeci, *The EU's Security Impact on Turkey*.

63   The German Marshall Fund of the USA, *Transatlantic Trends Survey 2007*.

64   Danish cartoonist Kurt Westergaard depicted the Prophet Mohammed with a bomb in his turban.

65   The Pope later apologized for these statements.

66   Heather Grabbe, Talk at European Studies Centre, Oxford, April 2007.

67   Servantie, "European public opinion on Turkey".

68   European Parliament, *EU Draft Report on Turkey's Progress Towards Accession*, 6 June 2006.

69   On 22 June 2009, following the 2009 European elections, the ED subgroup left the EPP-ED, when the British Conservatives

and the Czech Civic Democratic Party, together with the Polish Law and Justice Party formed their own group named 'European Conservatives and Reformists'. The ED subgroup was abolished from that date and the EPP-ED Group reverted to its original name, the EPP Group.

70   Interview with Jonathan Evans MEP, 5 April 2008

71   Quoted in Cebeci, *EU's Security Impact on Turkey.*

72   Quoted in B. O'Rourke, "Turkey: AKP tries to join European Conservative Group", EPP-ED website, June 2003.

73   Interview with Jonathan Evans MEP, 5 April 2008.

74   European Ideas Network "Summer University", *Conclusions*, Lyon, September 2006 and Warsaw, September 2007.

75   PES website, 24 February 2004.

76   Interview with Maria Eleni Koppa, 21 January 2008.

77   European Parliament website, "Duff welcomes Turkey decision and castigates EPP group", 15 October 2007.

78   IRNA, Brussels, 28 September 2006.

79   C. Çamlibel, *Turkish Daily News*, 10 March 2007.

80   The German Marshall Fund of the USA, *European Elites Survey*, Centre for the Study of Political Change, Campagnia di San Paolo, Italy, 7 September 2007.

81   Here I mean the official positions of governments of member-states.

82   See Barysch, *What Europeans Think About Turkey and Why.*

83   No other European government has been as reluctant as was the government led by Chancellor Wolfgang Schüssel to open the door to negotiations with Turkey (ESI, *The Austrian Debate on Turkey,* September 2005).

84   The second siege of Vienna, and the subsequent defeat and retreat of the Ottoman forces, marked an important turning-point in the history of Europe, as for about one thousand years (since the seventh century) prior to that date European Christendom had lived under the constant threat of Islam.

85   Katzenstein and Byrnes, "Trans-national religion in an expanding Europe", p. 686.

86   Not only successive Austrian governments, but also the two biggest Austrian political parties and much of the media are also openly against Turkish accession.

87   Quote from Nicolas Véron from "Bruegel", a Brussels think-tank

(quoted in Barysch, *What Europeans Think About Turkey and Why*, p. 3).

88 The issue of Muslim communities in Western Europe is discussed in detail in Chapter 5.2.

89 ESI, *The German debate on Turkey*, October 2006.

90 Angela Merkel, quoted in ESI, *The German Debate on Turkey*.

91 Corrado Pirzio-Biroli, "Does Muslim Turkey belong in Christian Europe?", Debate at the National Press Club, Washington DC, 13 January 2005.

92 Taspinar, "Does Muslim Turkey belong in Christian Europe?".

93 Asli Aydintasbas, "Turkey in full", *International Herald Tribune*, 8 April 2009.

94 Kathimerini, "Obama's support may boost Turkey bid for EU membership", Athens, 8 April 2009.

95 *Financial Times*, 2007.

96 Independent Commission on Turkey, "Turkey in Europe: Breaking the Vicious Circle", Second Report, 7 September 2009.

97 Baskin Oran, Lecture at European Studies Centre, Oxford, 2006.

98 Ibid.

99 Kathimerini, "Obama's support may boost Turkey bid for EU membership".

100 Fritz Bolkestein's farewell speech as a European Commissioner, September 2004.

101 Fritz Bolkestein, The Chancellor's Seminar at St Antony's College Oxford, 1 March 2007.

102 Quoted in Tarifa and Adams "Who's the sick man of Europe".

103 Quoted in Hurd, "Negotiating Europe", p. 406.

104 Ibid., p. 406.

105 Deutsche Welle, 9 November 2007.

106 Charles Bremner, *The Times*, 8 May 2007.

107 Kirsty Hughes, Talk at European Studies Centre.

108 The 'Club Med' summit was hosted by Sarkozy in Paris on 13 July 2008.

109 Interview with Jonathan Evans, 5 April 2008.

110 Enlargement Newsletter, 5 November 2007.

111 Barysch, *What Europeans Think About Turkey and Why*.

Chapter 5

1   Lewis, *The Crisis of Islam*, p. 27.
2   "Letter to America", published in November 2002.
3   It is said that the Muslim Brotherhood was created in 1928 principally as a reaction to the transformation of Turkey into a secular state in 1924 by Kemal Atatürk.
4   Cox and Marks, *The West, Islam and Islamism*, p. 61.
5   Martin Kramer, "Islam vs Democracy", in *Commentary*, January 1993, p. 38.
6   Cox and Marks, *The West, Islam and Islamism*, pp. 68–9.
7   Lewis, *The Crisis of Islam*, p. 154.
8   Kramer, "Islam vs Democracy", pp. 38–39.
9   The bomber's family and the sponsoring organisations celebrate his martyrdom with festivities, as if it were a wedding. Hundreds of guests congregate at the house to offer congratulations. Often the mother will ululate in joy over the honour that Allah has bestowed upon her family (Cox and Marks, *The West, Islam and Islamism*, p. 10).
10 Lewis, *The Crisis of Islam*, p. 39.
11 Fukuyama, "Identity, Immigration, and Liberal-democracy", p. 10.
12 Berger, *Desecularisation of the World*, p. 8.
13 Dutch filmmaker Theo van Gogh was murdered in Holland because of his film *Submission*, which denounced the violence to which many women are subjected in Muslim countries.
14 M. Evans and P. Webster, *The Times*, 6 November 2007.
15 Katzenstein and Byrnes, "Trans-national religion in an expanding Europe", p. 680.
16 Lewis, *The Crisis of Islam*, p. 137.
17 *Financial Times* Harris Poll, 23 August 2007.
18 Caldwell, *Reflections on the Revolution in Europe*.
19 Pew Forum on Religion and Public Life, "Mapping the Global Muslim Population: A Report on the Size and Distribution of the World's Muslim Population", October 2009. http://pewforum.org/newassets/images/reports/Muslimpopulation/Muslimpopulation.pdf
20 Roy, *Globalised Islam*, p. 101.
21 Ibid., p. 21.

22   Fukuyama, "Identity, Immigration, and Liberal-democracy", p. 9.
23   Ibid., p. 15.
24   Ibid., p. 16.
25   Siedentop, *Democracy in Europe*, p. 189.
26   Martin Beckford, "Radical Islam is filling void left by collapse of Christianity in UK", *Telegraph*, 29 May 2008.
27   Michael Burleigh, "The Christian Tradition, Islam and Contemporary Europe", *Hoover Digest* 3, 2006, p. 163.
28   Phyllis Chesler, *The Times*, 7 March 2007.
29   R. Leiken, "Europe's Angry Muslims", *Foreign Affairs*, vol. 84, no. 4, 2005, pp. 120–35.
30   Fukuyama, "Identity, Immigration, and Liberal-democracy", p. 6.
31   Roy, *Globalised Islam*, p.144.
32   As Huntington says, 'The West is now at an extraordinary peak of power in relation to other civilisations. Its superpower opponent has disappeared from the map. Western military and economic power is also unrivalled. There is also Western domination of the UN Security Council. The West in effect is using international institutions, military power and economic resources to run the world in ways that will maintain Western predominance, protect Western interests and promote Western political and economic values.' ("The clash of civilisations", p. 40).
33   Bernard Lewis, "The Roots of Muslim Rage", *Atlantic Monthly*, 1990, vol. 166.
34   Leiken, "Europe's Angry Muslims", p. 264.
35   W. Laquer, "Europe in the 21st century", *Society*, vol. 41, no. 1, p. 69.
36   Tarifa, *Facing Tomorrow's Global Challenges*, p. 7.
37   Policy Exchange, "Living Together Apart: British Muslims and the Paradox of Multiculturalism", UK, 2007.
38   In Austria there are more than 380 teachers of the Islamic religion.
39   Deutsche Welle, "Criticism towards teachers of Islam in Austria", 4 February 2009.
40   Johann Hari, *Independent*, 27 November 2007.
41   Cox and Marks, *The West, Islam and Islamism*, p. 72.
42   Bouyeri is reported as saying: 'If I had the opportunity to get out of prison, and I had the opportunity to do it again, what I did on November 2nd, Allah I would have done exactly the same', and then, 'My successors are ready' (Geert Wilders, *Fitna*).

43   Quoted in Tarifa, *Facing Tomorrow's Global Challenges*, p. 10.

44   Michael Evans and Philip Webster, *The Times*, 6 November 2007.

45   BBC News, "Profile: Islam4UK", 5 January 2010.

46   Muslim Issues 2007.

47   Ramadan, *To Be a European Muslim*.

48   BBC, TV Drama, *Britz*, November 2007.

49   Leiken "Europe's Angry Muslims", p. 265.

50   Cox and Marks, *The West, Islam and Islamism*, p. 73.

51   Siedontop, *Democracy in Europe*, p. 204.

52   Ramadan, *To Be a European Muslim*, pp. 121, 122, 145, 136.

53   Fukuyama "Identity, Immigration, and Liberal-democracy", p. 15.

54   Ibid., p. 18.

55   Burleigh, "The Christian Tradition, Islam and Contemporary Europe", pp. 162–72.

56   Nick Squires, "Muslims warned to integrate if they want to settle in Australia", 2007.

57   Ibid.

58   Ramadan, *To Be a European Muslim*, pp. 181–82.

59   According to Ramadan, Muslims in Europe can follow three possible processes:

1. Assimilation: A European Muslim without Islam. Ramadan argues that the fact that religion should be a private affair leads us to witness contradictory tendencies today: on one hand, an indifference towards religion and often a worrying phenomenon called religious illiteracy, but, on the other, a chaotic questioning of values. Our industrialised and modern society is, to a very great extent, irreligious, and the values associated with its culture, such as freedom, individualism or efficiency, do not echo directly any religious teachings. In the minds of many Europeans, their society has positively liberated them of the oppressive yoke of religion. For some, Muslims should be Muslims without Islam, for there exists a widespread suspicion that to be too Muslim means not to be completely integrated into the Western way of life and its values. This is shared by some Muslims in Europe, who say that to be part of Europe is to adopt oneself to Western way of life. By so arguing, they reduce the message of Islam to theoretical values. Such a concept is based on the belief that Western values are the sole universal ones and hence must

be followed…The public space in Europe has become non-religious, if not sometimes anti-religious and growing numbers of believers find it difficult to face this situation. They are told they are free to believe privately in whatever they want, but the public sphere is occupied with sacred values founded on individualism, money and entertainment. Surrounded by all this high technology, there arises a question: What about God? What about spirituality? The goal of human spirituality is to live constantly one's relationship with God.

2. Isolation: Living in Europe but out of Europe. They try to reproduce a social microcosm within which they live among themselves, with few contacts with the indigenous population, cutting themselves off and avoiding contacts with the external world and non Muslims. They apply the way of life of the Prophet, wearing turbans and visiting mosques frequently. Some of them are already citizens, or have been residents for more than 20 years, but they know nothing of the constitutional framework of their country.

3. Integration (the middle path): Muslim identity is a faith, a practice and spirituality. Muslim identity should be neither diluted within the European environment, nor in reaction (or violent opposition to) against it, but rather based on its foundations according to Islamic sources. This is the meaning of integration from a Muslim point of view. A co-existence which rejects both assimilation and isolation is possible (Ramadan, *To be a European Muslim*, pp. 183, 185, 188, 191, 196, 197, 216, 226, 231, 253).

60   Ramadan, *To Be a European Muslim*, pp. 99, 166, 252.
61   Ibid., pp. 41, 139, 171.
62   L. McLaren "Explaining Opposition to Turkish Membership of the EU", *European Union Politics*, no. 8, 2007.
63   This was also discussed in Chapter 3.
64   Pew Research Centre, *Europeans debate the scarf and the veil*, 20 November 2006.
65   ESI, *The German Debate on Turkey*.
66   Former European Commissioner Fritz Bolkestein warned of the 'Islamisation of Europe' if Turkey joins the Union, during his parting shot in September 2004.
67   On 11 September 2007, a number of organisations from various EU Member States wanted to hold a peaceful demonstration in

Brussels against the Islamisation of Europe. The organisers had no links to political parties. They wanted also to commemorate the victims of the terrorist acts of 11 September 2001. The mayor of Brussels banned the demonstration in view of the large numbers of Muslims living in Brussels.

68   Evan Osnos, *Chicago Tribune*, 19 December 2004.

69   Burleigh, "The Christian Tradition, Islam and Contemporary Europe", p. 166.

70   *Catholic World News*, "Curb mosque height, says German leader", 5 December 2007.

71   German Chancellor Angela Merkel has said that the domes of Islamic mosques should not be taller than the bell towers of Christian churches (ibid.).

72   Muslim Issues 2007.

73   Osnos, *Chicago Tribune*.

74   In 2007, the Bavarian Constitutional Court ruled that the headscarf, and, even more so, the burka, may be regarded as an expression of opposition to certain fundamental constitutional values and laws. The ban on the burka was opposed by the European Commissioner for Justice and Civil Liberties, Franco Frattini, but Wolfgang Schäuble, Germany's Interior Minister, said that he agreed with the criticisms of the burka expressed by Jack Straw, Britain's Justice Secretary.

75   Pew Forum on Religion and Public Life, *An uncertain road: Muslims and the future of Europe*.

76   Ramadan, *To Be a European Muslim*, pp. 120, 122, 136.

77   Seewald, "Interview with Georg Ganswein".

78   Oriana Fallaci was one of the most famous political interviewers in the world: her subjects were among the world's most powerful figures: the Dalai Lama, Henry Kissinger, the Shah of Iran, Ayatollah Khomeini, Deng Xiaoping, Willy Brandt, Zulfikar Ali Bhutto, Muammar al-Gaddafi, Federico Fellini, Yasir Arafat, Indira Gandhi, Alexandros Panagoulis, Golda Meir, Sean Connery, Lech Wałęsa etc. After 11 September, she became an outspoken critic of Islamism. In her best-selling books, *The Rage and the Pride* (considered as the 11 September Manifesto) and *The Force of Reason* (both of which sold over one million copies), Fallaci argues that 'The clash between us and them is not a military clash. It is a cultural one, a religious one. And our military victories do

not solve the offensive of Islamic terrorism. On the contrary, they encourage it. They exacerbate it, they multiply it. The worst is still to come'.

79   Fritz Bolkenstein, *Financial Times*, 31 May 2005.

80   Tarifa, *Facing Tomorrow's Global Challenges*, p. 5.

81   Ian Traynor, *Guardian*, 22 September 2004.

82   CBC News, "Swiss vote to ban new mosque minarets", 30 November 2009.

83   Alexander Higgins, "Swiss ban mosque minarets in surprise vote", *Associated Press,* 29 November 2009.

84   Ahmed Ghanim, "Understanding the Swiss Minarets Ban", Interview with Swiss Ambassador to the USA, *IslamOnline.net*, November 2009.

85   There are several types of headscarves and veils for Muslim women – those that cover the face being the niqab and the burka. The niqab usually leaves the eyes clear. It is worn with an accompanying headscarf and sometimes a separate eye veil. The burka covers the entire face and body with just a mesh screen to see through.

86   BBC News, "Sarkozy stirs French burka debate", 22 June 2009.

87   BBC News, "The Islamic veil across Europe", 26 January 2010.

88   BBC News, "France MPs' report backs Muslim face veil ban", 26 January 2010.

89   BBC News, "France refuses a citizenship over full Islamic veil", 3 February 2010.

90   In 2008, a French court denied citizenship to a Moroccan woman on the grounds that her 'radical' practice of Islam was incompatible with French values.

91   Farage said: 'I can't go into a bank with a motorcycle helmet on. I can't wear a balaclava going round the District and Circle line... What we are saying is, this is a symbol. It's a symbol of something that is used to oppress women. It is a symbol of an increasingly divided Britain...There is nothing extreme or radical or ridiculous about this, but we can't go on living in a divided society...And the real worry, and it isn't just about what people wear, the real worry is that we are heading towards a situation where many of our cities are ghettoised and there is even talk about Shari'a law becoming part of British culture'.

92   BBC News, "UKIP chief Nigel Farage calls for burka ban", 17 January 2010.

93   BBC News, "The Islamic veil across Europe", 26 January 2010.

94   India Knight, "Banning the burka unveils some nasty traits in us", *Sunday Times*, 10 January 2010.

95   The Associated Press, *International Herald Tribune*, 23 October 2007.

96   Tony Paterson, "Swiss government adverts warn Africans", *Independent*, 29 November 2008.

97   http://www.euro-islam.info/country-profiles/italy/

98   BBC News, "Dutch far right in poll triumph", 5 June 2009.

99   BBC News, "BNP wins two European seats", "UKIP beats Labour to second", 8 June 2009.

100   International Crisis Group, *Islam and Identity in Germany*, Europe Report no. 181, 14 March 2007.

101   Imogen Foulkes, "Swiss hold crunch citizenship vote", BBC News, Bern, 31 May 2008.

102   Candidates from Turkey, the former Yugoslavia and Africa are regularly rejected.

103   What is more, being born in Switzerland does not bring an automatic right to citizenship.

104   Switzerland has a large foreign community composing 21 per cent of the total population.

105   Siedentop, *Democracy in Europe*, p. 209.

106   Ibid., p. 214.

107   Burleigh, "The Christian Tradition, Islam and Contemporary Europe".

108   Martin Beckford, "Radical Islam is filling void left by collapse of Christianity in UK", *Telegraph*, 29 May 2008.

109   Ruth Gledhill, "Church and State", *The Times*, 7 June 2008.

110   ICN News, "Germania, chiese vendute ai musulmani", 11 October 2007.

111   "København får en rigtig moské", 28 August 2009.

112   "Islamic sect's plan to build mega-mosque next to Olympics site collapses", *The Times*, 18 January 2010.

113   "Islamic reprieve for pig tales", *Guardian*, 5 March 2003.

114   "Muslims win toy pigs ban", *Sun*, 1 October 2005.

115   WorldNetDaily.com, "English flag offensive to Muslims?", 5 October 2005.

116   BBC News, "Christians told not to preach", 1 June 2008.

117   "BA biased against Christians", *Metro*, 14 November 2007.

118   The court upheld a complaint filed by Soile Lautsi, a Finnish woman

who lives in Italy and has Italian citizenship, who complained that her children had to attend a state school in a town near Venice which had crucifixes in every classroom. The court awarded her €5,000 in 'moral damages', which will have to be paid by the Italian government unless it is successful in an appeal.

119 CNN World, "Italy vows to fight for classroom crucifixes", 4 November 2009.

120 Nick Squires, "Italians outraged as European court rules against crucifixes", *Christian Science Monitor*, 3 November 2009.

121 BBC News, "Greek Church acts on crucifix ban", 12 November 2009.

122 Oriana Fallaci, "A Sermon for the West", Speech held at the American Enterprise Institute, 10 January 2003. http://97.74.65.51/readArticle.aspx?ARTID=20339

123 Hillel Fendel, "Another Islam–Christian Blow-up on the horizon?", IsrealNationalNews.com, 29 July 2007.

124 BBC News, "UK's ban of Dutch MP criticised", 13 February 2009.

125 'Fitna' is an Arabic word, generally regarded as very difficult to translate, but at the same time considered to be an all-encompassing word referring to schism, secession, upheaval and anarchy at once. It is often used to refer to civil war, disagreement and division among people or a test of faith in times of trial.

126 Geert Wilders, *Fitna* the movie.

127 Al-Qaida has pronounced the death penalty for Geert Wilders, through a fatwa issued against him.

128 Minette Marrin, "Labour bares its appeaser's teeth to unbending Muslims", *The Times Online*, 15 February 2009.

129 Jerome Taylor, "How the flying Dutchman was stopped in his tracks", *Independent*, 13 February 2009.

130 On the flight to Britain, a Dutch journalist, in a somewhat surreal gesture, handed Wilders a pink burka, saying he should try to enter the UK wearing it, in order to fool immigration officers (ibid.).

131 Burleigh "The Christian Tradition, Islam and Contemporary Europe".

132 Javier Solana, Talk at Oxford University, 28 February 2006.

133 S. Ozel, "Turkey faces west", *The Wilson Quarterly*, vol. 31, no.1, 2007, p. 21.

134 Quoted in Tarifa and Adams "Who's the sick man of Europe", p. 63.

135 An-Na'im, "Political Islam in National Politics and International Relations", p. 103.
136 Except for the army, the secular establishment includes the judiciary, opposition secularist parties, urban elite and sections of civil society, especially women's organisations.
137 On the AKP's side are also the conservatives, the Islamic-oriented population, the lower middle-class, the liberals and the part of the left that does not agree with the aggressive nationalist attitude of the army.
138 Katzenstein and Byrnes, "Trans-national religion in an expanding Europe", p. 688.
139 Headscarves were banned in schools and universities in 1982 after a coup by the pro-secular armed forces.
140 Morton Abramowitz, *Newsweek*, 11 June 2007.
141 Stephanie Irvine, BBC News, 28 April 2007.
142 The military and secularists think that the First Lady of Turkey wearing a headscarf in public symbolises a victory for the Islamic Movement. On the other hand, wives of Turkish officers are not allowed to wear headscarves in public.
143 Vincent Boland, *Financial Times*, 30 April 2007.
144 Posch, "Crisis in Turkey?", p. 29.
145 Michael Binyon, *The Times*, 23 July 2007.
146 Power and Interest News Report "The AKP's Complex Victory in Turkey", 16 August 2007.
147 Posch, "Crisis in Turkey", p. 8.
148 Abramowitz, *Newsweek,* 11 June 2007. Abramowitz was the former US Assistant Secretary of State and US Ambassador to Turkey.
149 Sarah Rainsford, "Turkish women attack clothing law", BBC News, 5 July 2008.
150 Many sceptics think that this is about Islam and that the squeeze of the pork business is proof of this. On the other hand, the Agriculture Ministry denies the situation is anything to do with Islam, and refuses licences to operate this business on the grounds merely of their not meeting strict new regulations introduced to bring Turkey up to European standards (BBC News, "The demise of Turkey's pork butchers", 2008).
151 Andrew Purvis, "God and Country", *Time*, 28 July 2008.
152 Sarah Rainsford, "Turkish women attack clothing law", BBC News, 5 July 2008.

153 Pew Forum on Religion and Public Life, *Can secular democracy survive in Turkey?*

154 European Stability Initiative, *The headscarf and the constitution,* February 2008.

155 BBC News, 24 January 2008.

156 Guler Sabanci, Lecture at St Antony's College Oxford, 21 February 2008.

157 Enlargement Newsletter, 17 June 2008.

158 Hugh Pope, *"The EU–Turkey–Cyprus Triangle: Setting the Stage"*, ICG, 23 February 2009.

159 Anti-secular statements, activities and publications of AKP, except for the attempt to lift the headscarf ban in universities, include the publication by the AKP mayor of Istanbul of 'Our beloved Prophet Muhammad' in 2006, a book which included the phrase 'Not to cover [hair] means to be sinful'. Ten thousand copies were printed. Another publication is a booklet for newly-wed couples, issued by the AKP mayor of Tuzla municipality, which includes the suggestion that husbands can beat their wives if they do not obey (ESI Newsletter 2/2008).

160 Purvis, "God and Country".

161 The group was named 'Ergenekon' after a legend of Turks' Central Asian origins. It was formed in 2008, when the one-year old AKP government pushed through laws to help the country's EU accession talks get under way (N. Birch).

162 Nicholas Birch, "Defenders of Atatürk on trial for plotting to overthrow government", *Independent*, 21 July 2009.

163 Ibid.

164 European Commission, *Turkey 2009 Progress Report,* p. 8.

165 Pope, *"The EU–Turkey–Cyprus Triangle.*

Conclusion

1 Hurd, "Negotiating Europe", p. 402.

2 Pew Forum on Religion and Public Life, *An Uncertain Road: Muslims and the future of Europe.*

3 Hugh Pope, "EU support is needed for Turkey to progress", *Independent*, 21 July 2009.

BIBLIOGRAPHY

Books and Journal Articles

An-Na'im, A.A. "Political Islam in National Politics and International Relations", in Berger, P. (ed), *Desecularisation of the World: Resurgent religion and world politics*. Washington, DC: The Ethics and Public Policy Centre 1999, pp. 103–15.

Aberbach, J.D. and Rockman, B.A. "Conducting and Coding Elite Interviews", *PS: Political Science and Politics* 35 (4), 2002, pp. 673–78.

Berger, P. (ed). *Desecularisation of the World: Resurgent Religion and World Politics*. Washington, DC: The Ethics and Public Policy Centre, 1999.

Berger, P. "Religion and the West". *The National Interest* 8, 2005, pp. 112–19.

Burleigh, M. "The Christian Tradition, Islam and Contemporary Europe". *Hoover Digest* 3, 2006, pp. 162–72.

Bruce, S. *Politics and Religion*. Cambridge: Polity Press, 2003.

— *Religion in the Modern World: From Cathedral to Cults* (Oxford: Oxford University Press, 1996).

Bogdani, M. and Loughlin, J. *Albania and the European Union: The Tumultuous Journey towards Integration and Accession*. London and New York: I.B.Tauris, 2007.

Cox, C. and Marks, J. *The West, Islam and Islamism: Is Ideological Islam Compatible with Liberal-democracy?* London: Civitas: Institute for the Study of Civil Society, 2003.

Caldwell, C. *Reflections on the Revolution in Europe*. London: Allen Lane, 2009.

Cagaptay, S. *Islam, Secularism and Nationalism in Modern Turkey: Who is a Turk?* New York: Routledge, 2006.

Davie, G. "Europe: The Exception", in Berger, P. (ed). *Desecularisation of the World: Resurgent Religion and World Politics.* Washington, DC: The Ethics and Public Policy Centre, 1999.

Evans, J. "Europe's troubled Eastern Border". *European Voice.* 22 September 2006.

Fukuyama, F. "Identity, Immigration, and Liberal-democracy". *Journal of Democracy* 17/2, 2006, pp. 5–20.

Fukuyama, F. "The end of history". *National Interest,* 1989.

Huntington, S. "The clash of civilisations". *Foreign Affairs* 72. Summer 1993, pp. 22–49.

Hurd, E. "Negotiating Europe: The politics of religion and the prospects for Turkish accession to the EU". *Review of International Studies,* vol. 32 (3), July 2006, pp. 401–18.

Hughes, K. "Turkey and the EU: Just another enlargement?" A *Friends of Europe* Working Paper. June 2004.

Katzenstein, P.J. and Byrnes, T.A. "Trans-national religion in an expanding Europe". *Perspectives on Politics* vol. 4, no. 4. December 2006, pp. 679–94.

Kazancigil, A. "High Stateness in a Muslim Society: The Case of Turkey", in Dogan, M. and Kazancigil, A. (eds), *Comparing Nations: Concepts, Strategies, Substance.* Oxford: Blackwell, 1994, pp. 221–34.

Keyman, F. and Senem, A. "European Integration and the Transformation of Turkish Democracy". *CEPS Working Paper* 8, 2004.

Kramer, M. "Islam vs Democracy", in *Commentary,* January 1993.

Lewis, B. *The Crisis of Islam: Holy War and Unholy Terror.* London: Weidenfeld & Nicolson, 2003.

— "The Roots of Muslim Rage", *Atlantic Monthly,* 1990, vol. 166.

— *The Political Language of Islam.* Chicago: University of Chicago Press 1988.

Lipset, S. M. "The centrality of culture", in Larry Diamond (ed), *The Global Resurgence of Democracy.* Baltimore: Johns Hopkins University Press, 1996.

Laquer, W. "Europe in the 21st century", *Society* vol. 41, no. 1, pp. 67–74.

Leiken, R. "Europe's Angry Muslims". *Foreign Affairs,* vol. 84, no. 4, 2005, pp. 120–35.

Micklethwait, J. and Wooldridge, A. *God is Back: How the Global Rise of Faith is Changing the World.* London: Allen Lane, 2009.

Martin, D. "The Evangelical upsurge", in Berger, P. *Desecularisation of the World: Resurgent Religion and World Politics.* Washington, DC: The Ethics and Public Policy Centre, 1999.

Olsen, J. "The many faces of Europeanization". *Journal of Common Market Studies.* vol. 40, no. 5, 2002, pp. 927–39.

Ozel, S. "Turkey faces west". *Wilson Quarterly.* vol. 31, no. 1, 2007, pp.18–25.

Pope, H. "The EU–Turkey–Cyprus Triangle: Setting the Stage", ICG, 23 February 2009.

Peabody, R. L. et al. "Interviewing Political Elites". *Political Science and Politics,* 23 (3), September 1990.

Posch, W. "Crisis in Turkey: Just another bump on the road to Europe?" Occasional Paper, no. 67. Paris: European Union Institute for Security Studies, June 2007.

Ramadan, T. *To Be a European Muslim.* Leicester: Islamic Foundation, 1999.

Roy, O. *Globalised Islam: The Search for a New Ummah.* New York: Columbia University Press, 2004.

Siedentop, L. *Democracy in Europe.* Ch. 10, "Europe, Christianity, and Islam". Harmondsworth: Penguin Books, 2000.

Tarifa, F. and Adams, B. "Who's the sick man of Europe: A wavering EU should let Turkey in". *Mediterranean Quarterly.* A Journal of Global Issues, vol. 18, no. 1, 2007, pp. 52–74.

Van Evera, S. *Guide to Methods for Students of Political Science.* Ithaca: Cornell University Press, 1997.

Weigel, G. "Roman Catholicism in the Age of John Paul II", in Berger, P. (ed), *Desecularisation of the World: Resurgent Religion and World Politics.* Washington, DC: The Ethics and Public Policy Centre, 1999.

White, J. *Islamic Mobilisation in Turkey: A Study in Vernacular Politics.* Washington, DC: University of Washington Press, 2002.

Woliver, L.R. "Ethical Dilemmas in Personal Interviewing", *Political Science and Politics* 35 (4), 2002, pp. 677–78.

Yavuz, H. *Islamic Political Identity in Turkey.* New York: Oxford University Press, 2003.

EU and Other Organisations' Reports and Documents

Conference of the Representatives of the Governments of Member States. *Treaty of Lisbon.* 3 December 2007. http://www.consilium. europa.eu/uedocs/cmsUpload/cg00014.en07.pdf

European Commission. *Turkey 2009 Progress Report.* Brussels, 14 October 2009   http://ec.europa.eu/enlargement/pdf/key_documents/2009/ tr_rapp.ort_2009_en.pdf

— *Turkey 2008 Progress Report.* Brussels, 5 November 2008.

— *Turkey 2007 Progress Report.* 6 November 2007. http://ec.europa.eu/ enlargement/archives/pdf/key_documents/2007/package/sec_142 6_final_progress_report_tr_en.pdf

— *Enlargement Strategy and Main Challenges 2006-07.* 8 November 2006.

— Enlargement Newsletter. Monthly Electronic Newsletter. 2006–07. http://ec.europa.eu/enlargement/press_corner/newsletter/index_ en.htm#a1

— *2005 Enlargement Package.* 9 November 2005.

— *Turkey – Accession Negotiating Framework.* October 2005.

EU Council. *On the principles, priorities and conditions contained in the Accession Partnership with Turkey.* 6 November 2007.

— *Religious Freedom in Turkey.* 8 June 2006. http://epp.ed.org/Press/ showpr.asp?PRControlDocTypeID=1&PRControlID=4952&PRC ontentID=8914&PRContentLG=en

European Parliament. *Turkey, the Enlargement of the EU and the EU Constitutional Treaty.* Weekly Message. 18 December 2006.

— *EU Draft Report on Turkey's Progress Towards Accession.* 2006/2118 (INI). 6 June 2006.

— *Second Report on Women's Role in Social, Economic and Political Life in Turkey.* EP Women's Rights Committee. 20 December 2006, in Enlargement Newsletter, 12 January 2007.

European Ideas Network (EIN) Working Group on "Geographic Limits of the EU". *Speeches, conclusions and recommendations.* Lyon 2006 and Warsaw 2007. http://www.europeanideasnetwork.com/

European Stability Initiative (ESI). Newsletters and Reports 2007–08. http://www.esiweb.org/

— *The Austrian Debate on Turkey.* January 2008. http://www.esiweb. org/index.php?lang=en&id=156&document_ID=101

— *The German Debate on Turkey.* October 2006. http://www.esiweb. org/pdf/esi_turkey_germany_grand_coalition.pdf

— *The Battle for Turkey's Soul: Party closures, gangs and the state of democracy.* ESI Briefing. 2 April 2008. http://www.esiweb.org/index. php?lang=en&id=156&document_ID=104

— *The Headscarf and the Constitution.* February 2008.

— *Sex and Power in Turkey: Feminism, Islam and the Maturing of Turkish Democracy.* ESI Report. 2 June 2007. http://www.esiweb.org/index. php?lang=en&id=156&document_ID=90

— *Islamic Calvinists. Change and Conservatism in Central Anatolia.* ESI Report. 19 September 2005. http://www.esiweb.org/index. php?lang=en&id=156&document_ID=69

Foreign and Commonwealth Office. *The Annual Report on Human Rights,* March 2009.

International Crisis Group. *Solving the EU–Turkey–Cyprus Triangle,* Istanbul/Brussels, 23 February 2009.

— *Islam and Identity in Germany.* Europe Report No. 181, 14 March 2007.

Independent Commission on Turkey. "Turkey in Europe: Breaking the Vicious Circle", Second Report, 7 September 2009.

Power and Interest News Report. *The AKP's Complex Victory in Turkey,* 16 August 2007. http://www.pinr. com

Pew Forum on Religion and Public Life. "Mapping the Global Muslim Population: A Report on the Size and Distribution of the World's Muslim Population", October 2009.

— *Can secular democracy survive in Turkey?* 4 May 2007. http:// pewresearch.org/pubs/470/can-secular-democracy-survive-in- turkey

— *Does 'Muslim' Turkey belong in 'Christian' Europe?,* 13 January 2005. http://www.pewtrusts.org/news_room_ektid23054.aspx

— *An Uncertain Road: Muslims and the future of Europe.* Report. October 2005.

Opinion Polls and Surveys

Barysch, K. *What Europeans Think About Turkey and Why.* Centre for European Reform Briefing Note. August 2007. http://www.cer.org. uk/pdf/briefing_kb_turkey_24aug07.pdf

BBC News World Edition. "Britons backed Christian society". BBC Poll. 29 November 2005.

Deutsche Welle. "Study shows Turkish values don't coincide with EU ideals". 3 July 2007. http://www.dw-world.de/dw/article/0,2144,2666276,00.html

European Commission. *Attitudes towards European Union Enlargement:* Special Eurobarometer 255/65. July 2006. http://ec.europa.eu/public_opinion/archives/ebs/ebs_255_en.pdf

— Eurobarometer Survey No. 67: *Public Opinion in the European Union.* November 2007. http://ec.europa.eu/public_opinion/archives/eb/eb67/eb67_en.pdf

— Flash Eurobarometer 217: *Intercultural dialogue in Europe.* December 2007.

— Eurobarometer Survey No. 66: *Public Opinion in the European Union.* 2006.

Financial Times Harris Poll. *Attitudes toward Muslims mixed in Europe and the U.S.* 23 August 2007. http//www.harrisinteractive.com/news/allnewsbydate.asp?NewsID=1228

— *Religious views and beliefs vary greatly by country.* 20 December 2006

German Marshall Fund of the USA. *Transatlantic Trends Survey* 2007. http://www.transatlantictrends.org/trends/doc/TTToplineData2005.pdf

— *European Elites Survey.* Centre for the Study of Political Change. Campagnia di San Paolo, Italy. 7 September 2007. http://www.gips.unisi.it/circap/ees_overview

IRNA. "European Socialists accuse right-wing opponents of not wanting Muslim Turkey in EU". 28 September 2005.

Knight, I. "Banning the burka unveils some nasty traits in us", *Sunday Times*, 10 January 2010.

McLaren, L.M. "Explaining Opposition to Turkish Membership of the EU". *European Union Politics.* No. 8, 2007, pp. 251–78.

Pew Forum on Religion and Public Life. *Islamic extremism: Common concern for Muslim and Western publics.* Global Attitude Survey. 14 July 2005.

— *Europeans debate the scarf and the veil.* 20 November 2006. http://pewresearch.org/pubs/95/europeans-debate-the-scarf-and-the-veil

Policy Exchange. *Living Together Apart: British Muslims and the Paradox of Multiculturalism*, UK, 2007

Ruiz-Jiménez, A. and Torreblanca, J.I. *European Public Opinion and Turkey's Accession: Making sense of arguments for and against.* European Policy Institutes Network. 16 May 2007.

Servantie, A. "European public opinion on Turkey". *The Bridge: A Quarterly Review on European integration*, 2007. http://www.bridgemag.com/magazine/index.php?option=com_content&task=view&id=261&Itemid=31

UK Foreign and Commonwealth Office. *Annual Report on Human Rights*, March 2009

Newspaper Articles

Abramowitz, M. "A showdown in Ankara", *Newsweek*, 11 June 2007.

Akyol, M. "Welcome to Islamic Reformation 201", *Turkish Daily News*, 1 March 2008. http://www.turkishdailynews.com.tr/article.php?enewsid=97795

Ahmed, A. and Rosen, L. "Islam and freedom of thought", *Islam for Today*, 15 July 2008.

Aydintasbas, A. "Turkey in full", *International Herald Tribune*, 8 April 2009.

Çamlibel, C. "EU made up of Christian values, Turkey has no place in it, says far right EU politician", *Turkish Daily News*, 10 March 2007. http://www.turkishdailynews.com.tr/article.php?enewsid=67923

BBC News. "EU hardens tone on enlargement", "Brussels sets deadline for Turkey", "Cyprus may veto EU-Turkey talks", "Turks stoical about EU report", November–December 2006.

— "What impact will the murder of Turkish journalist have? Have your say", 20 January 2007.

— "Turkish secularists in new rally", 13 May 2007.

— "Muhammad teddy teacher arrested", 26 November 2007.

— "Christians told not to preach", 1 June 2008.

— "New move to lift Turkey scarf ban", 24 January 2008.

— "When Muslims become Christians", 21 April 2008.

— "The demise of Turkey's pork butchers", 2008.

— "UK's ban of Dutch MP criticised", 13 February 2009.

— "Europe gas pipeline deal agreed", 13 July 2009.

— "Sarkozy stirs French burka debate", 22 June 2009.

— "Greek Church acts on crucifix ban", 12 November 2009.

— "France refuses a citizenship over full Islamic veil", 3 February 2010.

— "The Islamic veil across Europe", 26 January 2010.

— "France MPs' report backs Muslim face veil ban", 26 January 2010.

— "UKIP chief Nigel Farage calls for burka ban", 17 January 2010.

— "Profile: Islam4UK", 5 January 2010.

Barber, T. "Europe's public figures press Turkey's case to join union", *Financial Times*, 2 October 2007.

Beckford, M. "Radical Islam is filling void left by collapse of Christianity in UK", *Daily Telegraph*, 29 May 2008.

Binyon, M. "World keeps watch on test case for political Islam", *The Times*, 23 July 2007.

Birch, N. "Defenders of Atatürk on trial for plotting to overthrow government", *Independent*, 21 July 2009

Boland, V. "Generals' veiled threat signals fight for religious or secular future", *Financial Times*, 30 April 2007.

Bolkestein, F. "France's verdict tells us that Europe has been oversold", *Financial Times*, 31 May 2005.

Bremner, C. "Sarkozy's tough agenda", *The Times*, 8 May 2007.

CNN World. "Italy vows to fight for classroom crucifixes", 4 November 2009.

CBC News. "Swiss vote to ban new mosque minarets", 30 November 2009.

Castle, S. "EU freezes talks on Turkey's membership", *Independent*, 12 December 2006.

Charter, D. "Ban on free speech still keeps Ankara out of EU", *The Times*, 7 November 2007.

Chesler, P. "Is it racist to condemn fanaticism? How my eyes were opened to the barbarity of Islam", *The Times*, 7 March 2007.

Catholic World News. "Curb mosque height, says German leader", 5 December 2007.

Coghlan, T. "Karzai backs down over abhorrent marital rape law", *The Times*, 28 April 2009.

Deutsche Welle. "EU says Turkey must improve freedom of speech", 9 November 2007.

— "Criticism towards teachers of Islam in Austria", 4 February 2009.

Daily Telegraph, "Nicolas Sarkozy pushes for burka ban in France", 12 November 2009.

Danish Affairs. "Why Europeans don't want Turkey in EU", 9 May 2008.

Dombley, D. and Boland, V. "EU holds to tough line on Turkey's membership talks", *Financial Times*, 11 December 2006.

Erdern, S. "Reformers battle for soul of Turkey", *The Times*, 16 July 2007.

Evans, M. and Webster, P. "MI5 report on terror threat", *The Times*, 6 November 2007.

Hari, J. "My life under a fatwa: Ayaan Hirsi Ali speaks out", *Independent*, 27 November 2007.

Higgins, A. "Swiss ban mosque minarets in surprise vote", Associated Press, 29 November 2009.

Fendel, H. "Another Islam–Christian Blow-up on the horizon?", IsrealNationalNews.com, 29 July 2007.

Foulkes, I. "Swiss hold crunch citizenship vote", BBC News, Bern, 31 May 2008.

Fedynsky, P. "Nabucco Pipeline Competition for Russian Gas", Voice of America News, 14 July 2009.

Guardian, "Islamic reprieve for pig tales", 5 March 2003.

Gledhill, R. "Church and State", *The Times*, 7 June 2008.

Independent, "In the name of God: The Saudi rape victim's tale", 29 November 2009.

Irvine, S. "Defending the secular faith", BBC News, 28 April 2007.

Jihad Watch, 18 October 2004.

Jones, T. "Secular fundamentalists are the new totalitarians", *Guardian*, 6 January 2007.

Kafadar, S. "The EU's Hypocrisy", *Daily Telegraph*, 14 December 2006.

Kettler, K. "Letter to the Editor", *Economist*, 21 December 2002.

Kiniklioglu, S. "Spurned by the West, Turkey looks eastward", *International Herald Tribune*, 7 September 2006.

Kathimerini, "Obama's support may boost Turkey bid for EU membership", Athens, 8 April 2009.

Heneghan, T. "Turkey not reforming Islam, but itself with Hadith review", *Washington Post*, 29 February 2008.

Lodge, T. "Turkey is key for the EU's energy-hungry states", *Independent*, 21 April 2009.

Meixler, L. "Turkey's future in question after EU vote", Associated Press Writer, 2 June 2005.

Metro, "BA biased against Christians", 14 November 2007.

Marrin, M. "Labour bares its app.easer's teeth to unbending Muslims", *The Times Online*, 15 February 2009.

Newsweek Magazine, "Letters to the Editor", 12 February 2007.

— "Letters to the Editor", 3 December 2007.

— "Interview with Erdogan on the passions and power politics currently rolling the Middle East", 9 February 2009.

International Herald Tribune, "A record Swiss vote for rightists", 23 October 2007.

ICN-News.com, "Germania, chiese vendute ai musulmani", 11 October 2007. http://www.icn-news.com/?do=news&id=1670

Osnos, E. "Islam shaping Europe", *Chicago Tribune*, 19 December 2004.

Parker, G. and Dombey, D. "EU freezes parts of Turkish accession talks", *Financial Times*, 12 December 2006.

Paterson, T. "Swiss government adverts warn Africans", *Independent*, 29 November 2008.

Parris, M. "A distant view of the hills and the news", *The Times*, 21 May 2009.

Piggott, R. "Turkey in radical revision of Islamic texts", BBC News, 26 February 2008.

Pope, H. "EU supp.ort is needed for Turkey to progress", *Independent*, 21 July 2009

Purvis, A. "God and Country", *Time*, 28 July 2008.

Rainsford, S. "Women condemn Turkey Constitution", BBC News, 24 January 2008.

Raisnford, S. "Turkish women attack clothing law", BBC News, 5 July 2008.

Rainsford, S. "MP breaks language law in Turkey", BBC News, 25 February 2009.

Seewald, P. "Interview with Georg Ganswein", *Sueddeutsche Zeitung Magazin*, 27 July 2007.

Siedentop, L. "Do you realise Europe is in the throes of civil war?" *The Times*, 27 February 2007.

Squires, N. "Muslims warned to integrate if they want to settle in Australia", 2007.

— "Italians outraged as European court rules against crucifixes", *Christian Science Monitor*, 3 November 2009.

Spillius, A. "Cyprus – the thorn in Turkey's EU foothold", *Daily Telegraph*, 14 December 2006.

Smith, J. "Islam and the modern world don't mix", *Independent*, 28 November 2007.

Sun, "Muslims win toy pigs ban", 1 October 2005.

Traynor, I. "In 1682 Turkey was the invader, in 2004 much of Europe still sees it that way", *Guardian*, 22 September 2004.

Taylor, J. "How the flying Dutchman was stopp.ed in his tracks", *Independent*, 13 February 2009.

The Times, "Islamic sect's plan to build mega-mosque next to Olympics site collapses", 18 January 2010.

Thompson, D. "Headquarters of Turkish campaign for EU membership is…a confiscated Christian building", Telegraph.co.uk, 12 December 2009.

Verma, S. "Mother of raped boy forces tourist paradise to confront its dark side", *The Times*, 13 December 2007.

Watt, N. "Turkey deal set to avoid EU summit row", *Guardian*, 12 December 2006.

Western Mail, "Turkey needs to make amends", Letters, 3 November 2007.

WorldNetDaily.com, "English flag offensive to Muslims?", 5 October 2005.

Interviews (semi-structured elite interviewing)

Maria Eleni Koppa: MEP from European Socialists Group, Vice-Chairwoman of the EU–Turkey Joint Parliamentary Committee, European Parliament. Oxford, 21 January 2008.

Jonathan Evans: MEP from EPP-ED Group, former Leader of British Conservatives at European Parliament. Cardiff, 5 April 2008.

Graham Avery: Formerly Director at the DG for Enlargement and DG for External Relations, European Commission. Oxford, 4 March 2008.

Fadi Hakura: Associate Fellow of the Europe Programme and Analyst on Turkey, Chatham House. London, 9 April 2008.

Lectures and Speeches

Akgunduz, A. *The Ottoman State as a Muslim State*. Lecture at Marmara University, 3 December 2006.

Cebeci, M. *The EU's security impact on Turkey: Democratisation as Desecuritisation*. Lecture at European Community Institute, 2006.

Fallaci, O. "A Sermon for the West", Speech held at the American

Enterprise Institute, 10 January 2003. http://97.74.65.51/readArticle. aspx?ARTID=20339

Ghanim, A. "Understanding the Swiss Minarets Ban". Interview with Swiss Ambassador to the USA. IslamOnline.net, November 2009.

Lugo, L., Davidson, J., Pirzio-Biroli, C. and Taspinar, O. *Does Muslim Turkey belong in Christian Europe?* Debate at the National Press Club, Washington DC, 13 January 2005. http://pewforum.org/ events/index.php?EventID=66

Tarifa, F. *Facing tomorrow's global challenges: What role for Social Science.* Paper presented at the 2006 Annual Conference of the Association for Applied and Clinical Sociology, San Jose, California, October 2006.

Internet Sites and Dictionaries

Alliance of Liberals and Democrats for Europe, "Duff welcomes Turkey decision and castigates EPP group". http://www.andrewduffmep. org.uk/news/000164/duff_welcomes_turkey_decision_ands_ castigates_epp_group.html

Almanac of World History (National Geographic), November 2003.

BBC, TV Drama, *Britz,* November 2007.

BBC News, "Muslims in Europe: Country Guide", 23 December 2005.

Delegation of the European Commission to the Republic of Turkey, Albania and Croatia website. http://www.delhrv.ec.europa.eu/en/ static/view/id/27

Muslim Issues 2007.

O'Rourke, B. "Turkey: AKP tries to join European Conservative Group". http://www.eurasianet.org/departments/insight/articles/eav040603. shtml

Readers Digest Universal Dictionary, 1994.

Websites of EPP-ED (http://www.eppgroup.eu/home/en/default.asp), Socialists (http://www.pes.org/) and Liberal-Democrats (http:// www.eldr.org/en/index.php and http://www.alde.eu/) groupings of the European Parliament.

Wikipedia. Figures, data and facts on Turkey, Poland, Albania, Bosnia-Herzegovina and Croatia. http://en.wikipedia.org/wiki/Turkey/ Poland/Albania/Bosnia/Herzegovina/Croatia

Wilders, G. *Fitna* the movie (YouTube).

Sultan, W. TV interview at Al Jazeera (Qatar), 21 February 2006. http://switch3.castup.net/cunet/gm.asp?ai=214&ar=1050wmv&ak

Relevant Conferences, Seminars, Workshops and Lectures

Summer Conference of European Ideas Network and its working group "'Geographic limits of the EU", Berlin 2004, Lisbon 2005, Lyon 2006 and Warsaw 2007.

Baskin Oran. "Some remarks by EU Statesmen concerning Turkish accession". Lecture at European Studies Centre, Oxford, 2006.

Fritz Bolkestein (Former EU Commissioner). The Chancellor's Seminar. 1 March 2007, St Antony's College, University of Oxford.

Heather Grabbe (Member of Cabinet of Olli Rehn, DG Enlargement, European Commission). "EU Transformative Power", April 2007, European Studies Centre, Oxford.

Graham Avery (Former Director at the European Commission). "Europe Enlargement: Return of a lost brother, or an invasion by a distant cousin?" May 2007, St Anne's College, University of Oxford.

Tariq Ramadan et al. "Europe's Muslim Neighbourhoods", 22–23 May 2007, Reuters Institute, Oxford.

Jose Manuel Barroso (President of the European Commission). Annual Lecture of European Studies Centre, 11 October 2007, St Antony's College, University of Oxford.

Costas Simitis (Former Prime Minister of Greece). "On the future of Europe". 7 October 2007, St Catherine's College, University of Oxford.

Tariq Ramadan (ESC, Oxford) and Denis McShane (MP). "Should we be afraid of Islamism?" October 2007, European Studies Centre, Oxford.

Dora Bokoyannis (Foreign Minister of Greece). "Does Europe have a message for the world?"Annual Lecture of South Eastern European Centre, 6 November 2007, St Antony's College, University of Oxford.

Marilena Koppa (MEP) and Kirsty Hughes (Freelance writer on international affairs). "Turkey and the European Union: Who is right, who is wrong?" 21 January 2008, European Studies Centre, Oxford.

Conference, "Turkish Politics since 2002". January 2008, Nuffield College, University of Oxford.
Javier Solana (EU High Representative for the CFSP). "Europe in the world: Next steps", February 2008, Examination School, Oxford.
Chris Patten (Chancellor, University of Oxford) and Güler Sabanci (Chairman, Sabanci Holdings and Founder of Sabanci University). "Bridging worlds". The Chancellor's Seminar, 21 February 2008, St Antony's College, University of Oxford.

INDEX

Numbers in *italics* refer to Appendix I.